AQA

Religiou Studies A
Judaism

GCSE

Marianne Fleming
Peter Smith
David Worden

Series editor
Cynthia Bartlett

OXFORD

UNIVERSITY PRESS

OXFORD
UNIVERSITY PRESS

Great Clarendon Street, Oxford, OX2 6DP, United Kingdom

Oxford University Press is a department of the University of Oxford. It furthers the University's objective of excellence in research, scholarship, and education by publishing worldwide. Oxford is a registered trade mark of Oxford University Press in the UK and in certain other countries

British Library Cataloguing in Publication Data
Data available

978-0-19-837036-9

(Kerboodle book: 978-0-19-837035-6)

10 9 8 7 6 5 4 3

Paper used in the production of this book is a natural, recyclable product made from wood grown in sustainable forests. The manufacturing process conforms to the environmental regulations of the country of origin.

Printed in India by Multivista Global Pvt. Ltd

Links to third party websites are provided by Oxford in good faith and for information only. Oxford disclaims any responsibility for the materials contained in any third party website referenced in this work.

Approval message from AQA

This textbook has been approved by AQA for use with our qualification. This means that we have checked that it broadly covers the specification and we are satisfied with the overall quality. Full details of our approval process can be found on our website.

We approve textbooks because we know how important it is for teachers and students to have the right resources to support their teaching and learning. However, the publisher is ultimately responsible for the editorial control and quality of this book.

Please note that when teaching the AQA GCSE Religious Studies course, you must refer to AQA's specification as your definitive source of information. While this book has been written to match the specification, it cannot provide complete coverage of every aspect of the course.

A wide range of other useful resources can be found on the relevant subject pages of our website: www.aqa.org.uk.

Please note that the Practice Questions in this book allow students a genuine attempt at practising exam skills, but they are not intended to replicate examination papers.

Contents

PART TWO: THEMATIC STUDIES

Chapter 3: Relationships and families

Chapter 4: Religion and life

Chapter 5: The existence of God and revelation

Chapter 6: Religion, peace and conflict

Chapter 7: Religion, crime and punishment

Chapter 8: Religion, human rights and social justice

Introduction

This book is written specifically for GCSE students studying the AQA Religious Studies Specification A, 3.1.6 Judaism and 3.2.1 Religious, philosophical and ethical studies.

Chapters 1 and 2 cover the beliefs, teachings and practices of Judaism, including beliefs about the nature of God, the Covenant and the mitzvot, or commandments, and the way Jews live out their faith, including worship, family life and festivals.

Chapters 3 to 8 cover religious, philosophical and ethical issues, including Relationships and families, Religion and life, the Existence of God and revelation, Religion, peace and conflict, Religion, crime and punishment, and Religion, human rights and social justice.

For the full course you must study two world religions, and four out of six of the philosophical and ethical themes. There are two examination papers, one on the religions and the other on the issues.

For a short course qualification you must study the beliefs and teachings of Christianity and either Judaism or Islam and two themes: Relationships and families and Religion, peace and conflict. There is one examination paper on these topics.

Assessment guidance

Each chapter has an assessment guidance section that helps you to familiarise yourself with the AQA paper. There are multiple choice questions worth 1 mark, short-answer questions worth 2 marks, and longer questions worth 4 and 5 marks that test your ability to retell and explain facts. There are longer evaluation questions worth 12 marks that test your ability to analyse and evaluate different viewpoints.

Examination questions will test two assessment objectives, each representing 50 per cent of the total marks:

AO1: Demonstrate knowledge and understanding of religion and beliefs including:

- beliefs, practices and sources of authority
- influence on individuals, communities and societies
- similarities and differences within and/or between religions and beliefs.

AO2: Analyse and evaluate aspects of religion and belief, including their significance and influence.

For AO1 questions, the grid below gives guidance on how marks will be allocated:

Marks	Question type	Criteria
1 mark	Multiple choice	The correct answer chosen from 4 options
2 marks	Short answer (asking for two facts)	One mark for each of **two** correct points
4 marks	Asking for two ways in which beliefs influence Jews today OR two contrasting ways in which religion is practised OR two contrasting beliefs in contemporary British society about an issue studied in the themes, including one from Christianity and one from another religion or in the case of theme C, non-religious perspectives	For each of the **two** ways / contrasts: • one mark for a simple explanation of a relevant and accurate way / contrast; • two marks for a detailed explanation of a relevant and accurate way / contrast
5 marks	Asking for two Jewish beliefs or teachings, OR two Jewish practices OR two religious beliefs about a philosophical or ethical issue PLUS reference to scripture or sacred writings	For each of the **two** beliefs / practices: • one mark for a simple explanation of a relevant and accurate belief / practice; • two marks for a detailed explanation of a relevant and accurate belief / practice; **PLUS** one mark for a relevant, accurate reference to scripture or sacred writing

The grid below gives you some guidance on different levels for the 12 mark evaluation question (testing AO2).

Levels	Criteria	Marks
4	A well-argued response, reasoned consideration of different points of view Logical chains of reasoning leading to judgement(s) supported by knowledge and understanding of relevant evidence and information	10–12
3	Reasoned consideration of different points of view Logical chains of reasoning that draw on knowledge and understanding of relevant evidence and information	7–9
2	Reasoned consideration of a point of view A logical chain of reasoning drawing on knowledge and understanding of relevant evidence and information OR Recognition of different points of view, each supported by relevant reasons/evidence	4–6
1	Point of view with reason(s) stated in support	1–3
0	Nothing worthy of credit	0

For the latest mark schemes, please also refer to the AQA website.

In modern Britain Jews practise their religion alongside people from many different faiths. The AQA GCSE specification requires that students understand Christian beliefs on three issues in each of the ethical and philosophical themes and are able to compare these with other faith perspectives, including Judaism (or between Christianity and non-religious viewpoints in the case of Theme C).

Theme	Students must be able to explain contrasting beliefs on the following:
A: Relationships and families	• Contraception • Sexual relationships before marriage • Homosexual relationships
B: Religion and life	• Abortion • Euthanasia • Animal experimentation
C: The existence of God and revelation	• Visions • Miracles • Nature as general revelation
D: Religion, peace and conflict	• Violence • Weapons of mass destruction • Pacifism
E: Religion, crime and punishment	• Corporal punishment • Death penalty • Forgiveness
F: Religion, human rights and social justice	• Status of women in religion • The uses of wealth • Freedom of religious expression

You should also bear in mind non-religious views such as atheism and humanism, and understand the influence of beliefs teachings and practices on individuals, communities and societies.

Spelling, punctuation and grammar (SPaG) is also important so it will be useful to practise the 12 mark extended writing questions. There are 5 marks available for SPaG: 1 mark for threshold performance, 2–3 marks for intermediate performance and 4–5 marks for high performance. You should aim to write correctly using a wide range of specialist religious terms.

Examination grades will be awarded on a scale of 9–1 rather than A* to G. Grade 9 will be the equivalent of a new grade for high performing students above the current A*. Grade 4 will be the same as a grade C pass. The aim of the new grading system is to show greater differentiation between higher and lower achieving students.

Kerboodle Book

An online version of this book is available for student access, with an added bank of tools for you to personalise the book.

Part 1: The study of religions

1 Judaism

1.1 The nature of God: God as One

■ The concept and nature of God

The belief in one God is the most basic principle in Judaism and so Judaism is a **monotheistic** religion. Jews believe that it is God who has had the major effect and influence on the world and their place within the world. Although there are important people in the history of the faith, there has never been any suggestion that any of them have been a part of God or a god themselves. It is God who is the source of all Jewish morality, beliefs and values, which affect Jews' decisions about how to live correctly.

Jews believe that this overwhelming importance and significance of God is seen in his role as the creator. In addition to being the creator, God also sustains his creation by caring for people and requiring loyalty in exchange. Jews believe that God has given laws to his people, and is the true judge of how people follow these laws.

Jews believe that they can see the work of God in history, and that by carefully studying history they can learn more about God. The historical content in the Tenakh (also commonly spelled Tanakh – the Jewish scriptures) is considered important for what it reveals about God. The idea of seeing God at work, and learning more about him, is also extended into the present and the future because Jews believe God is constantly at work.

While Judaism is a monotheistic religion, there is considerable diversity in how the faith is practiced and how the Jewish scriptures are interpreted. You will learn more about some of these differences in the following pages.

■ God or G-d?

Some Jews prefer not to write the word God. They use G-d instead as a sign of respect. When written in Hebrew, God's name can never be erased or destroyed. The Hebrew letters of the name for God are YHWH, and this is never said out loud by Jews. When it appears in scripture or liturgy, instead of saying it, Jews substitute the Hebrew word 'Adonai', which means 'my Lord'. Any book containing the Hebrew name of God is treated with respect and is never destroyed or thrown away. When it is too old to be used it is kept in a special place in the synagogue before being properly buried in a Jewish cemetery.

> ### Objectives
>
> - Understand the concept and nature of God for Jews.
> - Understand the Jewish belief that God is One.

> ### Key terms
>
> - **monotheistic:** a religion that believes there is only one God
> - **Shema:** a Jewish prayer affirming belief in the one God, found in the Torah

▲ *Old Jewish books containing the Hebrew name of God, stored in a synagogue in Israel*

Some Jews think it is acceptable to write the word God, as they view it as a title, not a name. It is important to note that God and G-d refer to exactly the same one God and not different gods or parts of God.

God as one

For Jews, monotheism is not just the belief there is only one God; it is a way of viewing the world and all the contents of the world that they believe God created. It is God who is ever present in people's lives; every sight they see, sound they hear, and experience they are aware of is regarded as a meeting with God. This is the true meaning of the idea that God is One and is best expressed in the first two verses of the **Shema**, an important Jewish prayer that derives from passages in the books of Deuteronomy and Numbers. It begins with an expression of the unity of God, and the way humankind should respond to this belief:

> ❝ Hear, O Israel! The LORD is our God, the LORD alone. You shall love the LORD your God with all your heart and with all your soul and with all your might. ❞
>
> *Deuteronomy 6:4–5*

The reference to loving God with all your heart implies that God requires total loyalty, just like loyalty is needed in a full loving relationship. The mention of the soul shows that Jews need to have spiritual dedication to the one God.

▲ *A Jew sits to recite the Shema. Many Jews put their hand over their eyes or cover their face while saying the first line, to avoid distractions.*

For Jews, God is a single, whole, indivisible entity who cannot be divided. He is infinite and eternal, beyond the full understanding of humankind. This makes him the only being who should be praised.

Activities

1 What does the term monotheism mean?

2 Explain fully the Jewish belief that God is One.

3 Write out the first two verses of the Shema.

4 Explain what you think the Shema means to Jews.

Discussion activity

'It is God who is the source of all Jewish morality, beliefs and values, which affect Jews' decisions about how to live correctly.'

With a partner, discuss what you think this means to individual Jews who are keen to follow their faith properly. After five minutes, compare your conclusions with two other people.

Extension activity

Read the next part of the Shema from Deuteronomy 6:7–9. What instructions does this give about ways in which the Shema should be used?

⭐ Study tip

You are allowed to write G-d rather than God in your exam and will not be penalised for doing so. Whichever version you choose, it is respectful to use an upper case G.

Summary

You should now understand key Jewish beliefs about the concept and nature of God, including the belief that God is one.

The nature of God: God as creator

■ Jewish beliefs about creation

The **Torah** begins with these words:

> **❝** When God began to create heaven and earth … **❞**
>
> *Genesis* 1:1

So right from the very start of the Torah, the belief that God is the **creator** is established. Jews believe that God created the universe out of nothing, exactly how he wanted it to be.

The book of Genesis tells how God took six days to create the universe and everything in it. Many **Orthodox** and **ultra-Orthodox Jews** believe that this is a literal truth and that it happened around 6000 years ago. They reject scientific theories of evolution. Other Jews accept that an evolutionary theory may be correct and that the universe is much older, but that God made everything happen. They still believe that God is the creator, but do not take the creation story in Genesis literally.

According to the creation story, it took four days for God to get the universe fit to support life and a further two days to create all living creatures. On the seventh day, God rested and made it a holy day. Jews remember this every week between sunset on Friday to night time on Saturday during the observance of **Shabbat**. In doing so, Jews are regularly reminded of God's importance and role in the creation of everything.

▲ *The earth seen from the moon*

■ Evil and free will

Jews believe that in order for God to have the ability and power to create the universe, it is essential he has characteristics that no other living being has. Jews believe that God is:

Objectives

- Understand the Jewish belief that God is the creator and the sustainer.
- Understand how this relates to the concepts of evil and free will.

Key terms

- **Torah:** (1) the five books of Moses, which form the first section of the Tenakh/Tanach (the Jewish Bible) (2) the Jewish written law
- **creator:** the one who makes things and brings things about
- **Orthodox Jews:** Jews who emphasise the importance of following the laws and guidance in the Torah; they believe the Torah was given directly by God to Moses, so should be followed as closely as possible
- **ultra-Orthodox Jews:** Jews who are even more committed than Orthodox Jews to strictly following the laws and guidance in the Torah
- **Shabbat:** the Jewish holy day of the week; a day of spiritual renewal starting shortly before sunset on Friday and continuing to night time on Saturday
- **omnipotent:** almighty, having unlimited power; a quality of God
- **omniscient:** knowing everything; a quality of God
- **omnipresent:** being everywhere at all times; a quality of God

- **omnipotent** – all powerful
- **omniscient** – all knowing
- **omnipresent** – being everywhere at all times.

Jews believe that God is the creator of everything; there is no concept in Judaism that evil was created by the devil. They believe that God, as the only creator, must have created evil himself. However, he also gave people the free will to choose what they know is right, and to reject evil as being completely against God.

Jews believe that in order for people to have free will, they have to be able to make their own choices between good and bad, which is why evil needs to exist. Being able to *choose* to do good also makes the act of doing good more significant.

Some find it difficult to accept that God created the potential for evil – particularly when remembering events such as the Holocaust (Shoah), when Jews faced extreme persecution – but it is considered to be a necessary consequence of giving humans free will.

The belief in one God who creates everything, including the potential for evil, is reinforced in Isaiah 45:6–7.

▲ *'God saw all that He had made, and found it very good' (Genesis 1:31)*

■ God the sustainer

Jews believe that God not only created the universe but also sustains it. This means that God provided sufficient resources on the planet to feed and provide for all species. The fact that resources are distributed unequally, so that some have less than they need, is a result of human free will, granted by God. Those who follow Jewish teaching by helping to provide resources for others who have too little are helping to fulfil God's plan for the world he created.

⭐ Study tip

The three words beginning with omni, meaning 'all' – omnipotent, omniscient and omnipresent – are important words to remember when referring to Jewish beliefs about the nature of God.

Activities

1 Carefully explain the Jewish belief that God is the creator.

2 Why can it be difficult to accept that God created evil as well as good?

3 Explain what it means when Jews call God 'the sustainer'.

> ❝ I am the LORD and there is none else, I form light and create darkness, I make weal and create woe – I the LORD do all these things. ❞
>
> *Isaiah 45:6–7*

Discussion activity

With a partner, discuss what Isaiah 45:6–7 means in regards to the Jewish belief in one God.

Summary

You should now understand what it means when Jews call God 'the creator' and 'the sustainer'. You should also understand Jewish beliefs about evil and free will.

The nature of God: God as lawgiver and judge; the divine presence

■ God as lawgiver

In order to help people to exercise their free will in the way he would like them to, God gave the Jews many laws that he expects them to obey. The foundation for these laws are the **Ten Commandments**. God gave these to Moses after he rescued the Jewish slaves from Egypt, probably in the thirteenth century BCE. They were originally inscribed on two tablets of stone and Jews still consider these laws to be of great importance.

Altogether the Torah contains 613 laws that govern how people should behave. These are called **mitzvot** and they form the basis of the Halakhah, which is the accepted code of conduct for Jewish life. By obeying these various laws, Jews believe they are doing what God requires of them and fulfilling his will on earth.

In providing the Ten Commandments and the other mitzvot, Jews believe that God has set the basis of his relationship with his people, and that that is the purpose of God being the lawgiver.

▲ *Studying and obeying the mitzvot in the Torah is very important to Jews*

■ God as judge

Jews believe that God not only gave them laws to follow, but also judges them for how well they follow those laws. They believe that God judges everyone – whether they are a Jew or not – based on their actions, behaviour and beliefs. Jews believe that God's judgements are fair and always tempered by his loving, **merciful** nature; the qualities of justice and mercy are perfectly balanced.

For Jews there are two main times when God's judgement happens. The first is once a year during the festival of Rosh Hashanah (the Jewish new year), when God judges people for their actions over the past year and decides what the coming year will bring them. This festival offers Jews

Links

For more on Moses and the Ten Commandments see pages 20–21.

Links

For more on mitzvot see pages 26–27.

the chance to reflect on their behaviour over the year, repent for their wrongdoings and pray for goodness and happiness for themselves and their families.

Many Jews also believe they will be judged after death, when God determines where they will spend their afterlife.

◼ The divine presence (Shekhinah)

The word **Shekhinah** does not appear in the Tenakh, but its meaning is present in many passages. Shekhinah means 'God's manifested glory' or 'God's divine presence'. It refers to the presence of God on earth.

Many Jewish writings refer to the Tabernacle – a portable structure, similar to a tent – as being the early dwelling place for the divine presence of God. The Jews carried the Tabernacle with them on their journey after their exodus from Egypt, through the wilderness, to the conquering of the land of Canaan.

At times, the Tenakh mentions that the Jews were led on this journey by a pillar of fire or a cloud, which were also possible manifestations of the Shekhinah. So the Shekhinah is associated with God's presence among his people and their experience of the Spirit of God. It is seen as a sign of his power and glory.

After Canaan was conquered, the Tabernacle was replaced with Solomon's **Temple** in Jerusalem in the tenth century BCE. Several of the prophets, including Isaiah, Jeremiah and Ezekiel, made reference to the presence of God in the temple.

> ❝ In the year that King Uzziah died, I beheld my LORD seated on a high and lofty throne; and the skirts of His robe filled the Temple. Seraphs stood in attendance on Him. ❞
>
> *Isaiah 6:1–2*

▲ *An early twentieth-century model of Solomon's Temple*

A small number of Jews believe that the Shekhinah is the feminine presence of God, because in Hebrew Shekhinah is a feminine word.

Research activity

Over the centuries, there were two temples built or rebuilt on Temple Mount: Zerubbabel's Temple and Herod's Temple. Find out when and why they were built, and who built them. Then find out about the Holy of Holies.

Discussion activity

With a partner, discuss what might be meant by the feminine presence of God.

Activities

1 Carefully explain God's role as lawgiver.

2 Explain how laws help people to use their free will responsibly.

3 Explain the Jewish belief in the Shekhinah. Exodus 40:34–35 gives an example that will help you.

Summary

You should now understand how Jews view God as the lawgiver and judge, and understand the meaning of Shekhinah.

1.4 Life after death, judgement and resurrection

■ Jewish customs surrounding death

Jews believe that because it is part of God's plan, death is an inevitable part of life. Judaism teaches that Jews should not die alone, although of course this is not always possible to achieve. The dying person's family should make every effort to visit and look after them, and ensure there is always somebody with them. It is considered to be an act of great kindness to be present at the time of death and to close the dead person's eyes. Upon hearing of a death of a loved one, Jews make a blessing to God:

> **❝** Blessed are You, Lord our God, King of the universe, the True Judge. **❞**

Intense mourning follows a person's death, especially while waiting for their burial, then for seven days after the burial, followed by a further 30 days of lesser mourning.

Jews follow these traditional customs to show respect to the dying person, and to show they accept that God has taken their loved one's life.

■ Jewish beliefs about the afterlife

There is little teaching about life after death in the Jewish holy books, and beliefs about it have developed over the centuries. This has led to differences between Jews in their ideas about what happens after death. Some believe that life after death will be a physical life, while others believe it will be spiritual.

Heaven and Sheol

Teachings about the afterlife imply that the good will enter paradise (Gan Eden) while others will go to a place sometimes referred to as Sheol. This is seen as a place of waiting where souls are cleansed. Even though many Jews believe that those who follow their faith properly will be judged good enough for paradise, there is no clear teaching about what paradise is like. It is believed that heaven will be with God, but it is not known whether it is a state of consciousness, or an actual physical or spiritual place.

Judgement and resurrection

Some Jews believe they will be judged by God as soon as they die; this view is supported for example by Ecclesiastes 12:7, which suggests that **judgement** happens upon or shortly after death.

▲ Graves in a Jewish cemetery marked with the Star of David – a symbol commonly used to represent Judaism

---

Objective

- Understand what Jews believe about what happens after death.

Key terms

- **judgement:** the belief that God judges a person based on their actions, and either rewards or punishes them as a result
- **resurrection:** the belief that after death the body remains in the grave until the end of the world, before rising again when God will come to judge
- **rabbi:** a Jewish religious leader and teacher

Links

To learn more about mourning rituals see pages 52–53.

Some believe that God will judge everyone on the Day of Judgement, after the coming of the Messiah. This is when God will decide who goes to heaven and who goes to hell. This is the view taken in Daniel 12:2.

Daniel looks forward to a time of **resurrection** at some point in the future. In Judaism, resurrection is the idea that at some point after death, people will rise from their graves to live again. However, many Jews reject the idea of resurrection, whether physical or spiritual. They have no firm view on what happens after death.

One of the reasons for the lack of agreement about the afterlife is that Jews believe the present is more important, and they should focus on living in a way that is pleasing to God. The idea that it is best to focus on the present rather than the afterlife is told in the following story by Rabbi Benjamin Blech (a contemporary American **rabbi**):

> ❝ A very wealthy man, not known for his piety, stood in a long line of those waiting to have their lives assessed by the heavenly court. He listened attentively as those who were being judged before him recounted both their spiritual failings and achievements. A number of them seemed to have the scales weighted against them until they suddenly remembered acts of charity they had performed, which dramatically tipped the scales in their favour. The rich man took it all in and smiled to himself.
>
> When it was his turn, he confidently said, 'I may have committed many sins during my lifetime, but I realise now what has the power to override them. I am a very wealthy man and I will be happy to write out a very large cheque to whatever charity you recommend.'
>
> To which the court replied, 'We are truly sorry, but here we do not accept cheques – only receipts.' ❞
>
> Rabbi Benjamin Blech, 'Life after death', www.aish.com

> ❝ Many of those that sleep in the dust of the earth will awake, some to eternal life, others to reproaches, to everlasting abhorrence. ❞
>
> *Daniel* 12:2

> ❝ And the dust returns to the ground As it was, And the lifebreath returns to God Who bestowed it. ❞
>
> *Ecclesiastes* 12:7

Activities

1 Why do you think Jews prefer to focus on this life rather than the next?

2 Do you agree that this is a good idea? Explain your reasons.

3 Explain different Jewish views about judgement after death.

4 Why do you think there are few references to life after death in the Tenakh?

Discussion activity 💬

With a partner, discuss what, if anything, you think happens after death.

⭐ Study tip

If you are writing about a topic like resurrection or judgement, try to include different views to show that some Jews believe one thing while others believe differently.

Summary

You should now understand what Jews believe about life after death, including different views on judgement and resurrection.

▲ *Jews believe they should focus on living in a way that is pleasing to God, for example by observing the mitzvot or helping the poor; here Jewish volunteers are putting together kosher food packages*

1.5 The nature and role of the Messiah

◼ Origins of the Messiah

In the twelfth century Rabbi Moses ben Maimon, also known as Maimonides, compiled the 'Thirteen Fundamental Principles of Jewish Faith', based on the Torah. The twelfth principle is 'The belief in the arrival of the **Messiah** and the Messianic era.' The nature and role of the Messiah is the cause of great debate among many in the Jewish community.

The word Messiah means 'anointed one', and was originally used in the Tenakh to refer to the kings of Israel. The first king of Israel was Saul, who lived around the eleventh century BCE. In anticipation of Saul being made king, the prophet Samuel anointed him to show that he was chosen by God:

> ❝ Samuel took a flask of oil and poured some on Saul's head and kissed him, and said, 'The LORD herewith anoints you ruler over His own people.' ❞
>
> *1 Samuel* 10:1

Samuel also made a prediction about Saul which came true immediately:

> ❝ The spirit of the LORD will grip you, and you will speak in ecstasy along with them; you will become another man. And once these signs have happened to you, act when the occasion arises, for God is with you. ❞
>
> *1 Samuel* 10:6–7

▲ *Saul is anointed by Samuel*

Objectives

- Understand the nature and role of the Messiah.
- Consider different beliefs about the Messiah.

Key terms

- **Messiah:** 'the anointed one'; a leader of the Jews who is expected to live on earth at some time in the future
- **Messianic age:** a future time of global peace when everyone will want to become closer to God, possibly through the intervention of the Messiah

Activities

1. Explain different Jewish beliefs about the role of the Messiah.
2. What do Jews believe the Messianic age will be like?
3. If the Messiah came this year, what do you think Jews would want him to do? Explain your reasons.
4. Explain why the belief in the Messiah might provide comfort to Jews in bad times.

■ The nature of the Messiah

Today, many Jews use the term 'Messiah' to refer to a future leader of the Jews. There is no suggestion in Judaism that Saul is connected to the coming Messiah, especially as he disobeyed God once he became king. However, the way that God changed Saul is also likely to apply to the future Messiah. The Messiah is expected to be a future king of Israel – a descendent of Saul's successor, King David – who will rule the Jews during what is known as the **Messianic age**.

Jews who believe in the future Messianic age debate about what it will be like and when it will come. Some believe the dead will be resurrected and live in a time of peace in a restored Israel. The prophet Micah describes it as a time when war will end and people will live in universal peace and harmony:

> ❝ And they shall beat their swords into plowshares, And their spears into pruning hooks. Nation shall not take up, Sword against nation; They shall never again know war. ❞
>
> *Micah 4:3*

Orthodox Jews believe that in every generation there is a descendent of King David who has the potential to be the Messiah. If the Jews are worthy of redemption, this person will be directed by God to become the redeemer and will rule over all humanity with kindness and justice. He will also uphold the law of the Torah and will be the ultimate teacher of it. In addition, he will rebuild the temple in Jerusalem and gather all Jews back to the land of Israel. He will usher in world peace and unite humanity as one. Each of these expectations is outlined in the Tenakh.

In contrast, many in Reform Judaism reject the idea of a Messiah. Instead of believing in one specific person who will unite the world in peace, they believe that everyone should work together to achieve that peace. They still believe in a future Messianic age, but one that is achieved through people's collective actions, including observance of religious obligations, rather than as the result of the leadership of one person.

▲ *The star of David appears on the flag of Israel and is named after the king from whom the Messiah will be descended*

While Christians believe that Jesus was the Messiah, Jews firmly do not. This is because Jesus did not fulfill the expectations that the Jews have for their Messiah, especially in his observance of Torah law and because Jews do not believe he established the Messianic age.

The belief in the coming of the Messiah has provided some hope and comfort for Jews facing persecution and hardship. Many Jews murdered in the death camps during the Second World War went to their deaths proclaiming their belief in God and in the coming of the Messiah.

> **Discussion activity**
>
> 'People should work together to establish peace on earth rather than waiting for the Messiah to do it.'
>
> With a partner, discuss whether you agree with this statement and give reasons that support and oppose your opinion.

Summary

You should now understand the nature and role of the Messiah. You should also have considered different Jewish beliefs about the Messiah.

⭐ **Study tip**

When writing about the Messiah, remember that different groups of Jews have different beliefs about the Messiah's role and importance.

1.6 The Promised Land and the covenant with Abraham

■ Abraham and the Promised Land

According to Jewish tradition, Abraham was born in the city of Ur in Mesopotamia, probably in the twentieth or nineteenth century BCE. At that time, it was common for people to worship idols of many different gods. From an early age, Abraham became convinced that there could be only one God who created everything, and that worshipping idols was wrong. He tried to spread this message to the people of Ur but with little success. The belief that there is only one God is called **monotheism**.

▲ The city of Ur was excavated in 1929

Abraham, together with his wife Sarah, father Terah and some other family members, left Ur to travel to Canaan. However, they did not reach Canaan, choosing instead to settle on the way at Haran in Northern Mesopotamia where, sometime later, Terah died.

The book of Genesis tells that God told Abraham to continue the journey to Canaan and made a promise to him:

> **‟** The LORD said to Abram [Abraham], 'Go forth from your native land and from your father's house to the land that I will show you. I will make of you a great nation, And I will bless you; I will make your name great, And you shall be a blessing. I will bless those who bless you, And curse him that curses you; And all the families of the earth, Shall bless themselves by you.' **”**
>
> *Genesis 12:1–3*

Once Abraham and Sarah reached Canaan, God told Abraham to look all around him and said that, 'for I give all the land that you see to you and your offspring forever' (Genesis 13:15).

God's promises to Abraham mean that Canaan (which includes present-day Israel) has become known as the **Promised Land**.

The covenant with Abraham

The word **covenant** means agreement. A covenant benefits both parties; it includes promises and sometimes responsibilities that should be undertaken. Jews believe that the covenants that God has made in history with people such as Adam, Abraham and Moses were binding for those individuals, the people they represented and God. Jews believe the covenants still apply to them today. Even though in the past some people have broken their side of the covenant (indeed some Jews broke the covenant between God and Moses soon after it had been agreed), Jews believe that God never has and never will break his side.

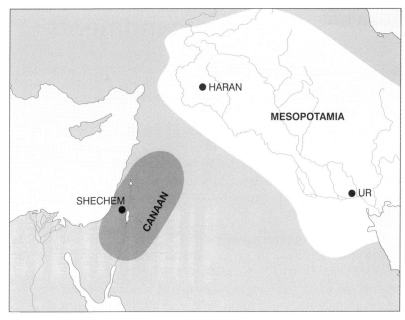

▲ *Map of the area around Canaan in Abraham's time*

The existence of covenants between the Jews and God has led to a belief that Jews were specially chosen by God to be his people (see Deuteronomy 14:2).

Although some have interpreted statements such as this as meaning that Jews believe they are in some way superior to all others, this is a misunderstanding. Jews themselves focus on the responsibilities of being chosen by God with no thought of superiority.

Covenants are sealed by oaths, often supported by a special action such as a sacrifice. In the case of the covenant with Abraham, it was supported by the action of **circumcision**. Once God had told Abraham the terms of the covenant, which was that he would make Abraham the father of many nations if Abraham would 'walk in My [God's] ways and be blameless' (Genesis 17:1), Abraham proved his acceptance by being circumcised himself and by circumcising all the males in his household.

To make it possible for Abraham to become the father of a great nation, God enabled Abraham's wife Sarah to conceive despite the fact that she was very elderly and had previously been unable to conceive. Coming so soon after the covenant was established, Sarah's pregnancy and the birth of a son, Isaac, may be seen as a gift from God to mark the covenant between God and Abraham.

> **❝** For you are a people consecrated to the Lord your God: of all the peoples on earth the Lord your God chose you to be His treasured people. **❞**
>
> *Deuteronomy 7:6*

Links

For more about circumcision in present-day Judaism see pages 46–47.

⭐ Study tip

If you are referring to a particular covenant, try to remember to include the name of the person with whom God made the covenant (most likely Abraham or Moses).

Summary

You should now know about Abraham's journey to the Promised Land, and understand the covenant that was made between Abraham and God.

Activities

1 Explain the meaning of the term covenant.

2 Explain the promise God made to Abraham as his side of the covenant.

3 How did Abraham support the oath he made to God?

4 How did God make it possible for Abraham to be the father of a great nation?

The covenant at Sinai and the Ten Commandments

■ The escape from Egypt

About 400 years after God established the covenant with Abraham, the Jews found themselves as slaves in Egypt. For many it was difficult to follow the faith established by Abraham. The Torah tells the story of Moses, who was rescued from the river Nile as a baby and brought up in the royal palace. He was chosen by God when he fled to escape being put to death for killing an Egyptian who was ill-treating a Jewish slave. God gave instructions to Moses by speaking to him through a bush that appeared to be on fire.

God told Moses to approach the Egyptian pharaoh and ask him to release the Jews from slavery so they could leave Egypt to return to Canaan, the Promised Land. Eventually, after God sent a number of plagues to Egypt, the final and worst one being the death of the firstborn child in every Egyptian family, the pharaoh was persuaded to allow them to leave. They travelled across the Sea of Reeds (also referred to as the Red Sea), once God had parted the waters to allow them through. Estimates of the number of Jews who escaped from Egypt range from several thousand to around 3 million (the latter number is more consistent with the story in the Torah, which refers to around 600,000 men, most of whom probably had wives and children travelling with them).

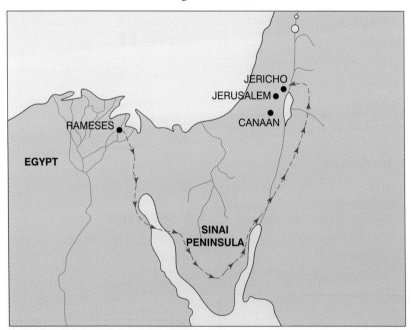

▲ *Map of the possible route taken by the Jews as they escaped Egypt*

■ The Ten Commandments

Once across the Sea, the Jews wandered for many years in the desert in the Sinai region between Egypt and Canaan. When they arrived

Objectives

- Know about the covenant at Sinai, including the role and importance of Moses in establishing the covenant.
- Know the Ten Commandments and understand their importance.

Key term

- **Ten Commandments:** ten laws given by God to Moses over 3000 years ago

Discussion activity

The Jews have developed a belief that they are God's chosen people. With a partner, discuss how you think the story of Moses and the covenant has contributed to this belief.

at Mount Sinai, Moses ascended the mountain, leaving the Jews at the base. While on Mount Sinai, God gave Moses ten laws, four of them concerning the relationship between the Jews and God and six concerning their relationships with each other. These were carved on two tablets of stone that Moses carried down the mountain. In this way the **Ten Commandments** were given to the Jews.

The Ten Commandments are recorded in Exodus 20:1–17 and also in Deuteronomy 5:6–21.

> **I the Lord am your God** who brought you out of the land of Egypt, the house of bondage.
>
> **You shall have no other gods beside Me**. You shall not make for yourself a sculptured image or any likeness of what is in the heavens above, or on the earth below, or in the waters under the earth. You shall not bow down to them or serve them …
>
> **You shall not swear falsely by the name of the Lord your God;** for the Lord will not clear one who swears falsely by His name.
>
> **Remember the sabbath day and keep it holy**. Six days you shall labor and do all your work, but the seventh day is a sabbath of the Lord your God … For in six days the Lord made heaven and earth and sea, and all that is in them, and He rested on the seventh day; therefore the Lord blessed the sabbath day and hallowed it.
>
> **Honor your father and your mother**, that you may long endure on the land that the Lord your God is assigning to you.
>
> **You shall not murder. You shall not commit adultery. You shall not steal. You shall not bear false witness against your neighbor.**
>
> **You shall not covet** your neighbor's house: you shall not covet your neighbor's wife, or his male or female slave, or his ox or his ass, or anything that is your neighbor's. **"**
>
> *Exodus* 20:1–17

Activities

1 Explain why Moses asked the pharaoh to allow the Jews to leave Egypt.
2 What special event happened to Moses on Mount Sinai? (See Exodus 19:16–25.)
3 Explain why God gave the Ten Commandments to Moses.

★ Study tip

When referring to the Ten Commandments, it is acceptable to use a simplified version rather than the full version from Exodus 20:1–17.

Summary

You should now understand how the Ten Commandments were given to the Jews, and why they are important. You should also understand the terms of the covenant between God and the Jews.

The Ten Commandments form the basis of the covenant between God and the Jews. The terms of the covenant were that God would be the God of the Jews and would protect them from harm, provided they obeyed his laws in return. This is the basis of the belief that the Jews are the chosen people of God. The Ten Commandments gave the Jews important guidance on how to create a society where people had basic rights and were able to live in peace with each other.

Moses died in Moab, just before the Jews reached the Promised Land of Canaan. He was succeeded by Joshua, who led the Jews across the River Jordan into the Promised Land. After winning several battles, including a famous one at Jericho, the Jews settled into their new home.

▲ *The possible location of Mount Sinai, in the Sinai Peninsula in Egypt*

As with all religions, most Jews see Judaism as a complete way of life. In addition to providing opportunities and methods to acknowledge and worship God, it also provides guidance to help believers to live in a way that is pleasing to God. The last six of the Ten Commandments outline ways in which this can be achieved, and they are further developed in other Jewish teachings.

■ Justice

For Jews, pursuing **justice** is a sacred duty that can only be achieved when accompanied by truth and peace. It can be defined as bringing about what is right and fair, according to the law, or making up for a wrong that has been committed. According to the prophet Micah, God requires his people 'to do justice and to love goodness, and to walk modestly with your God' (Micah 6:8).

The prophet Amos expresses the wish that people should:

> ❝ But let justice well up like water, Righteousness like an unfailing stream. ❞
>
> *Amos* 5:24

Jews believe that the Torah and the prophets were sent by God to help people understand and bring about justice in a way that demonstrates mercy. The laws in the Torah give important guidance on the treatment of the poor and vulnerable, in order that justice can be achieved for them as well as for the rich and powerful. For Jews there is never any reason to ignore justice or the suffering of others. Creating a just society requires all individuals to contribute by living their lives correctly, following the laws of the Torah.

■ Healing the world

The concept of **healing** (or repairing) **the world** (tikkun olam) is very important in Judaism. While Jewish scholars have debated it widely, many see it simply as an action that draws people closer to God. For many Jews it motivates them to get involved in work designed to increase social justice, for example by volunteering for a **charity** that helps the poor or protects the environment.

Some Jews believe this understanding of healing the world by doing charity work or similar actions is too limited. They believe the term should encompass much more, including obeying the mitzvot and trying to become closer to God spiritually, for example through prayer.

Objective

- Understand the Jewish moral principles of justice, healing the world, and kindness to others.

Key terms

- **justice:** bringing about what is right and fair, according to the law, or making up for a wrong that has been committed
- **healing the world (tikkun olam):** being involved in God's work to sustain the world; it can involve work to increase social justice or to preserve the environment
- **charity:** (1) providing help and love to those in need (2) an organisation that does not make a profit, whose main purpose is to help those in need
- **kindness to others:** positive, caring actions that should be shown to all living things

▲ *Jewish and Muslim volunteers prepare Christmas day meals for the homeless*

▲ *Young Jews in Israel plant trees to help the environment*

GIFT

GIFT (Give It Forward Today) is a Jewish charity which was started in 2003. Its aim is to inspire and educate young people to become givers, while also helping those in need in society. It is based on the premise that in a generation largely focused on the individual, the value and importance of giving is often forgotten. The purpose of GIFT is to shift attitudes and practical behaviour towards giving. GIFT is driven by the belief that all relationships in society, from friendship and marriage to parenting and community involvement, will be enhanced as a result of nurturing this particular value and trait in the individual. GIFT's educational workshops are designed to lead to practical initiatives, such as:

- collecting, packaging and delivering food parcels to hundreds of needy families each week
- twinning young people with a wide array of volunteer opportunities
- running creative, interactive and educational sessions in schools, youth groups and communities across the UK
- organising celebratory parties which benefit children and those in need
- encouraging fundraising and a sense of personal and social responsibility in support of all worthy causes
- organising hospital and retirement home visits.

■ Kindness to others

Kindness to others is an important concept in Judaism. Many of the laws of the Torah spell out how to be kind to others and this is something Jews must aim to achieve. The Torah laws not only forbid murder and other negative actions, but also provide positive laws to encourage acts of kindness. These should be shown to all living things, both Jews and non-Jews alike. Leviticus 19 twice instructs Jews to love people as they love themselves:

> ❝ You shall not take vengeance or bear a grudge against your countrymen. Love your fellow as yourself. ❞
>
> *Leviticus* 19:18

> ❝ The stranger who resides with you shall be to you as one of your citizens; you shall love him as yourself, for you were strangers in the land of Egypt. ❞
>
> *Leviticus* 19:34

Research activity

Find out about how the charity World Jewish Relief helps the healing of the world. You could start by reading about an example of their work in Chapter 8, page 169.

Extension activity

Leviticus 19 contains a large number of laws that are designed to help people show kindness to others. Read Leviticus 19:1–18 and write down five laws that you think show kindness to others most strongly.

Activities

1. Explain what justice is.
2. Explain how Judaism interprets the moral principle of justice.
3. Choose the quote from either Micah or Amos and explain what it says about justice.
4. Explain the meaning of healing the world.
5. Explain how the Torah law shows the importance of showing kindness to others.

★ Study tip

You may find it helpful to consider and refer to the concepts of justice, healing the world and kindness to others in other sections of your course, especially in the ethical themes.

Summary

You should now understand the moral principles of justice, healing the world and kindness to others.

Sanctity of life

■ What does the 'sanctity of life' mean?

Belief in the **sanctity of life** is important in many faiths, including Judaism. For Jews, the belief stems from the story of creation in Genesis, when humans were created in the image of God. The story tells that God breathed life into Adam and into the whole of creation. Life is therefore seen to be holy and sacred because it is given by God. This is the meaning of the phrase 'sanctity of life'. It particularly applies to humans (rather than animals) because they were made in God's image.

How this affects Jewish beliefs about ending life

Believing in the sanctity of life helps Jews to work out whether an action is moral and acceptable to God. It is a key consideration in such areas as war, murder, abortion, euthanasia and capital punishment. Put simply, belief in the sanctity of life means that life is sacred, special and valuable because it belongs to God. God gives life to humans and that means only he has the right to take it away.

As life belongs to God, preserving life is a duty in Judaism. Death cannot be made to come more quickly than it would from natural causes. For Jews this rules out such practices as active euthanasia and murder.

However, advances in medical technology mean that making life and death decisions is more complex today than it was in the past. While Jewish law states that people have a duty to preserve life, there are different opinions among scholars about what this means in practice.

Some Jews think that patients should be kept alive at all costs, while others believe that you shouldn't prolong a natural death if the patient is in great pain. For example, if a dying patient is being kept alive with a ventilator, some Jews believe it would be acceptable to remove the ventilator as it is preventing a natural death.

An important teaching about preserving life is found in the **Talmud**:

> **❝** He who destroys one soul of a human being, the Scripture considers him as if he should destroy a whole world, and him who saves one soul of Israel, the Scripture considers him as if he should save a whole world. **❞**
>
> *Sanhedrin 4:5*

The first half of this quote is engraved on the Medal of the Righteous, which the Yad Vashem organisation in Jerusalem awards to those who rescued Jews and saved their lives during the Second World War.

Objectives

- Understand the Jewish belief in the sanctity of life.
- Understand the Jewish concept of saving a life (pikuach nefesh).

Key terms

- **sanctity of life:** all life is holy as it is created and loved by God; human life should not be misused or abused
- **Talmud:** a commentary by the rabbis on the Torah – it consists of the Mishnah and Gemara together in one collection
- **pikuach nefesh:** the obligation to save a life, even if doing so breaks Jewish law

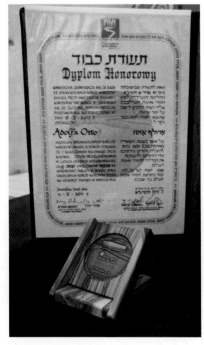

▲ *The Medal of the Righteous presented in 2011*

■ Saving a life (pikuach nefesh)

> **❝** Do not profit by the blood of your fellow. **❞**
>
> *Leviticus* 19:16

Although life is sacred and only God can give or take it, there are circumstances in which Jews believe that humans have a responsibility to take part in preserving life. In Judaism, the obligation to save life – **pikuach nefesh** – emphasises how valuable human life is for Jews, as it takes precedence over other responsibilities and most Jewish laws.

Transplant surgery is a way of preserving life in cases of disease or failure of certain organs. Many Jews agree with transplant surgery and feel it is a great honour to donate organs to save another person's life, although some disagree because they believe that the body should be complete when buried and donated organs make this impossible.

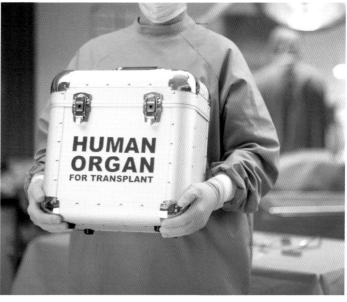

▲ *Some Jews believe that transplant surgery respects the sanctity of life and pikuach nefesh*

Jews are required to observe Shabbat, which means they are not allowed to do certain types of 'creative' work from sunset on Friday until night time on Saturday. Logically this would prevent saving life if it involved work. However, the principle of pikuach nefesh allows Shabbat law to be set aside if it is in order to save a life.

The Talmud contains several instances where it is permissible to break Shabbat law in order to save life. These include rescuing a child from the sea, breaking apart a wall that has collapsed on a person and putting out a fire that is endangering life. In more modern times, it might include driving a sick or injured person to hospital or performing a life-saving operation.

Activities

1 Referring to the belief in the sanctity of life, explain why ending life early is against Jewish beliefs and teachings.

2 How does believing in the sanctity of life help Jews to live in the way God wants them to?

3 Explain why deciding how to respect the sanctity of life may be more difficult today than in the past.

4 Explain how believing in pikuach nefesh helps Jews to respect the sanctity of life.

Extension activity

Find out what some people did to be awarded the Medal of the Righteous.

★ Study tip

You will not be expected to know many Hebrew terms, but pikuach nefesh is one that may be helpful for you to know and use.

Summary

You should now understand what belief in the sanctity of life means, and why it is important to Jews. You should also understand the concept of pikuach nefesh.

1.10 Free will and mitzvot

■ Free will

The story of Adam and Eve's disobedience in Genesis 3 teaches Jews that God has allowed them to choose how they can live their lives. This is called **free will**. However, these choices will always have consequences. Choosing to act in a way that pleases God should bring about a life of fulfilment, and a guarantee that God will judge Jews favourably on the Day of Judgement. However, Jews believe that using free will to justify actions that are wrong – such as stealing or worshipping different gods – will not bring them closer to God in life or after death. In the story of Adam and Eve, it is made clear that when Eve disobeyed God and persuaded Adam to do the same, the consequences were severe and continue to affect humankind today.

▲ *Young Jewish women studying the Torah*

Objectives

- Understand the relationship between free will and mitzvot.
- Understand the different types of mitzvot: mitzvot between man and God and mitzvot between man and man.
- Understand the importance of the mitzvot.

Key terms

- **free will:** belief that God gives people the opportunity to make decisions for themselves
- **mitzvot:** Jewish rules or commandments

Links

To read more about Jewish beliefs in life after death, see pages 14–15.

■ Mitzvot

Mitzvot is the plural of mitzvah, which literally means commandment. However in modern times it is also used as a term for a good deed or a charitable act.

There are 613 mitzvot in the Torah and others in the Talmud, which cover such things as the correct way to worship, family issues and conduct in society. It is generally accepted that there are 248 positive mitzvot (traditionally corresponding to the number of bones in the male human body). Obeying these helps Jews to strengthen their bond with God. The 365 'negative' mitzvot (corresponding to the number of days in the year), which tell people what not to do, attempt to prevent the bond between God and humans from being damaged.

★ Study tip

Try not to think of the idea of free will as a way to justify people choosing and being allowed to do whatever they want.

As the Torah mitzvot are believed to have been given by God to the Jews while they were in Sinai under the leadership of Moses, following them carefully makes it impossible to disobey God. The mitzvot help Jews to use their free will correctly by providing divine guidance on how to live. They help Jews to make responsible choices, and ensure that the results of their choices are good and pleasing to God. This is why Jews believe they are important.

Mitzvot between man and God

The first four of the Ten Commandments govern a person's relationship with God. They tell Jews that God is the only God and that they should not make images of him or any other god, nor should they misuse his name. On the seventh day of every week they should have a day of rest and worship to honour God. Many of the mitzvot that are based on the first four commandments give further guidance on how an individual can improve their relationship with God, including in the areas of ritual, worship, sacrifice, food laws and the observance of festivals.

Mitzvot between man and man

In the Torah there are instructions that a person must love God and also love their neighbour; for Jews these are very important and cannot be separated. They believe that obeying the mitzvot that involve people's relationships with each other is pleasing to God. Indeed, a person who does not love other people cannot be said to be showing love for God.

The mitzvot between man and man cover areas such as the treatment of workers, how to settle disputes, and the types of food that can and cannot be eaten. They are not just rules telling Jews what not to do; many of them give positive advice and guidance that will help them to live as true members of their faith and their community.

Discussion activity

'People should only do what they want if the results are good and pleasing to God.' With a partner, discuss what this quote means and whether you agree with it. Give your reasons.

Activities

1 Explain why Jews do not see free will as an excuse to do whatever they want.
2 Explain how free will is linked to consequences.
3 How many mitzvot are there and what do the number of positive and negative ones correspond to?
4 Why is it important that Jews observe the mitzvot?
5 Explain in detail the difference between mitzvot between man and God and mitzvot between man and man.
6 Why do you think Jews consider the mitzvot to be so important? Give as many reasons as you can.

▲ *Observing mitzvot regarding the types of food that can be eaten helps Jews to obey God*

Summary

You should now understand how the mitzvot help Jews to use their free will. You should also understand the different types of mitzvot and why they are important to Jews.

1 Assessment guidance

Beliefs and teachings – summary

You should now be able to:

✔ explain about the nature of God, specifically the belief that God is one, the creator, the lawgiver and judge, loving and merciful

✔ explain the divine presence (Shekhinah)

✔ explain beliefs about life after death, including judgement and resurrection

✔ explain the nature and role of the Messiah, including different views on the role and importance of the Messiah.

The covenant and the mitzvot – summary

You should now be able to:

✔ explain about the promised land and the covenant with Abraham, Genesis 12:1–3

✔ explain about the covenant at Sinai and its importance, including the role of Moses and the Ten Commandments, Exodus 20:1–17

✔ explain key moral principles, including justice, healing the world, charity and kindness to others

✔ explain the importance of the sanctity of human life, including the concept of 'saving a life' (pikuach nefesh)

✔ explain the relationship between free will and the 613 mitzvot

✔ explain mitzvot between man and God and mitzvot between man and man, including the difference between them and their importance.

Sample student answer – the 4 mark question

1. Write an answer to the following practice question:

    Explain two ways in which Jewish beliefs about the life after death influence Jews today.

    [4 marks]

2. Read the following student sample answer:

    "Jews are unclear about what happens to them after death. Therefore it is difficult for them to be influenced by them. They do believe in life after death so whatever form it takes, they do try to make sure it is good for them. This means they follow the mitzvot because this means they are doing what God wants them to. This also means they treat people properly. So even though they don't know what may happen, it does influence their lives and makes them better."

3. With a partner, discuss the student answer. Can you identify two different ways beliefs influence behaviour? If so, are they simple or detailed? How accurate are they? Is there any information that is not required? Can the answer be improved? If so, how?

4. What mark (out of 4) would you give this answer? Look at the mark scheme in the Introduction (AO1). What are the reasons for the mark you have given?

5. Now swap your answer with your partner's and mark each other's responses. What mark (out of 4) would you give the response? Refer to the mark scheme and give reasons for the mark you award.

Sample student answer – the 5 mark question

1. Write an answer to the following question:

    Explain two Jewish teachings about God the Creator.

    Refer to scripture or sacred writings in your answer.

    [5 marks]

2. Read the following student sample answer:

    "Jews believe that God is the creator and that he created the earth and all living things. This information is in Genesis.

    The creation was God's choice. He created humans with a job to do. Genesis says that this job is to look after the earth for him."

    With a partner, discuss the student answer. Can you identify two different pieces of relevant and accurate teaching? If so, are they simple or detailed? Are there any errors? Is there anything important missing from the answer? Is the reference to scripture or sacred writings worth a mark? How can this answer be improved?

3. What mark (out of 5) would you give this answer? Look at the mark scheme in the Introduction (AO1). What are the reasons for the mark you have given?

4. Now swap your answer with your partner's and mark each other's responses. What mark (out of 5) would you give the response? Refer to the mark scheme and give reasons for the mark you award.

Sample student answer - the 12 mark question

1. Write an answer to the following question:

   'The covenant at Sinai is more important to Jews today than the covenant with Abraham.'

   Evaluate this statement. In your answer you should:
   - refer to Jewish teaching
   - give detailed arguments to support this statement
   - give detailed arguments to support a different point of view
   - reach a justified conclusion.   **[12 marks]**

2. Read the following student sample answer:

   "The covenant with Abraham included a promise that he would become the father of a great nation. It also made it clear that Abraham was blessed by God and that if people cursed him, God would curse them. Everybody would be blessed through Abraham. This was very important to Abraham, even though he found it difficult to believe because he was old and had no children. In order for the covenant to be made real, Abraham had to leave his country and travel to a country that God would show him. Abraham actually did this and the fact he became a father seems to have shown that God was also keeping his side of the covenant.

   However, although this is an interesting story, it doesn't really affect the lives of Jews today. They can learn lessons about things like faith and obedience but there are many other examples in the Tenakh of the importance of faith and obedience.

   On the other hand, the covenant at Sinai really is important today. Without this covenant between God and the Jews represented by Moses, we would not have the Ten Commandments and the itzvoth. This covenant was not just with an individual person like the covenant with Abraham was,. but it was with thousands of people at Sinai of whom Moses was the leader.

   Therefore, this covenant affects the way Jews live today through the laws from the Torah that they have to obey. This makes it much more important."

3. With a partner, discuss the sample answer. Consider the following questions:
   - Does the answer refer to Jewish teachings and if so what are they?
   - Is there an argument to support the statement and how well developed is it?
   - Is a different point of view offered and how developed is that argument?
   - Has the student written a clear conclusion after weighing up both sides of the argument?
   - What is good about the answer?
   - How do you think it could be improved?

4. What mark (out of 12) would you give this answer? Look at the mark scheme in the Introduction (AO2). What are the reasons for the mark you have given?

5. Now swap your answer with your partner's and mark each other's responses. What mark (out of 12) would you give the response? Refer to the mark scheme and give reasons for the mark you award.

Practice questions

1 How many mitzvot are there in the Torah?
A) 513   B) 563   C) 613   D) 663   **[1 mark]**

2 Give two people who had covenants with God in the Tenakh.   **[2 marks]**

 Study tip

If you do not know the answer, write down the names of two people from the Tenakh that you have studied – you may be correct.

3 Explain two ways in which a belief in the sanctity of human life influences Jews today.   **[4 marks]**

 Study tip

The question asks about how a belief influences Jews today. You should make sure you apply the belief to the present day, rather than just explaining it.

4 Explain two Jewish beliefs about the divine presence (Shekinah).

Refer to scripture or sacred writings in your answer.   **[5 marks]**

 Study tip

If you can't think of two beliefs, explain one belief with good reference to scripture or sacred writings.

5 'The mitzvot help Jews to use free will properly.'

Evaluate this statement. In your answer you should:
- refer to Jewish teaching
- give detailed arguments to support this statement
- give detailed arguments to support a different point of view
- reach a justified conclusion.   **[12 marks]**

 Study tip

It is a good idea to spend a couple of minutes organising your thoughts and maybe jotting down some ideas before you start your answer.

 Study tip

Your answer to question 5 will also be assessed for the quality of your spelling, punctuation and grammar. You should try not to make careless errors in the way you write.

■ What is a synagogue?

A **synagogue** is a house of assembly (the Hebrew term is Beit K'nesset) where Jews meet for prayer, worship and study. Jews can pray anywhere but there are certain prayers that can only be said in the presence of a **minyan** – a group of at least 10 adults. (In Orthodox Judaism, this needs to be 10 men over the age of 13; in Reform Judaism women can be part of the minyan as well.) Jews believe that it is good to pray together in a group, and the synagogue provides the facility to do so. As a result it is sometimes called Beit T'filah (House of Prayer).

▲ *The Star of David in the wall of a synagogue*

Synagogues are usually rectangular in shape but they can be any shape and size. There are no rules about what the building should look like from the outside, but there are usually symbols associated with Judaism that make it recognisable as a synagogue. There is sometimes a representation of a **menorah** or the **Star of David**. There are often stained glass windows showing patterns or pictures in coloured glass. The second of the Ten Commandments forbids making and worshipping idols of humans or animals, so images of humans or animals are not usually found in synagogues.

> **Objective**
>
> ● Explore the importance of the synagogue in Judaism.

> **Key terms**
>
> ● **synagogue:** a building for Jewish public prayer, study and gathering
> ● **minyan:** a group of at least 10 adults; the minimum number of Jews required for a Jewish religious service
> ● **menorah:** a many-branched candlestick that holds either seven or nine candles
> ● **Star of David (Magen David):** a symbol of Judaism said to represent the shield of King David, who ruled Israel in the tenth century BCE

▲ *A young Jew lighting a menorah*

Various names are used for the synagogue. Many Orthodox Jews often refer to the synagogue as 'shul', which means 'school' or 'place of study'. Some Reform Jews use the word 'temple' because they consider the synagogue to be a replacement for the Temple in Jerusalem, which was an important centre of worship for Jews before it was destroyed by the Romans in 70 CE.

■ The importance of the synagogue

Links

To learn about Bar and Bat Mitzvahs see pages 48–49.

The synagogue is important because it forms the centre of the Jewish religious community. It is a place of prayer, study and education, social and charitable work, as well as a social centre. It provides a focal point for the celebration of festivals and rites of passage such as a Bar Mitzvah, Bat Mitzvah or a marriage.

An important function of the synagogue is to provide a house of study (Beit Midrash). Some synagogues provide classes for the learning of Hebrew. This is important if Jews are to take a full part in study, prayer and worship, and it helps young Jews to prepare for their Bar or Bat Mitzvahs. The importance of education, however, spans the whole life of those who follow the Jewish faith. Most synagogues have a well-stocked library to enable adults to improve their knowledge and understanding of the Jewish faith, its sacred texts and its culture.

▲ *A synagogue can also be a place of study*

Most synagogues have a social hall that is used for religious and non-religious activities. The synagogue often functions as a sort of town hall where matters of importance to the community, both religious and non-religious, can be discussed. It also provides a venue for collecting money or other items to be distributed to the poor and needy, both at a local and international level. For example, Jews frequently support the work of organisations such as World Jewish Relief, and they often hold charity events to provide aid in the time of a natural disaster. The social hall can be used for a variety of activities for young children, teenagers and adults. Youth clubs, music, drama and sports groups, lunch clubs and other clubs for senior citizens may all meet there.

Discussion activity

In small groups or in pairs discuss the following statements:

'The synagogue is so important to Jews that without it the religion might not survive.'

'Jewish worship does not need to be in a synagogue.'

★ Study tip

If you are asked to explain the importance of the synagogue to the Jewish community, don't forget to include both worship and all the other activities which take place there.

Summary

You should now be able to explain the importance of the synagogue for Jews, and describe the activities that happen in a synagogue.

Activities

1 What is meant by Beit K'nesset?

2 How might a synagogue be recognised from the outside?

3 Explain why pictures of animals or humans are not usually found in synagogues.

4 Why do some Jews use the word 'shul' when referring to a synagogue?

5 Explain the importance of the synagogue to the Jewish community.

■ The prayer hall

The prayer hall of a synagogue is usually rectangular in shape, often with seats on three sides facing inwards towards the **bimah**. The fourth side includes the focal point of the synagogue – the holy Ark (**Aron Hakodesh**). The prayer hall will contain a seat for the **rabbi** and a pulpit from where sermons are delivered. Most halls also have a seat for the chazzan (a trained singer) who leads the prayers.

Patterns, Jewish symbols or extracts from the scriptures may be used as decoration, but pictures of the prophets or other human beings are not, as that would break the second commandment not to have idols.

■ The Ark (Aron Hakodesh)

The Ark (Aron Hakodesh) is regarded as the holiest place in the synagogue. This is because it is where the sacred Torah scrolls are kept and because it represents the original Ark of the Covenant. Jews believe that the original Ark was created to hold the stone tablets which contained the Ten Commandments that God gave Moses at Mount Sinai. This Ark was eventually taken to Jerusalem and placed in the Temple built by King Solomon, and was the focus of Jewish worship. In many synagogues Jews are reminded of this because above the ark there are two stone tablets on which the start of each of the Ten Commandments is written.

▲ *The Ark when opened, showing the Torah scrolls inside*

The Ark is situated at the front of the synagogue, usually set into the wall facing Jerusalem (the eastern wall in British synagogues). This means that when worshippers face the Ark, they are facing towards the city where the Temple once stood. The Aron Hakodesh is usually reached by climbing up steps, as a reminder to worshippers that God is above his people and that the sacred Torah is above humanity.

Objective

- Understand the design and religious features of a synagogue, including their importance and their use in worship.

Key terms

- **bimah:** a platform in a synagogue from where the Torah is read
- **Aron Hakodesh:** the Ark – the holiest part of the synagogue, which contains the Torah scrolls
- **rabbi:** a Jewish religious leader and teacher
- **ner tamid:** eternal light; a light that is kept burning in the synagogue above the Ark

Activities

1 Name three features that can be found in the prayer hall of a synagogue.
2 Explain the importance of the Aron Hakodesh (Ark) in the synagogue.
3 Explain why the ner tamid is kept burning at all times.
4 Describe the bimah and explain its purpose in worship.
5 Explain how features in the synagogue's prayer hall are reminders of the Temple in Jerusalem.

The Ark itself is an ornamental container or cupboard that houses the handwritten Torah parchment scrolls (Sefer Torah). It is only opened during special prayers and when removing the Torah to read during services. The remainder of the time it is covered with a curtain called the Parochet. This symbolises the curtain that was in the Temple in Jerusalem.

> ❝ [He] brought the ark inside the Tabernacle. Then he put up the curtain for screening, and screened off the Ark of the Pact – just as the LORD had commanded Moses. ❞
>
> *Exodus* 40:21

Every action involving the Ark is full of ceremony and it is considered an honour to be the person who climbs the steps, opens the doors and parts the inner curtain so that the Torah scroll may be removed.

■ The ever-burning light (ner tamid)

Each synagogue has a light that is kept burning at all times. It is placed in front of, and slightly above the Ark, and is called the **ner tamid** (eternal flame or ever-burning light). It symbolises God's presence and so is never put out. It is also a reminder of the menorah that was lit every night in the Temple in Jerusalem. Originally synagogues used an oil lamp, but now most use electric lights with an emergency power source in the event of an electricity cut.

▲ *A synagogue with the bimah in the centre*

■ The reading platform (bimah)

The bimah is a raised platform situated in most synagogues in the very centre. It is used when reading from the Torah and often by the person leading services. When the Torah scrolls are being read, the bimah is the focus of worship, and the raised platform makes it easier for the congregation to hear what is being said. To some it is a reminder that the altar was the central feature of the courtyard of the Temple in Jerusalem.

Research activity
Look up Exodus 25:10–22 to find details of the original Ark of the Covenant.

Extension activity
Find out about the connection between the ner tamid and the Jewish festival of Hanukkah.

★ Study tip
Make sure you are familiar with the Jewish terms used to describe the features in a synagogue, and are able to use them appropriately.

Discussion activity
In pairs or a small group discuss and evaluate the following statement: 'The ner tamid is the most important feature of a synagogue.' Give reasons for and against this statement.

Summary
You should now be able to describe the interior features of a synagogue, and explain their function and importance.

Worship in Orthodox and Reform synagogues

■ Different Jewish groups

Within modern Judaism there are different religious groups who have their own interpretation of the faith and ways of worshipping. The main groups in Britain today are the **Orthodox** and **Reform Jews**.

Orthodox Judaism

Orthodox Judaism is the traditional branch of the Jewish religion and was the only form of Jewish practice until the eighteenth century. Orthodox Jews emphasise the importance of obeying God's instructions as laid down in the Torah and the Talmud. They also believe that there are different roles for men and women, which result in different religious duties and responsibilities.

Reform Judaism

Reform Judaism, which is a type of Progressive Judaism, emphasises the importance of individual choice in deciding how to worship and practise the faith. Reform Jews believe that their religion should change its practices to become more relevant to modern life. They believe that it is the overall spiritual and moral code within the Torah and Talmud that must be obeyed, rather than each individual law. They also believe in equality for men and women.

■ Public worship

Jews are expected to pray three times a day and often this takes place in a synagogue. The services in the synagogue are led by either a rabbi, a **cantor** (chazzan) or a member of the congregation.

Orthodox synagogue services

In an Orthodox synagogue, the person leading the service has his back to the congregation so he is facing the Ark (Aron Hakodesh), and prays facing the same direction as the congregation. The service is conducted in Hebrew and the singing is unaccompanied. Men and women sit separately; traditionally the women sat in an upstairs gallery or at the back of the synagogue. Nowadays this arrangement is often replaced by a symbolic dividing structure between men and women sitting at the same level. Orthodox Jews believe that when men and women pray separately, they avoid distractions or sexual thoughts and it enables the focus to be on the prayers and coming close to God. They believe that a greater level of personal connection with God can be achieved in this way.

Within the Orthodox tradition, women have been working towards change in recent times, promoting greater equality, looking at ways of expanding their roles in prayer services, and taking greater community leadership roles. Currently Orthodox rabbis are all male.

> **Objective**
> - Understand some of the differences between worship in Orthodox and Reform synagogues.

> **Key terms**
> - **Orthodox Jews:** Jews who emphasise the importance of following the laws and guidance in the Torah; they believe the Torah was given directly by God to Moses, so should be followed as closely as possible
> - **Reform Jews:** Jews who believe the laws and guidance in the Torah can be adapted for modern times; they believe the Torah was inspired by God but written by humans, so can be interpreted according to the times
> - **cantor (chazzan):** a person who leads or chants prayers in the synagogue

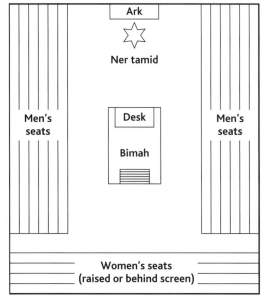

▲ *An example of the layout of an Orthodox synagogue*

▲ *A service in a Reform synagogue, where women and men sit together*

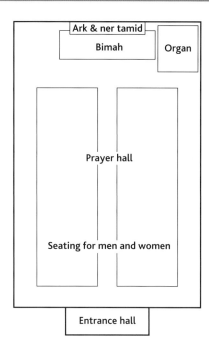

▲ *An example of the layout of a Reform synagogue*

Orthodox Jewish men always cover their heads when attending the synagogue, and some cover their heads at all times. They wear a skull cap known as a kippah or yamulkah. Some also wear a hat over the kippah. The covering of the head is a sign of respect for and fear of God; it shows that the worshipper recognises that God is above humankind. Married women also cover their heads by wearing a scarf or a hat.

Reform synagogue services

Many Reform synagogues do not hold daily services, but concentrate instead on celebrating Shabbat and festivals. In Reform synagogues the men and women sit together and the person leading the service faces the congregation most of the time. The Reform communities allow women to take a more active part than in the Orthodox tradition. Women can perform all rituals traditionally reserved for men such as becoming a rabbi, publicly reading the Torah, being a cantor and being part of the minyan. Reform services are shorter than Orthodox ones but tend to be more rigidly structured; there is a set time and all worshippers are usually present at the beginning.

Reform services are conducted in both Hebrew and the country's own language (English in the UK), and the singing may be accompanied by musical instruments. In larger synagogues in America, there is often a choir to lead the singing, but this is not common in the UK.

In a Reform service, most men wear a head-covering and some female worshippers wear a kippah or a hat.

Activities

1 Name two different groups or movements within Judaism in Britain today.
2 Explain the reasons why these groups have some different practices in worship.
3 Who leads worship in the synagogue?
4 Explain the major differences in worship between Orthodox and Reform Jews.
5 Give two reasons why Jews cover their heads in worship.

Extension activity

Look up Psalm 150, which is used as part of morning worship. Explain what it says about God and how God should be worshipped.

★ Study tip

Make a chart to show the differences between Orthodox and Reform beliefs and practices. It will help you to learn the differences.

Summary
You should now be able to explain some of the differences between the worship of Orthodox and Reform Jews.

Daily services and prayer

▪ Tallit and tefillin

During morning prayers Orthodox Jewish men wear the **tallit** and, on weekdays, the **tefillin**, and in the Reform tradition some men and women wear them as well. The tallit is a prayer shawl made from wool or silk, with a long tassel called a tzitzit attached to each corner. It is usually white with blue or black stripes. The tallit reminds Jews that they are obeying God's word whenever they wear it.

The tefillin are a pair of black leather boxes (phylacteries) containing passages of scripture, including some of the words of the Shema. One is fastened with leather straps to the centre of the forehead. The other is wound around the upper arm in line with the heart. This reminds Jews that during prayers their total concentration should be on God and the prayers should be completely from the heart.

> ❝ And this shall serve you as a sign on your hand and as a reminder on your forehead – in order that the Teaching of the LORD may be in your mouth – that with a mighty hand the LORD freed you from Egypt. ❞
>
> *Exodus* 13:9

Objectives

- Understand how Jews worship in public.
- Understand the significance of prayer for Jews, including the Amidah.

Key terms

- **tallit:** a prayer shawl
- **tefillin:** small leather boxes containing extracts from the Torah, strapped to the wearer's arm and forehead for morning prayers
- **Amidah:** also known as the 'standing prayer', it is the central prayer of Jewish worship

▪ The format of Jewish services

Prayer is extremely important to Jews as they believe that it builds the relationship between God and humankind. Devout Orthodox Jews pray three times a day. Formal prayer services are held in Orthodox synagogues in the morning, afternoon and evening, although such services need not take place in a synagogue. For Sabbath and daily services all that is required is a minimum of ten adult males (in the Orthodox tradition) or ten men and women (in the Reform tradition) to be present. Daily prayers are taken from a book called a siddur, which sets out the order of the prayers.

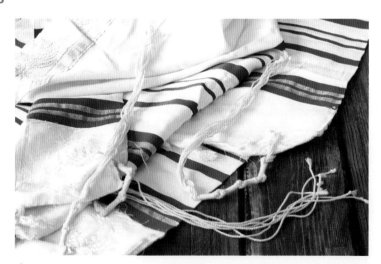

▲ *The tzitzit tassels on a tallit represent the 613 Jewish laws*

The opening prayers vary depending on the service, but might consist of a series of prayers and psalms that praise and give thanks to God.

The Shema is the Jewish statement of belief, which begins, 'Hear O Israel, the Lord our God, the Lord is One'. It is accompanied by blessings (prayers), which are said before and after the Shema.

Research activity

Use the internet to find out more about the Jewish daily prayers and how the three services differ.

The **Amidah** is also called the 'standing prayer' or the 'eighteen blessings' (although the blessings now number nineteen). On a weekday it forms the core of all Jewish prayer services, and is prayed in silence while standing and facing Jerusalem. It consists of a series of blessings:

▲ *Tefillin are fastened to the forehead and the upper arm*

- The first three blessings in the Amidah praise God; they also inspire the worshipper and ask for God's mercy.

- The middle thirteen blessings are prayers of petition and intercession (requests for God's help): they consist of six personal requests, six requests for the community, and a final request that God accept the prayers.

- The final three blessings thank God for the opportunity to serve him and pray for peace, goodness, kindness and compassion.

The Amidah is sometimes followed by a reading from the Torah.

The final prayers include the closing Aleinu prayer. This prayer is recited at the end of each of the three daily services and gives praise and thanks to God.

■ The importance of prayer

Jews believe that prayer is vital for communicating with God. They believe that prayer brings them closer to God as it enables them to focus their hearts, minds and souls on him. It reinforces their faith by helping them find new insights into their relationship with God. Formal prayer in the synagogue also helps them to remember what their faith is all about and strengthens the sense of Jewish community.

Extension activity

Look up Deuteronomy 6:4–9 and write down what this passage is telling Jews to do. Explain why these instructions are important to Jews.

Discussion activity

In small groups or in pairs evaluate the following statements:

'Jews can pray whenever they wish so they don't need set times.'

'Jews should wear the tallit and tefillin for all their prayers.'

Activities

1 Why do Jews wear the tallit and tefillin at morning prayers?

2 How many times a day is an observant Jew expected to pray?

3 Describe what happens during a typical morning prayer service in the synagogue.

4 What is the Amidah?

5 Explain why prayer is seen as very important in Judaism.

Summary

You should now be able to describe the main features of daily prayer in Judaism, and explain why prayer is important to Jews.

★ Study tip

When learning about Jewish prayer, it is important not only to know how Jews pray but also to understand why it is a central part of their religion.

Shabbat in the synagogue

■ What is Shabbat?

Every week Jews celebrate a special holy day called **Shabbat** (the Sabbath day). It is seen as a gift from God of a day of rest and renewal. Described in Jewish literature, music and poetry as a bride or queen, Shabbat provides the opportunity to relax and temporarily forget the concerns of everyday life. It is also a time to worship God and enjoy family life.

Shabbat begins just before sunset each Friday and lasts until an hour after sunset on Saturday, approximately 25 hours in total. All the shopping, cooking and cleaning is done in advance – such work isn't allowed during Shabbat itself, which is a day of rest – and Jews look forward to a very special time. It is considered the most important holy day as it was explicitly commanded by God in the Ten Commandments:

> **❝** Remember the sabbath day and keep it holy. Six days you shall labor and do all your work, but the seventh day is a sabbath of the LORD your God: you shall not do any work. **❞**
>
> *Exodus* 20:8–10

Celebrating Shabbat is a reminder of the agreement (covenant) made between God and the Jewish people, and is an occasion to rejoice that God has kept his promises. The idea of rest comes from the Genesis story in which God created everything in six days and rested on the seventh day. So Shabbat is seen as a time when the demands of a busy life can be replaced by an oasis of calm, when no work should be done. It is a time to forget distractions such as the television and internet, and instead relax and worship together as a family. Shabbat is observed and celebrated in different ways in Judaism; the following pages describe customs that are common to many Jews.

■ Shabbat services

On the Friday evening there is a brief service (which lasts around 45 minutes) in the synagogue. Shabbat is welcomed like a bride coming to meet her husband, the Jewish people. Some synagogues hold services specially designed for families with children on either Friday evening or Saturday morning. These include storytelling, discussion, games and music. At the end of the Friday service, the prayer leader takes a cup of wine and recites a blessing (Kiddush) thanking God for having given Shabbat to the Jewish people.

The Saturday morning service is longer than the weekday services and includes not only the prayers and blessings, but also a reading from the Torah and often a sermon. The Torah is divided into sections so that each week a different part is read, meaning that the entire five books of Moses are completed in a year.

▲ *A yad is used as a pointer when reading the Torah scroll*

■ The Torah

During the Saturday morning service, when the doors or curtains of the Ark (Aron Hakodesh) are opened to reveal the Torah scrolls, it is customary for the congregation to stand. This is a reminder of how the Israelites stood at the bottom of Mount Sinai when Moses returned with the Ten Commandments. The congregation chants Numbers 10:35, and the Torah is taken from the Ark and dressed with a cover and various ornaments, such as a breastplate, crown or belt. This reminds Jews of the vestments worn by the priests in early Judaism.

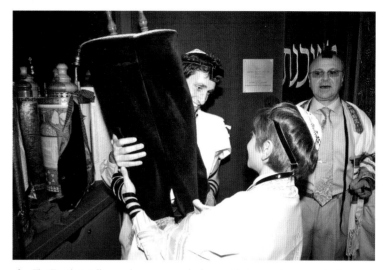

 The Torah scrolls are always covered when not being read, as a mark of respect

The Torah is held in front of the congregation while verses from scripture are chanted, after which it is paraded around the synagogue. This represents the march through the wilderness, when the Jews carried the holy Ark (containing the Ten Commandments) from Mount Sinai to Jerusalem. It also gives the congregation an opportunity to be close to the Torah and give thanks for having God's word. As it passes, many touch it with their tzitzit or siddur and then touch their lips. This is done to show that God's words should be on their lips and that his words are sweet like honey (Ezekiel 3:3).

The reading for the day (the sidra) is read from the bimah. Once this is finished the Torah scrolls are dressed again, then paraded around the synagogue once more before being placed back in the Ark.

The rabbi or visiting speaker then gives a sermon, which may be based on the sidra or something important in the news. On leaving the synagogue, Jews wish each other 'Shabbat Shalom' ('have a peaceful Shabbat').

Research activity

Use the Internet or a library to find out some of the particular things that Orthodox Jews are not allowed to do during Shabbat.

Activities

1 What is Shabbat?
2 Give three reasons why Shabbat is very special to Jews.
3 Describe what Jews do to get ready for the Shabbat celebrations.
4 What services take place in the synagogue during Shabbat?
5 Explain what happens to the Torah during the Shabbat synagogue service.

⭐ Study tip

Remember that Shabbat is both a day of rest and a day devoted to God.

Discussion activity

In small groups or in pairs discuss the following statement: 'Shabbat is a luxury that is not necessary in the modern world.'

Summary
You should now understand some of the reasons why Shabbat is special to Jews, and know how it is celebrated in the synagogue.

Shabbat preparations

In Jewish homes, all the work is done and the home is prepared before Shabbat begins on Friday evening. The house is cleaned, the food is prepared, and the family washes and changes into clean, smart clothes.

Shabbat is often seen as being like welcoming a special bride or queen into the home. The table is set with the best cutlery and crockery, and at least two candles: these represent the two commandments to remember and observe Shabbat. Many homes also have an additional candle for each member of the family.

▲ *Welcoming in the Shabbat*

Wine or grape juice and two loaves of challah bread are also placed on the table; the loaves are covered with a special cover whenever possible. (Challah bread is a type of bread made with eggs that is usually braided before baking; it is eaten on Shabbat and other special occasions.) Shabbat wine is sweet and is usually drunk from a special goblet known as the Kiddush cup. Drinking this wine on Shabbat symbolises joy and celebration. The loaves represent the two portions of manna (a type of food) that God provided for the Israelites on Shabbat while they were in the wilderness.

Lighting the candles

A female member of the family (usually the wife and mother) has the honour of lighting the candles. She lights them about eighteen minutes before sunset and once they are lit she welcomes in the Shabbat. She does this by waving or beckoning with her arms around the candles, and then covers her eyes to recite a blessing: 'Blessed are You, Lord, our God, King of the Universe, who sanctifies us with his commandments, and commands us to light the candles of Shabbat'. She also says a prayer asking God to bless the family. (If no women are present, a man lights the candles instead.)

The Friday meal

After the evening service in the synagogue, once a family has returned home, the parents bless their children and the head of the household recites the Kiddush blessings while holding up the Kiddush cup. The family say 'Amen' at the end of each blessing. Each family member then washes their hands as an act of purification before taking their place ready for the meal.

Activities

1 Describe four things that are done to prepare the home for Shabbat and explain why these actions are taken.

2 Describe how Shabbat is welcomed into the home.

3 Explain what happens at the Friday meal.

4 Why do you think that the Friday meal takes a long time?

5 Explain what happens in the ceremony that ends Shabbat.

Once everyone is seated, the head of the household removes the cover from the challah loaves and lifts them up while saying a blessing. The bread is cut into slices or broken into pieces, dipped or sprinkled in salt and passed around to each person so that everyone has a piece. Then the meal begins, which might last for a few hours. After each course, stories from the scriptures might be told to the children or songs might be sung. There is no rush as it is a time to relax and enjoy the company of the family and any friends whom they have invited. The meal ends with a prayer of thanksgiving for the food.

■ Saturday

After the morning service in the synagogue, the family enjoys another special meal in their home. During the afternoon parents may spend time with their children and study the Torah. Then there is another smaller meal before sunset.

The end of Shabbat is marked by the havdalah service. This is performed in the home after nightfall, once three stars can be seen in the sky.

▲ *A Jewish family performing the havdalah service*

Celebrating Shabbat

Ruth Cohen, an Orthodox Jew, describes how Shabbat ends:

'As the Shabbat finishes there is a bittersweet atmosphere – excitement for the coming week mixed with sadness that Shabbat has just finished. We mark the end of Shabbat with a ceremony called Havdalah. Havdalah consists of blessings performed over a cup of wine, sweet smelling spices, and a candle with several wicks. The besamim is meant to soothe the soul now that the Shabbat queen has left, and the candle is to provide a light now that the light of Shabbat has left the home.

▲ *The Havdalah candle, Kiddush cup and spices*

After the ceremony normal weekday activities may be resumed, although some Jews remain dressed in their Shabbat finest and have a meal.'

Discussion activity 💬

In pairs or small groups discuss the following statement: 'Getting prepared, as if to welcome royalty into the home, is a good way to get everything ready for Shabbat.'

⭐ Study tip

Make sure you know, in the right order, what happens when Jews celebrate Shabbat in the home. A simple diagram or flowchart might help you to remember the different steps.

Summary

You should now be able to describe how Jews observe Shabbat in the home, and explain the significance of their actions.

Worship in the home; the written and oral law

■ Worship in the home and private prayer

Jews believe that every day brings the opportunity to worship God. Prayers are said three times each day either in the home or in the synagogue. Jews traditionally stand to pray, and if they are alone they pray silently. Each house has reminders to obey God's commandments, such as a kitchen that is designed to meet the requirements of the Jewish food laws, and mezuzot. The mezuzah is a small box that contains a handwritten scroll of verses from the Torah, which is fixed to a doorpost. Jews touch the mezuzah as a sign of respect and a reminder of God's laws.

Objectives

- Understand how Jews worship and pray in the home.
- Understand what the Tenakh and Talmud contain, and why they are important to Jews.

Worshipping in the home

Janet Berenson describes what happens in her home:

'I am a member of Finchley Reform Synagogue and a Jewish Renewal community, the Ruach Chavurah, so prayer and mindfulness are important to me. I start each day with the Modeh Ani prayer, giving thanks that my soul has been returned to me, followed by the blessing thanking God that my body works as it should. I say the Shema every morning and at night. It doesn't matter where I am when I pray, as I believe that it is the practice that matters, and God hears my prayers wherever I may be.

I have a mezuzah on my front doorpost and on my bedroom door, and every time I leave and come home, I touch it to remind myself of the words of the Shema and to live my day in a way that demonstrates loving God with all my heart, soul and strength. Daily prayer helps me to stay conscious of the way I treat people, animals and the planet, and reminds me to live responsibly and ethically as a steward of God's world.'

▲ A mezuzah on the doorpost of a house

■ Study of the sacred writings

Tenakh: the written law

The Jewish sacred scriptures are known as the **Tenakh**. The Tenakh consists of 24 books (which can all be found in what Christians call the Old Testament), grouped into three main parts. The word TeNaKh is formed from taking the first letter of the Hebrew names for each of these three parts. They are:

1. the **Torah**: the five books of Moses, which form the basis of Jewish law
2. the **Nevi'im** (the Prophets): eight books that continue to trace Jewish history and expand on the laws in the Torah
3. the **Ketuvim** (the Writings): eleven books that contain a collection of poetry, stories, advice, historical accounts and more.

Activities

1. What is a mezuzah and what is its purpose?
2. Why do you think some Jews pray at home rather than in the synagogue?
3. Name the three parts of the Tenakh and explain what each part contains.
4. Explain why and how the Mishnah and Gemara were formed.
5. Explain the importance of the Talmud to Orthodox Jews.

Talmud: the oral law

Understanding the Torah (the law) is an important part of Jewish life. For the early Jews, teachings on how to interpret the Torah and apply its rules to life were passed from generation to generation by word of mouth, and became known as oral law. There was a danger that these teachings would get altered or misinterpreted and so it was important that they were written down. Rabbi Judah Hanassi did this in 200 CE by bringing together all the oral law into one document known as the Mishnah. It was formed of six sections, each one of which is known as a 'seder', dealing with subjects such as dietary laws, marriage and divorce, and laws of Shabbat.

The Mishnah caused much debate. These discussions were written down, organised and brought together in 500 CE and became known as the Gemara. The Mishnah and Gemara were then combined to form the Talmud.

The Torah and the Talmud are studied extensively by Orthodox Jews, as they are regarded as the source for all Jewish laws, legal teachings and decisions that affect their daily life. Regular lessons and lectures are held to help with this, including in colleges of advanced Jewish studies called Yeshivot. Reform Jews regard the authority of the Torah and the Talmud in a different way and may not study them as much.

▲ *Studying the sacred writings is important for many Jews*

Key terms

- **Tenakh:** the 24 books of Jewish scriptures
- **Torah:** (1) the five books revealed by God to Moses (2) the first section of the Tenakh/Tanach (the Jewish Bible), and the Jewish written law
- **Nevi'im:** the second section of the Tenakh; the prophets
- **Ketuvim:** the third section of the Tenakh; the writings
- **Mishnah:** the first written version of Jewish oral law; part of the Talmud
- **Gemara:** a commentary on the Mishnah; part of the Talmud
- **Talmud:** a commentary by the rabbis on the Torah – it consists of the Mishnah and Gemara together in one collection

⭐ Study tip

To help you remember how Jews worship in the home, make a bullet-point list of everything this involves (including at Shabbat).

Summary

You should now know how Jews worship in the home. You should also know what the Tenakh and Talmud contain, and understand their importance for Jews.

Discussion activity 💬

In pairs or in a small group discuss the following statements:

'Both the written law (Tenakh) and the oral law (Talmud) were written so long ago that they cannot be very relevant for daily life today.'

'The Talmud teaches Jews all they need to know to follow the Jewish way of life.'

Ceremonies associated with birth

■ The importance of rituals in Jewish family life

For Jews, family life is very important. The family is where the Jewish faith is preserved and passed on to the next generation. Four important events in the life of the family are celebrated with religious **rituals**. These stages in life are sometimes called 'rites of passage' because they involve moving from one phase of life to another. These are birth, coming of age, marriage and death. The wider Jewish community helps families to celebrate and observe these rites of passage.

■ Ceremonies associated with birth

For Jews the birth of a child is a happy event, especially because it fulfils the commandment in Genesis 1:28 to have children:

> ❝ God blessed them and God said to them, 'Be fertile and increase, fill the earth and master it.' ❞
>
> *Genesis* 1:28

There are three Jewish rituals associated with birth: naming, circumcision, and the redemption of the firstborn son.

Naming ceremony

Nowadays it is common for both boys and girls born into Orthodox families to be blessed in the synagogue on the first Shabbat after their birth. The father goes forward to recite the Torah blessing, and to ask God for the good health of his wife and baby. A baby girl's name will be announced at this point, but a boy will be named eight days after his birth at his circumcision. In Reform synagogues both parents will take part in the ceremony, which may not necessarily happen on the first Shabbat after the child's birth.

▲ *Strictly Orthodox Jews preparing for a Brit Milah ceremony*

Brit Milah

Circumcision recalls the covenant that God made with Abraham. It is a lifelong reminder of membership of God's chosen people.

Links

To read more about the covenant with Abraham see page 19.

> 66 You shall circumcise the flesh of your foreskin, and that shall be the sign of the covenant between Me and you. And throughout the generations, every male among you shall be circumcised at the age of eight days … any male who is uncircumcised … shall be cut off from his kin; he has broken My covenant. 99
>
> *Genesis* 17:11–14

Activities

1 Explain why rituals are important in Jewish family life.

2 Explain how the birth of a baby girl is announced in the synagogue.

3 In your own words, describe what happens at the Brit Milah ceremony, and explain why it is important to Jewish families.

Baby boys have the **Brit Milah** ceremony when they are eight days old. Traditionally, a close friend or relative is given the honour of placing the baby on an empty chair that symbolises the presence of the prophet Elijah. A trained circumciser (the mohel) picks up the baby and places him on the knee of a person chosen to be the 'companion of the child' (sandek). This is an honoured role often given to the baby's grandfather or a respected member of the synagogue congregation. The boy's father blesses his son with the words: 'Blessed are you Lord our God, King of the Universe, who sanctified us with his mitzvot and commanded us to enter my son into the covenant of Abraham.'

The others respond, 'Just as he has entered into the covenant, so may he enter into Torah, into marriage, and into good deeds.'

A blessing is said over wine and the baby is formally named. The foreskin of the baby's penis is removed in a simple operation that quickly heals. The family and guests then enjoy a festive meal to celebrate.

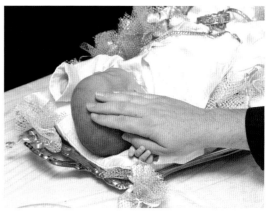

▲ *A Jewish boy is presented for redemption*

Redemption of the firstborn son

Some Orthodox Jews give a small amount of money 31 days after the birth of their firstborn son, to 'redeem' him from Temple service. The Temple in Jerusalem no longer exists, but some Orthodox parents keep up the tradition in a ceremony known as Pidyon Ha-Ben. Five silver coins are given to a kohen: a descendent of the priests who used to work in the Temple. Prayers are also said asking that the child may 'enter into Torah, into marriage, and into good deeds.'

This tradition comes from a command in Numbers 18:15–16:

> 66 The first issue of the womb of every being, man or beast, that is offered to the LORD, shall be yours; but you shall have the first-born of man redeemed … Take as their redemption price, from the age of one month up, the money equivalent of five shekels. 99
>
> *Numbers* 18:15–16

 Research activity

Find out how Reform Jews celebrate the birth of a child, including whether there are differences between celebrations for boys and girls.

Discussion activity

Discuss whether circumcision should be permitted in Britain today.

Summary

You should now be able to explain the importance of rituals in Jewish family life, and the purpose and meaning of ceremonies associated with birth, including Brit Milah.

⭐ **Study tip**

It is helpful to note the similarities and differences in the way rituals are carried out in different Jewish communities, and the importance of these rituals for each community.

2.9 Bar and Bat Mitzvah

■ Coming of age for Jews

When Jewish boys reach 13 and girls reach 12, they are considered old enough to take full responsibility for practising their faith. Boys have their **Bar Mitzvah** ceremony at 13 and become a 'son of the commandment'. Girls aged 12 may also have a **Bat Mitzvah** ceremony and become a 'daughter of the commandment'. Although there is no mention of ceremonies to mark coming of age in the Torah or Talmud, they are implied elsewhere, for example in Mishnah Berurah 225:6.

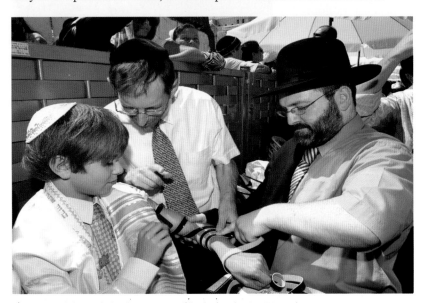

▲ *A Jewish boy is helped to put on tefillin before his Bar Mitzvah*

Celebrating a Bar Mitzvah

At the first opportunity after his thirteenth birthday (usually the first Shabbat), the boy is called to read from the Torah at the normal service in the synagogue. Many synagogues hold classes to prepare boys for this occasion. He will wear a tallit for the first time, may lead part of the service or prayers, and make a short speech. His father thanks God for bringing his son to maturity and declares that he is now responsible for his own actions. Many Jewish families then hold a celebratory meal or party in honour of the Bar Mitzvah boy and he receives gifts.

Celebrating a Bat Mitzvah

Reform Jews often have a Bat Mitzvah ceremony and celebrations for girls that are very similar to a Bar Mitzvah. The girl will read from the Torah, give a short speech, and may lead part of the prayer service. This will often be followed by a celebratory meal or party.

Since Orthodox Jewish women do not take an active role in leading synagogue worship, Orthodox Jews sometimes mark a girl's Bat Mitzvah with a family meal and small religious gifts. The girl may make a speech or give a brief Torah lesson at the end of a synagogue service. The girl's future role in keeping a Jewish home is part of Bat Mitzvah preparation for girls.

Giving a Bar Mitzvah speech

Sam Podolsky, a young American Jew, made a speech at his Bar Mitzvah explaining what it meant to him. Here is part of what he said:

'Thank you all for coming and sharing this special day with me – the day I become a Bar Mitzvah. My Torah portion … includes some of the most fundamental principles of the Jewish faith. It talks about the unity of Israel, future redemption, freedom of choice and the practicality of the Torah. It is this last principle that stands out to me … the Torah is not some far-off ideal that is beyond our reach. Rather, it is something down here on earth – that we all can relate to in our day-to-day lives … Becoming a Bar Mitzvah doesn't only mean I am becoming an adult in the Jewish religion. It also means that I am taking on the responsibilities of the Torah. Preparing for my Bar Mitzvah, such as studying, putting on tefillin and writing this speech has been meaningful to me, and I have learned so much from it. Also, becoming a Bar Mitzvah has helped me strengthen my relationship with Hashem [God] and the Torah. It has also brought me closer to my family, who were involved in my studies and have helped bring me to this day. I also found that my heritage is very important to me. I hope one day to pass along my knowledge of Judaism to my future children.'

▲ *A Jewish girl practises reading from the Torah in preparation for her Bat Mitzvah in a Reform synagogue*

Discussion activity

With a partner or in a small group, discuss the different ages when people are allowed to do certain things in Britain, such as drive, vote, watch certain films or drink. When do you think a young person 'comes of age'?

Activities

1 Explain the different ways in which Orthodox and Reform Jews mark boys' and girls' coming of age.

2 Read the case study. In your own words explain what Sam's Bar Mitzvah meant to him.

3 'Bar Mitzvah and Bat Mitzvah celebrations are no longer relevant in modern Britain.' Evaluate this statement. Be sure to include different points of view and refer to Jewish teachings in your answer.

⭐ Study tip

It is important to be able to explain the impact of a Bar or Bat Mitzvah on an individual and for the Jewish community as a whole.

Research activities

1 Find out more about how Jewish girls prepare for their Bat Mitzvah in Reform Judaism.

2 Some Jews travel to Israel with their families to celebrate their Bar or Bat Mitzvah. Use the internet to find out what might happen on these trips, and explain how a trip to Israel could make a Bar or Bat Mitzvah particularly special.

Summary

You should now be able to explain how Jews celebrate their coming of age, and why the Bar and Bat Mitzvah ceremonies are important to them.

2.10 Marriage

■ The importance of marriage for Jews

According to Jewish law, **marriage** is a two-step process. The first stage is betrothal: a period of time, traditionally the 12 months before the wedding ceremony, when the couple are engaged or promised to each other. The second stage is the wedding itself.

It was traditional for Jewish parents to choose a partner for their children, often with the help of a matchmaker. Some Orthodox Jews still do this because they believe the matchmaker is working on God's behalf to find a soulmate for each person. For Jews, marriage is more than just two people choosing to spend their lives together: it is a spiritual bond, where two souls are fused to become one. Marriage is the way of experiencing holiness in everyday life.

> ❝ Hence a man leaves his father and mother and clings to his wife, so that they become one flesh. ❞
>
> *Genesis* 2:24

■ Betrothal

The Hebrew word for betrothal is 'kiddushin'. It comes from a word meaning 'made holy' or 'set aside'. The couple are set aside for each other and no other. Betrothal has legal status in Jewish law and cannot be broken except by death or divorce.

Traditionally a special kiddushin ceremony was held a year before the wedding, but now this ceremony is held at the wedding itself. During the year of betrothal the couple will not live together, but they do prepare for their future lives together.

During the betrothal part of the ceremony, a wedding contract (ketubah) is drawn up. For Orthodox Jews this covers aspects

Objectives

- Know what happens during a Jewish marriage ceremony.
- Consider the meaning and importance of the ceremony.

Key term

- **marriage:** a legal union between a man and a woman (or in some countries, including the UK, two people of the same sex) as partners in a relationship

Discussion activity

Discuss what takes place when a couple get engaged in Britain today. Are there special celebrations or certain rituals involved?

▲ *Jewish weddings take place under a canopy (chuppah) that symbolises the couple's home*

such as the husband's duties to his wife, the conditions of inheritance upon his death, how the couple's children will be supported, and how he will provide for his wife if they get divorced. For Reform Jews the ketubah usually focuses on spiritual aspirations rather than legal rights. It often describes mutual hopes for the marriage, which are the same for both husband and wife. It might also include a promise not to oppose divorce if the couple should separate.

At the last Shabbat service in the synagogue before the wedding day, the husband-to-be takes part in the Torah blessing and announces his intention to marry. The congregation joins in a small celebration after the service with food, drink and wine. The couple and their families may then have a celebratory lunch together. This may be the last time the couple see each other before the wedding day.

■ The wedding

Weddings take place in the synagogue, or elsewhere such as in a hotel, on any day except Shabbat or a festival. The ceremony is led by a rabbi and held under a canopy called a chuppah, which symbolises the couple's home.

The couple may fast on their wedding day to cleanse themselves of sin and come to the ceremony with the right attitude. The betrothal ceremony takes place first. While the groom stands under the chuppah facing Jerusalem, the bride is brought to join him by her mother. The bride circles the groom seven times, which symbolises the bride and groom making personal space for each other every day of the week. They recite two blessings over wine, and the groom places a plain ring on the bride's finger, saying 'Behold, you are consecrated to me by means of this ring, according to the rituals of Moses and Israel.' Reform couples usually both exchange rings.

After the betrothal ceremony, the marriage contract is signed in the presence of witnesses, then read out and given to the bride. An important wedding guest, family member or the rabbi recites seven wedding blessings, then the rabbi makes a short speech and blesses the couple in front of the congregation.

The groom breaks a glass (wrapped in paper or cloth for safety) under his heel to show regret for the destruction of the Temple in Jerusalem. This symbolises that in life there is hardship as well as joy. The congregation shout 'Mazel Tov', which means 'good luck'. Finally the couple spend a short time together in a private room to symbolise their new status as a married couple. A joyous wedding reception follows that includes music and dancing.

Summary

You should now know what happens during a Jewish betrothal and wedding, and be able to explain its significance.

Activities

1 Explain why marriage is so important for Jews.

2 How is the Jewish community involved in a couple's marriage rituals?

3 Write down three conditions you would want in a marriage contract. Explain why.

4 Explain two symbols used in a Jewish wedding ceremony.

Research activity

Look up more detailed information about Jewish wedding ceremonies on the BBC Religion website. Make a note of any other customs mentioned.

▲ *The groom breaks a glass with his heel*

⭐ Study tip

Remember that marriage customs can vary depending on local traditions, and whether the couple are Orthodox or Reform Jews.

■ Customs surrounding death

When a Jew is nearing death, their family tries to visit them and makes sure someone stays with them so they do not die alone. Just before they die, the person makes a final confession and recites the Shema if they are able to do so.

When Jews first hear of the death of a close family member, they follow the example of Jacob by making a small tear in their clothes. For a parent, they make a tear over their hearts; for any other close relative they make a tear on the right side of the chest. When Jews hear of a death, they say a blessing that refers to God as the true judge ('Blessed are You, Lord, our God, King of the Universe, the True Judge'). This shows that they accept God's taking of the person's life.

> ❝ Jacob rent his clothes, put sackcloth on his loins, and observed mourning for his son many days. ❞
>
> *Genesis* 37:34

■ Mourning

For Jews there are clear set periods for **mourning** that decrease in intensity. This allows a family to grieve fully but also helps them to get back to normal life.

Jews believe that the soul does not fully leave the person until the burial takes place. It is important for the soul to feel the comfort and support of family members before this happens. During this first period of mourning, close family are left to grieve without having to follow certain religious rules.

Once the burial takes place, a meal of condolence consisting of bread and eggs (symbols of new life) is prepared by a close friend or relative. This marks the end of the immediate mourning period.

Shiva (seven days of intense mourning) begins on the day of burial. The mourners stay at home and sit on low stools or on the floor rather than on chairs. They do not wear leather shoes, shave or cut their hair, wear make-up or do work. Mirrors are covered so they cannot focus on their appearance, and they wear the clothes they tore. Prayer services are held three times a day in the home. Relatives, friends and neighbours make up the minyan (ten people required for certain prayers). The mourners recite the **kaddish** to praise God and pray for the coming age of eternal peace.

▲ *Orthodox Jews holding a prayer service in a mourner's home*

Objective

- Know about Jewish practices associated with death and mourning, and understand their importance.

Key terms

- **mourning:** a period of time spent remembering a person who has died
- **shiva:** an intense period of mourning that lasts for seven days
- **kaddish:** a prayer said by Jewish mourners that praises God and asks for peace

Links

To read more about Jewish beliefs in the afterlife see pages 14–15.

After shiva has finished, the lesser period of mourning begins and lasts until 30 days after the person's death. During this time, normal life resumes but mourners do not listen to music, go to parties or shave or cut their hair. Male mourners say the kaddish daily in the synagogue.

The final period of mourning lasts for 11 months. Mourners do not attend parties and children continue to say the kaddish for a parent that has died. Formal mourning stops when this final period is over, but sons continue to mark the anniversary of a parent's death by reciting the kaddish and, if possible, making a Torah blessing. As a memorial, both sons and daughters light a candle that burns for 24 hours.

■ The funeral

While some Reform Jews accept cremation, most Jews are buried as soon after death as possible, usually within 24 hours. Before the burial, someone stays with the body and candles are lit beside it. The body is prepared for burial by being carefully washed. It is wrapped in a plain linen cloth, as well as a tallit for men. A corner fringe of the tallit is removed to show it will no longer be used in this life. The body is placed in a simple coffin to show that everyone is equal in death.

Funerals do not usually take place in the synagogue, which is considered a place of the living. The body is transported directly to the cemetery for burial. The service lasts about 20 minutes. Psalms are recited, prayers are said, scriptures are read and a rabbi says a few words about the person. Once the coffin is lowered, mourners shovel earth on top of it. After offering condolences, everyone washes their hands before leaving the cemetery to show that they are leaving death behind.

In Jewish law, a tombstone must be placed on the grave so that the person is remembered. Some families wait until the end of the 12-month mourning period, and may have a small ceremony to mark the unveiling of the headstone. Jews do not use flowers to remember the dead but visitors often place a small stone to show they have visited the grave.

Discussion activity

With a partner or in a small group, discuss whether you think having fixed periods of mourning is helpful. Give reasons for your opinions.

Research activity

Use the internet to read the mourners' kaddish prayer. What is the prayer asking for?

Activities

1 What does a Jewish family do before and just after the death of a loved one?

2 Explain what happens in a Jewish home during shiva.

3 Describe what takes place at a Jewish funeral.

⭐ **Study tip**

Remember that customs may vary between Orthodox and Reform Jews.

Summary

You should now know how Jews mourn a death and understand the importance of Jewish mourning practices.

▲ *Jews often mark their visit to a grave by placing a small stone there*

2.12 Dietary laws

■ Jewish dietary laws

Jews have strict rules (**dietary laws**) about what they can and cannot eat. Food that is permitted is called **kosher**. Food that is unacceptable is called **trefah**, which means 'torn'. Trefah originally described animals whose flesh had been torn by a predator and so couldn't be eaten.

The kosher laws are found in the Torah, particularly in Leviticus 11 and Deuteronomy 14. The Talmud explains in more detail how Jews should put these laws into practice.

Although the Torah itself gives no logical reason for the dietary laws, some people think that the rules seem to have originally been for hygiene or health reasons, or because an animal was more valuable for uses other than food. For example, the prohibition against pork was sensible in a hot climate where pigs could carry many diseases. Camels were more valued for transporting goods across deserts than as a source of food. Not eating animals that had been killed by predators or that were already unconscious reduced the chances of getting a disease.

Orthodox Jews follow the dietary laws strictly. They believe the laws have come from God to test their obedience and mark out the Jewish people as different from others. The laws are also a call to holiness that helps people to develop self-control and reminds them daily of their faith. However, many Reform Jews think the laws are outdated in modern British society and it should be up to the individual whether or not they follow them.

■ Kosher butchers

Meat that is permitted must be killed in the prescribed way. The animal must be healthy and slaughtered with a very sharp knife by a trained Jew. The animal's throat is cut so that the animal does not suffer. However, the animal is not stunned first as then it would be unconscious. Blood is drained from the animal as it is forbidden to Jews. Certain parts of the animal, like the intestines and kidneys, must also be removed.

> **Objective**
> - Know about Jewish dietary laws and understand their significance.

> **Key terms**
> - **dietary laws:** rules that deal with foods permitted to be eaten, food preparation, food combinations, and the utensils and dishes coming into contact with food
> - **kosher:** food that meets the requirements of Jewish laws
> - **trefah:** food that Jews are forbidden to eat; means 'torn'

▲ *Jews have to be careful about how they prepare food in kitchens to make sure it is kosher*

> **Discussion activity** 💬
>
> 'The Jewish food laws are no longer relevant in modern British society.' Discuss this statement. Be sure to include more than one point of view and refer to Jewish beliefs and teachings in your answer.

Examples of kosher food	Examples of trefah food
Cows, sheep, goats, deer	Pork, camel, rodents, reptiles
Fish that has scales and fins, such as salmon, tuna, carp, herring and cod	Seafood without fins and scales, such as crabs, prawns, lobsters, oysters and clams
Cheese that has been officially certified as kosher	Cheese that has not been declared kosher
Any fruit and vegetables, so long as they are free of insects	Any insects or amphibians such as frogs

> But make sure that you do not partake of the blood; for the blood is the life, and you must not consume the life with the flesh.
> *Deuteronomy* 12:23

■ A Jewish kitchen

Certain combinations of foods, particularly dairy products and meat, are not allowed to be eaten at the same time. After eating meat, several hours must pass before anything containing milk is eaten. Jews debate the reasons for this, but most believe it stems from the instruction in Exodus 23:19: 'You shall not boil a kid in its mother's milk.'

Many Orthodox homes have kitchens with two sinks and two food preparation areas. This is so they can keep milk and meat separate. They may also colour-code their utensils, cutlery and crockery so that the ones used for meat dishes stay separate from the ones used for dairy products.

Most synagogues have kosher kitchens in which food can be prepared according to the dietary laws for functions held there. It can be difficult for Jews who live in non-Jewish communities to ensure that when they eat out, not only is the food kosher but it is also prepared with kosher crockery and utensils. To make it easier when buying food at a supermarket, a number of Jewish authorities will certify foods as kosher and put a label on the packaging.

Activities

1 Explain the terms kosher and trefah.
2 Explain how kosher meat is prepared. Why might some animal welfare groups oppose this method?
3 Make up a menu that would be permitted for a Jewish family dinner.
4 How is a Jewish kitchen organised to follow the dietary laws?

Summary You should now understand Jewish dietary laws and be able to explain how they affect Jewish life today.

Research activities

1 Find out what the RSPCA has said about kosher methods of butchering meat in an information sheet called 'Slaughter without pre-stunning (for religious purposes)'. Consider how the Jewish community might respond to this report. The Shechita website (www.shechitauk.org) might help you.

2 Many Reform Jews believe that the eco-Kashrut movement, demanding the ethical treatment of animals and workers in the food industry, is a modern way of approaching the dietary laws. Use the internet to find out more about the eco-Kashrut movement and make a note of some of the issues it raises about food production.

3 Divide the class in half: one group to look in Leviticus chapter 11 and the other in Deuteronomy chapter 14 for rules about clean and unclean food. Compare your findings. Do you think these rules were helpful to the Jewish people at the time they were written?

★ Study tip

It is helpful to know several examples of kosher and trefah foods.

Rosh Hashanah is a festival that is celebrated over two days to mark the start of the Jewish new year. The ten days beginning with **Rosh Hashanah** and ending with **Yom Kippur**, the Day of Atonement, are sometimes called 'Days of Awe'. It is a time when Jews think seriously about their lives, consider their actions over the past year, and ask for forgiveness for their sins.

■ Origins of Rosh Hashanah

Rosh Hashanah recalls the creation story from the book of Genesis; it is considered to be the anniversary of the day on which God created humans. It is also a day of judgement. Some Jews believe that God keeps a record of people's good and bad deeds, and on Rosh Hashanah God weighs them up, judges them and makes a decision about what people's fortune will be in the coming year. The judgement can be influenced by the actions taken during the festival, so Jews pray, do works of charity and try to atone for (make up for) any harm or upset they have caused another person. Other Jews see God's record-keeping as representing the idea that all actions have consequences, so people should reflect on and take responsibility for their own actions.

▲ *Giving to charity is an important way that Jews can show repentance before Yom Kippur*

■ Celebrating Rosh Hashanah in Britain today

The month before Rosh Hashanah, a ram's horn (shofar) is blown daily in the synagogue (except on Shabbat) to announce the coming day of judgement. Special prayers for forgiveness are said all month. On the day before, preparations are made similar to those made for Shabbat, including buying fruit that the family has not eaten for a long time to symbolise renewal. Candles are lit just before sunset. At the usual evening synagogue

> **Objective**
> - Consider the origins and importance of Rosh Hashanah and Yom Kippur.

> **Key terms**
> - **Rosh Hashanah:** the Jewish new year
> - **Yom Kippur:** the Day of Atonement; a day of fasting on the tenth day after Rosh Hashanah

> **66** Despite the fact that repentance and crying out to G-d are always timely, during the ten days between Rosh Hashanah and Yom Kippur it is exceedingly appropriate, and is accepted immediately. **99**
>
> Rabbi Moses Ben Maimon, *Mishneh Torah*

> **Links**
>
> To read more about how Shabbat is celebrated see pages 38–41.

service, prayers are focused on asking God to continue to be the king of the world for the coming year. The service ends with a Kiddush blessing over wine.

At home a festive meal begins with the Kiddush blessing, and apples dipped in honey are eaten: a symbol of hope for a sweet new year. A fish head is sometimes eaten to show the desire for good deeds to grow in number like fish. Other symbolic foods, such as pomegranates, may also be eaten.

Next morning at the synagogue the shofar is blown 100 times. The service is longer than usual with special prayers for the occasion and it attracts a large congregation. Many Jews who do not regularly go to the synagogue will attend on this special day.

▲ *The shofar calls Jews to repentance*

◼ Origins of Yom Kippur

Yom Kippur is the holiest and most important day in the Jewish calendar. Its origins come from Leviticus 16, which describes how it must be observed. One original custom involved symbolically putting the people's sins on a goat and driving it into the desert.

> ❝ You shall practise self-denial; and you shall do no manner of work … For on this day atonement shall be made for you to cleanse you of all your sins; you shall be clean before the LORD. It shall be a sabbath of complete rest for you, and you shall practise self-denial; it is a law for all time. ❞
>
> *Leviticus* 16:29–31

This Day of Atonement is when God seals the Book of Judgement, so it is the last chance to repent for any sins. It is expected that Jews will have already mended relationships with other people in the days before Yom Kippur. Atonement that takes place on this day concerns the Jews and God; it is an occasion when Jews repent of their sins and God forgives them, enabling the relationship between them and God to be restored.

◼ Observing Yom Kippur in Britain today

- No work is done.
- Jews fast (have no food or drink) for 25 hours.
- Bathing, wearing leather shoes, and sexual intercourse are forbidden.
- Jews wear white as a symbol of purity. (Isaiah 1:18 speaks of sins becoming 'like snow'.)

Many Jews spend much of Yom Kippur in the synagogue, where services will be held throughout the day. One of the most important parts is a general confession of sins as a community. The word 'we' is used rather than 'I' in expressing sorrow for sins. During the final service the doors of the Ark are open, requiring all to stand. This is the last chance for people to make confession before the door of the Ark is closed to show that God's judgement is now sealed. The service ends with the blowing of the shofar to signal the end of the fast.

Activities

1 Write down three actions Jews take to influence God's judgement upon their lives.

2 Explain how Rosh Hashanah is celebrated in the home and in the synagogue in Britain today.

3 Why is Yom Kippur such an important holy day for Jews?

4 Explain the impact of these festivals on individual Jews and on the Jewish community.

Discussion activity

With a partner or in a small group, discuss whether you have ever gone without food and drink for 25 hours. How difficult do you think it would be? Why do you think fasting is part of the observance of Yom Kippur?

⭐ Study tip

When studying festivals in Judaism it is important to consider their influence both on individual Jews and on the Jewish community as a whole.

Summary

You should now understand the origins and meaning of Rosh Hashanah and Yom Kippur, and know how they are celebrated in Britain today.

2.14 Pesach

■ Origins of Pesach

Pesach is also called 'Passover' because it recalls the night when God 'passed over' the houses of the Jewish slaves but killed the firstborn children and animals of the Egyptians. The story is found in Exodus 12:1–30.

God told Moses to ask the Pharaoh (ruler of Egypt) to let the Israelites go into the desert for three days to make offerings to God (Exodus 3). The Pharaoh refused, so God sent a series of plagues on Egypt. The final plague, the death of the firstborn, including Pharaoh's own son, finally succeeded in persuading him to allow the Israelites to leave. They miraculously crossed the Sea of Reeds to escape and eventually, after 40 years wandering in the desert, entered the land of Canaan that God had promised them.

■ Preparations for Pesach

God commanded the Jews to celebrate their escape from Egypt by eating unleavened bread (bread without yeast) for seven days each year (Exodus 12:15). The most important preparation for Pesach is to remove leaven (chametz) from the home. This includes wheat, barley, oats, or any grain that has been allowed to ferment or rise. Some Jews also avoid rice, corn, peanuts and beans. Removing leaven recalls how the escaping Israelites did not have time to let their bread rise.

Jews clean their homes thoroughly so that not a trace of leaven can be found. Usually the house is so clean that either parents or children deliberately hide some bread crumbs to find and burn to show that all leaven has been removed. Some firstborn males fast on this day in thanksgiving for their escape from death.

■ The Passover Seder

Pesach lasts for seven or eight days. On the first evening of Pesach, families hold a Seder service and celebrate with a special meal.

The mother lights candles to welcome the festival into the home. Often some family members visit the synagogue to offer thanks to God. When they return, the meal begins with the Kiddush blessing over the wine. On the table there is red wine, three pieces of matzo (unleavened bread), the Seder plate, and a copy of a special book (the Haggadah) which should be read during the Seder service. The middle matzo is broken and the largest piece is hidden for children to hunt for later. The finder receives a small prize.

On the Seder plate there is usually:
- a green vegetable, often parsley, to dip in salt water
- bitter herbs made from horseradish

▲ *The story of the exodus is told when the youngest child asks four questions about the meaning of Pesach rituals*

- a second bitter herb, such as romaine lettuce
- charoset (a paste of chopped apples, walnuts and wine)
- a roasted egg
- a lamb bone.

▲ *A Seder plate holds symbolic foods*

The different elements of the meal symbolise different things:

- Red wine reminds Jews of the lambs' blood the Israelites smeared on their doorposts to save their children from the final plague.
- The unleavened bread fulfils God's command, and recalls that the Israelites did not have time to let the bread rise before their escape.
- The salt water represents the bitter tears shed in slavery.
- The green vegetable may symbolise new life in the Promised Land.
- Bitter herbs, representing the bitterness of slavery, are dipped in the sweet charoset that symbolises the mortar used by the Jewish slaves. It reminds Jews that life is now sweet by comparison.
- The roasted egg and lamb bone are two reminders of sacrifices made in the Temple of Jerusalem.

Usually the youngest family member asks four questions and in reply the story of the escape from Egypt is retold from the Haggadah. During the meal, four small glasses of wine are blessed and shared to represent the four freedoms God promised in Exodus 6:6–7.

A fifth cup of wine is poured out and the door left open for the prophet Elijah, who is expected to reappear at Pesach to announce the coming of the Messiah. The Passover Seder ends with a wish that those present may celebrate next year in Jerusalem.

■ The importance of Pesach

Pesach has great significance for the Jewish community in the UK and elsewhere. It is a joyful festival as it celebrates the birth of the Jewish nation, freedom from slavery, entering the Promised Land and being given the law that made the Jews God's chosen people. The celebration of Pesach with their families gives Jews a chance to show gratitude to God for their redemption. The retelling of the Passover story to the next generation ensures Jewish faith and traditions are passed on. Jews are encouraged to relive the exodus through the Seder rituals and feel empathy with those who still live under political or religious oppression.

> ❝ I am the LORD. I will free you from the labours of the Egyptians and deliver you from their bondage. I will redeem you with an outstretched arm and through extraordinary chastisements. And I will take you to be My people, and I will be your God. ❞
>
> *Exodus* 6:6–7

Research activity 🔍

Read the story of Moses and the exodus in Exodus 3:1–12:42. What do you think the Jews learned about God through these events?

⭐ **Study tip**

You can use either the term 'Pesach' or 'Passover' when referring to this festival.

Summary

You should now understand the origins and importance of Pesach, and be able to describe how Jews celebrate Pesach.

Activities

1 Explain how Jewish families prepare for Pesach.
2 Give two ways that Jews involve their children in Passover celebrations.
3 Draw a table with three columns. List all the foods and actions from the Seder meal in the first column, explain what they represent in the second column, and draw a picture or symbol to help you remember these in the third column.

The synagogue and worship – summary

You should now be able to:

✔ explain the meaning and importance of the synagogue for Jews

✔ explain the design and religious features of synagogues, including the reading platform (bimah), ark (aron hakodesh), ever burning light (ner tamid)

✔ explain religious practices associated with these features of synagogues

✔ explain differences between Orthodox and Reform synagogues

✔ explain the meaning and significance of synagogue services in both Orthodox and Reform synagogues

✔ explain the significance of prayer in public acts of worship, including Amidah, the standing prayer

✔ describe the celebration of Shabbat in the home and in the synagogue

✔ explain the significance of Shabbat

✔ describe and explain worship in the home and private prayer

✔ describe what is meant by the written law (the Tenakh) and the oral law (Talmud)

✔ explain the use and significance of the written law and the oral law and their study in daily life.

Family life and festivals – summary

You should now be able to:

✔ explain the importance of rituals in Jewish family life

✔ describe and explain ceremonies associated with birth, including Brit Milah, and their importance

✔ describe and explain the ceremonies of Bar Mitzvah and Bat Mitzvah and their importance

✔ describe and explain the marriage ceremony and its importance

✔ describe and explain Jewish rituals associated with death and mourning and their importance

✔ explain Jewish dietary laws and their significance, including different Jewish views about their importance and their effect on Jewish life today

✔ explain what is meant by kosher and trefah and the separation of milk and meat

✔ explain the importance of festivals for Jews in Britain today

✔ explain the origins and importance of Rosh Hashanah and Yom Kippur and how they are celebrated

✔ explain the origins and importance of Pesach and how it is celebrated.

Sample student answer – the 4 mark question

1. Write an answer to the following practice question:

   Explain two contrasting Jewish views on the importance of following dietary laws. **[4 marks]**

2. Read the following student sample answer:

   "Some Jews follow very strict laws about food. For example, they cannot eat milk and meat together. There are certain foods like pork or lobster that they are not allowed to eat. These foods are called 'trefah' or forbidden. Foods they can eat are called 'kosher' as they are permitted. These include most meats and fish that have scales. They can also eat vegetables as long as there are no insects on them. Many Jews have kitchens with two sinks and two different sets of cutlery and dishes so that they don't mix up meat and milk.

   Other Jews think these rules are old-fashioned so they just eat whatever they want."

3. With a partner, discuss the sample answer. Is the focus of the answer about following the dietary laws? Is anything missing from the answer? How do you think it could be improved?

4. What mark (out of 4) would you give this answer? Look at the mark scheme in the introduction (AO1). What are the reasons for the mark you have given?

5. Now swap your answer with your partner's and mark each other's responses. What mark (out of 4) would you give the response? Refer to the mark scheme and give reasons for the mark you award.

Sample student answer – the 5 mark question

1. Write an answer to the following practice question:

   Explain two reasons why private prayer is important for Jews.

   Refer to Jewish teaching in your answer. **[5 marks]**

2. Read the following student sample answer:

   "One reason why Jews believe that private prayer is important is because it is a way of keeping up a close relationship with God. They think that God will hear what they say and answer their prayers. Jews are taught to pray three times a day – in the morning, afternoon and evening.

   Jews may pray to thank God for something. At other times they may want to ask God to help them or to help someone else. Jews often pray in the morning to thank God for another day. Jewish men often wear a tallit and tefillin when they pray. Sometimes they use prayers that have been written by someone else or on other occasions they make the prayer up as they pray."

3. With a partner, discuss the sample answer. It makes some good points but it fails to do something which is important. How do you think the answer could be improved?

4. What mark (out of 5) would you give this answer? Look at the mark scheme in the Introduction (AO1). What are the reasons for the mark you have given?

5. Now swap your answer with your partner's and mark each other's responses. What mark (out of 5) would you give the response? Refer to the mark scheme and give reasons for the mark you award.

Sample student answer – the 12 mark question

1. Write an answer to the following practice question:

   'The most important religious festival for Jews is Yom Kippur.'

   Evaluate this statement. In your answer you should:
   - refer to the teaching of Judaism
   - give developed arguments to support this statement
   - give developed arguments to support a different point of view
   - reach a justified conclusion.   **[12 marks]**

2. Read the following student sample answer:

   "Yom Kippur is the holiest day of the Jewish year therefore it is the most important religious festival. It is the Day of Atonement for sin. In olden times the Hebrews used to put the people's sins on a goat and drive it into the desert. This showed that the people were cleansed of their sins and could begin a new year with a clean slate. Nowadays Yom Kippur comes at the end of a time of repentance when people try to mend relationships with other people whom they may have hurt in the previous year. On Yom Kippur God will seal the book of judgement and so it is the last chance for Jews to tell God they are sorry for their sins. This is very important because it is the way Jews restore their relationship with God and avoid his judgement in the future.

   However some Jewish families might think that Pesach is more important because it is celebrated with their families. It is also a reminder of the most important part of Jewish history, their escape from slavery in Egypt. Pesach lasts eight days and involves eating special foods. The seder meal is a joyous occasion, although tinged with sadness because of the oppression of the Jewish people, which has continued into the present day. There are also fun activities for children like searching for a piece of matzot. The youngest child gets to ask important questions about the importance of the festival."

3. With a partner, discuss the sample answer. Consider the following questions:

   - Does the answer refer to Jewish teachings and if so what are they?
   - Is there an argument to support the statement and how well developed is it?
   - Is a different point of view offered and how developed is that argument?
   - Has the student written a clear conclusion after weighing up both sides of the argument?
   - Are there logical steps in the argument?
   - What is good about this answer?
   - How do you think it could be improved?

4. What mark (out of 12) would you give this answer? Look at the mark scheme in the introduction (AO2). What are the reasons for the mark you have given?

5. Now swap your answer with your partner's and mark each other's responses. What mark (out of 5) would you give the response? Refer to the mark scheme and give reasons for the mark you award.

Practice questions

1 Which one of the following is the written law in Judaism?

A) Torah   B) Tefillin   C) Tzitzit   D) Talmud   **[1 mark]**

2 Give two features of an Orthodox synagogue.   **[2 marks]**

 Study tip

This question only requires the naming of the two features and one mark will be given for each correct answer. Don't waste time by answering in sentences.

3 Explain two contrasting ways in which Jews mourn for the dead.   **[4 marks]**

 Study tip

Remember to develop the points you are making. This may be done by giving detailed information, such as referring to examples. Try to include contrasting ways in your answer. The contrasts could be between ways in which Orthodox Jews carry out mourning rituals and the way Reform Jews mourn the dead.

4 Explain two ways in which Shabbat is celebrated in the home. Refer to Jewish teaching in your answer.   **[5 marks]**

 Study tip

Remember this is about the celebration of Shabbat in the home, not in the synagogue. Two marks in each case are for detailed explanation of a way in which Shabbat is celebrated in the home and the fifth mark is for a reference to Jewish teachings.

5 'The most important duty of Jews is to attend the synagogue.'

Evaluate this statement. In your answer you should:

- refer to the teaching of Judaism
- give developed arguments to support this statement
- give developed arguments to support a different point of view
- reach a justified conclusion.   **[12 marks]**

 Study tip

Read the statement carefully and make sure that your answer is fully focused on what it is saying. Check that you have followed the guidance in the bullet points under the statement.

 Study tip

You should aim to develop two different points of view. Contrasting viewpoints can show differences between those who think the most important duty of Jews is to attend the synagogue and those who think other duties are more important. You should aim to refer to Jewish teaching in your arguments, for example scripture, religious writings or the teaching of religious leaders.

Part 2: Thematic studies

3 Relationships and families

3.1 Religious teachings about human sexuality

■ Jewish attitudes to human sexuality

Human sexuality refers to the way people express themselves as sexual beings. It is natural for young people to begin to have an interest in sex when they reach puberty. They are going through physical and psychological changes, which in most cases lead to forming a **heterosexual** relationship (between a man and a woman) and to reproduction (having children).

In Judaism, sex is seen as a wonderful creation of God, not just for having children but also for giving pleasure and expressing love, companionship and intimacy within a marriage. In the Torah, God created Eve as a companion and sexual partner for Adam.

▲ *Most Jews think physical attraction is important between married couples*

> ❝ The LORD God said, "It is not good for man to be alone; I will make a fitting helper for him." ❞
>
> *Genesis* 2:18

For most Jews, sex is part of God's plan but is only permissible within the context of marriage. Jewish law recognises that couples must have a mutual physical attraction for each other. Sex should be joyful and should not take place if the couple are quarrelling or drunk. A woman's right to sexual fulfilment is recognised and her husband is expected to know her needs and give her pleasure. Equally, a wife should not deny her husband sexual relations. To do so over a period of time may lead to a divorce.

■ Jewish attitudes towards homosexuality

A **homosexual** relationship is a sexual relationship with a member of the same sex, either between a man and another man or a woman and another woman. The Torah is clear that sex between men is forbidden:

Objectives

- Understand Jewish teachings about human sexuality.
- Understand the meaning of the terms heterosexual and homosexual relationships.
- Consider contemporary British attitudes towards these relationships.

Key terms

- **human sexuality:** how people express themselves as sexual beings
- **heterosexual:** sexually attracted to members of the opposite sex
- **homosexual:** sexually attracted to members of the same sex

Activities

1. Explain Jewish attitudes towards human sexuality.
2. How does Jewish law support a wife's sexual happiness in marriage?
3. Explain one reason why Orthodox Jews consider homosexual relationships to be wrong.
4. 'There is too much sexual freedom in contemporary British society.' Evaluate this statement.

64

> " Do not lie with a male as one lies with a woman; it is an abhorrence. "
>
> *Leviticus* 18:22

Neither the Torah nor the Talmud specifically forbids homosexual relationships between women, but Orthodox Judaism considers both male and female homosexual relationships to be wrong. However, it is important to remember that Jewish teaching does not condemn a person's sexual orientation. It is acting upon these desires that is considered wrong.

> " All human beings are created in the image of God and deserve to be treated with dignity and respect [...] Embarrassing, harassing or demeaning someone with a homosexual orientation or same-sex attraction is a violation of Torah prohibitions that embody the deepest values of Judaism. "
>
> *Statement of Principles on the Place of Jews with a Homosexual Orientation in Our Community,* signed by over a hundred Orthodox rabbis, Jewish educators and community leaders in July 2010

All branches of Reform and Liberal Judaism emphasise the loving relationship of homosexual couples and think that what they do in private is up to them. Judaism teaches that all people were created in the image of God, so most Jews oppose any forms of discrimination. Reform and Liberal Jews are against discrimination of any kind. Some Reform movements accept homosexuals as rabbis and cantors and many conduct same-sex marriages.

Contemporary British attitudes

Today, sex before marriage, multiple sexual partners, children born outside of marriage, affairs (adultery) or open homosexual relationships are more common. In Britain, homosexual relationships are legal and homosexual couples can now marry or convert civil partnerships into marriage if they wish.

Like many Jews, many British Christians believe that the only place for sex is within marriage and that heterosexual relationships fulfil God's purposes for humanity. But within Christianity, as within Judaism, there are those who accept homosexual relationships as part of life and as valid as heterosexual relationships.

The age of consent

In the UK, the age of consent for anyone to have sex, meaning the age at which you are legally old enough to freely agree to have sex, is 16 years old. The law tries to protect anyone under 16 from exploitation and abuse. Some people think that as long as people freely consent and are over 16, any kind of sexual behaviour is acceptable. Religions disagree, and most teach that because sex is a powerful force and can result in new life, it should be reserved for the commitment of marriage. Traditionally, the minimum age for marriage under Jewish law is 13 for boys and 12 for girls; however, the Talmud recommends that a man marry at age 18, or somewhere between 16 and 24. It is important to remember that Jews follow the laws of the country in which they live, so British Jews obey the UK law about the age of consent.

Links

For more information about same-sex marriages, see page 71.

▲ *Lionel Blue, Britain's first openly homosexual rabbi*

Contrasting beliefs

Find out more about Christian attitudes to homosexual relationships that contrast with those of Judaism.

Discussion activity

In a small group discuss this statement: 'Religions should not try to control people's sex lives.'

⭐ **Study tip**

Remember that there are diverse views about human sexuality within Judaism. Try to learn the attitudes of both Orthodox and Reform Jews on these issues, and be prepared to provide a contrasting viewpoint from Christianity on homosexuality.

Summary

You should now be able to explain Jewish and non-religious attitudes to human sexuality, including heterosexual and homosexual relationships.

3.2 Sexual relationships before and outside marriage

Sexual relationships before marriage

As we have seen, most Jews consider marriage to be the most appropriate place for a sexual relationship. The issue of pre-marital sex is debated within Judaism but the traditional view is that it is irresponsible and immoral, as it undermines the importance of creating a family through which Jewish religion and culture is passed down, can lead to unwanted pregnancy or the spread of sexually transmitted diseases, and can cheapen sex, lowering a person's self-respect and their respect for others – who are all created in God's image (Genesis 1:27). The Torah warns against promiscuity and sexual conduct that harms others. Orthodox Jews, following mitzvot from Leviticus and further guidance in the Talmud, believe that premarital sex is forbidden.

Jews believe that modesty, respect for others and faithfulness are important qualities that should apply to all relationships. In ultra-Orthodox Jewish families a chaperone (a responsible adult, usually a relative or family friend) accompanies an engaged couple when they meet.

Sexual relationships outside marriage

Like all religions, Judaism teaches faithfulness in marriage. **Adultery** or **sex outside marriage** is considered a serious sexual offence, and is against one of the Ten Commandments. In ancient times it was punishable by death. The commandments in the Torah prohibit adultery and desiring another man's wife, which can lead to adultery. Adultery in this case refers to sex between a married woman and a man who is not her husband. Jewish law does not apply the word 'adultery' to a married man who has sex with an unmarried woman, but nowadays Jews would be as critical of a man committing adultery as a woman. It is considered one of the most serious sins, along with murder and idolatry (worshipping false gods).

▲ Adultery is a betrayal of trust that can lead to divorce

Objectives

- Understand Jewish beliefs and teachings about sexual relationships before marriage and outside marriage.
- Consider contemporary British attitudes towards sexual relationships before marriage and outside marriage.

Key terms

- **adultery:** voluntary sexual intercourse between a married person and a person who is not their husband or wife; in Jewish law, adultery is defined as voluntary sexual intercourse between a married woman and a man who is not her husband
- **sex outside marriage:** sex between two people where at least one or both of them is married to someone else; adultery; having an affair
- **sex before marriage:** sex between two unmarried people

Links

For more information on marriage, see Chapter 2, pages 50–51.

Contrasting beliefs

Find out more about Christian beliefs on sex before marriage that might provide a contrast with Jewish attitudes to this issue.

> **❝** You shall not commit adultery; […] You shall not covet your neighbour's wife **❞**
>
> *Exodus* 20:12, 14

For Jews, marriage is a spiritual bond. Adultery breaks that bond and risks the happiness and security of the whole family. It is considered so wrong that Jewish law requires a man whose wife has been unfaithful to him to divorce her even if he is willing to forgive her.

■ Contemporary British attitudes

In contemporary Britain, **sex before marriage** is now widely accepted. Many magazines, films and television programmes reflect the common belief that it is usual for couples that are dating to have sex. There is often peer pressure on young people to have sexual experiences before marriage and it is often argued that couples should see whether they are sexually compatible before they marry. Some young British Jews might feel caught between the values of their religion and the values of the culture in which they live.

Jewish views on sex before marriage are similar to those held by Christians and other religions

Links

For more information on divorce, see pages 72–73.

▲ *Some young people in Britain sometimes feel pressured into having sex before marriage*

in Britain today. However, some liberal Christians and Jews are more tolerant of loving, committed sexual relationships that are conducted ethically and responsibly, even if the partners are not married.

Adultery is often reflected in the media and popular culture too. But many people, both religious and non-religious, would regard unfaithfulness in marriage as wrong. They would argue that commitment to be faithful and loyal is important and helps to develop a relationship built on honesty and trust. The lies and deception that adultery brings to a relationship often lead to divorce. Almost all British Jews would consider sex outside marriage (adultery) to be wrong.

Activities

1 Explain the difference between 'sex before marriage' and 'sex outside marriage'.
2 Explain two ways in which sex before marriage could harm the people involved.
3 Explain why Jews believe that adultery is a serious sin.

★ Study tip

Try to remember that there is a diversity of views within Judaism about sex before marriage but not about adultery, which all Jews think is wrong.

Summary

You should now be able to explain Jewish and non-religious beliefs about sex before and outside marriage, and the reasons for these beliefs.

■ What is contraception?

Contraception is a way of preventing pregnancy when a couple have sex. There are three main forms: artificial, natural and permanent.

- Artificial forms include the pill, diaphragm, condom, spermicidal jellies, coil and morning after pill.
- Natural contraception, for example the rhythm method, usually involves having sex only at certain times of the month in order to reduce the chance of pregnancy. The withdrawal method (withdrawing the penis before ejaculation) is also a natural form.
- Sterilisation (a surgical operation) of the man or the woman is more permanent.

■ Jewish beliefs about contraception and family planning

Like Catholic and Orthodox Christianity, Orthodox Judaism teaches that sex before marriage is wrong, so contraception is only considered in the case of married people. Reform Jews accept that some couples may choose to use contraception before marriage.

For some Jews, a large family is a blessing from God. Traditionally, Jewish men were expected to have at least one son and one daughter. However, Jews accept that **family planning** is sometimes helpful, as long as it is not used to prevent having children altogether. Jews recognise that the use of contraception is a complicated issue and there is much debate about it, especially as scientific and technological advances have provided more questions to consider. It is understood that each couple has their own unique situation in which they will need to weigh up priorities carefully before making decisions. Reform Jews allow contraception to be used for many reasons, including social and financial reasons, but many Orthodox Jews only allow contraception to be used to:

- prevent risk to the mother's health
- delay having children or to space them out, bearing in mind financial issues
- limit the number of children if this is thought to benefit the family.

Jewish law says that men should not destroy or waste their 'seed' (sperm) (see the sin of Onan in Genesis 38:9–10), so methods of contraception that damage sperm or stop it reaching its intended

▲ *The pill is the preferred method of contraception for most Jewish couples*

destination are usually forbidden. Many Orthodox Jews prefer the contraceptive pill as it does not interfere with the sexual act (as do the rhythm and withdrawal methods) or destroy semen (as do condoms). Orthodox Jews believe that a woman may use contraception if a pregnancy would cause harm. Permission to use contraception is 'non transferable' and 'non-expendable', meaning that each individual case needs to be brought to an Orthodox rabbi for consideration.

Sterilisation is forbidden because it damages the body God created.

Reform Jewish couples are free to choose a method of contraception that suits them. Unlike some Christians who oppose the use of the morning after pill because they believe it causes an abortion, Jewish authorities do not oppose it if the mother's health is at risk. However, they would not wish to see it used in normal circumstances. Some Jewish authorities also accept the use of condoms to prevent the spread of a sexually transmitted disease. There are some Orthodox Jews who do not believe in the use of contraception at all because they believe that the size of their family is for God alone to decide.

> ### Contrasting beliefs
>
> Try to find out more about Christian beliefs on different forms of contraception, both natural and artificial, and note any beliefs that contrast with Jewish views on this issue.

▲ *Some Orthodox couples consult their rabbi when deciding about contraception*

■ Contemporary British attitudes

Most people in Britain, religious and non-religious, accept the use of contraception for family planning. Some believers, such as Catholic and Orthodox Christians, oppose artificial methods but accept natural ones. Many people think that the medical advances in preventing unwanted pregnancies should be welcomed and used responsibly, perhaps for less personal reasons such as to help control population growth and to prevent the spread of sexually transmitted diseases. Most British Jews would generally agree that, if used for the right reasons, some forms of artificial contraception within marriage are acceptable.

⭐ Study tip

Remember that not all Jews agree on contraception. Try to use phrases such as 'some Jews believe…' and 'other Jews believe…' or 'Orthodox Jews believe…' and 'Reform Jews believe…' when describing Jewish beliefs about this issue.

Activities

1 Explain one social reason and one financial reason why a Jewish couple might wish to use contraception.
2 Give three circumstances in which Orthodox couples are permitted to use contraception.
3 'Jews should be allowed to use any method of contraception they wish in modern Britain.' Evaluate this statement. Be sure to discuss more than one point of view and refer to Jewish teaching in your answer.

Summary

You should now be able to explain Jewish beliefs and non-religious attitudes to family planning and the use of different methods of contraception within marriage.

Marriage in contemporary Britain

Marriage is a serious, lifelong, public commitment. It is a legal contract that brings security to a relationship and protects the rights of each partner. Until recently, marriage in the UK was defined as the legal union of a man and a woman. In 2004, same-sex couples were allowed to register their union in a **civil partnership** which gave them the same legal rights as married couples. **Same-sex marriages** became legal in England, Wales and Scotland in 2014, and in Ireland in 2015. The number of couples who marry is declining. Some couples choose to live together without getting married. This is called **cohabitation**.

Jewish beliefs about the nature and purpose of marriage

For Jews, marriage is more than just a social contract; it is the spiritual binding together of a man and a woman in love and a lifelong commitment to each other. It is part of God's plan at creation (Genesis 2:24). Jews think of their marriage partner as their soulmate and their marriage relationship reveals the love of God for his people of Israel (as shown in the covenant). An ideal marriage is one in which the qualities of each partner complements and fulfils the other so that they are a complete whole.

▲ Like many other people, some Jews use online dating sites to meet someone who shares their faith and values

The purpose of a Jewish marriage is to provide a secure foundation for raising a family in a stable, loving home. This is important for passing on Jewish traditions and values to the next generation. It is also the proper place for a couple to express sexual desires exclusively with one person in intimacy and dignity. Companionship is an important purpose of marriage. The first woman was created because it was not good for man to be alone (Genesis 2:18). Marriage helps couples to grow spiritually in their faith and draw closer to God. It enables them to show commitment and love for each other in a binding contract (ketubah). The contract protects the woman's financial security and sometimes sets out the responsibilities of each partner.

Objectives

- Consider Jewish beliefs about the nature and purpose of marriage.
- Explore Jewish and non-religious responses to same-sex marriage and cohabitation.

Key terms

- **marriage:** a legal union between a man and a woman (or in some countries, including the UK, two people of the same sex) as partners in a relationship
- **civil partnership:** legal union of same-sex couples
- **same-sex marriage:** marriage between partners of the same sex
- **cohabitation:** a couple living together and having a sexual relationship without being married to one another

Links

For more information on the covenant, see Chapter 1, pages 18–19.

Discussion activity

With a partner or in a small group, discuss the qualities you think are important for a marriage to succeed.

> ❝ Hence a man leaves his father and mother and clings to his wife, so that they become one flesh. ❞
>
> *Genesis* 2:24

■ Cohabitation

Many young couples in Britain choose to cohabit, although they may decide to marry when they want to start a family. Some live together for financial reasons, or because they want to see if the relationship will work. Others never marry but live in committed relationships throughout their lives. Same-sex couples may cohabit until they decide to seek a civil partnership or get married.

Many Jews do not approve of cohabitation because they believe a sexual relationship should only occur within marriage. However, some Reform Jews think that cohabitation, while not the ideal, is not wrong if the couple's commitment to each other is long term and if it is conducted responsibly with love and respect for each other.

■ Same-sex marriage

Traditional Jewish teachings make it clear that heterosexual marriage is intended by God and is the natural state in which people should live. Male homosexual acts are condemned in the Torah (Leviticus 18:22), so many Orthodox Jews, like some other religious believers, were opposed to the changes in the law that made same-sex marriages legal.

However, Reform Jews, like some liberal Christians, value the love and commitment of couples who wish to marry, whatever their gender. Liberal and Reform Jews accept the validity of civil marriages between same-sex couples, and some groups are willing to bless or conduct same-sex marriages in a religious ceremony.

> ❝ Marriage, by definition in Jewish (biblical) law is the union of a male and a female. While Judaism teaches respect for others and condemns all types of discrimination, we oppose a change to the definition of marriage that includes same-sex relationships. Jewish (biblical) law prohibits the practice of homosexuality. ❞
>
> Statement by the London Beth Din (the Chief Rabbi's court) and the Rabbinical Council of the United Synagogue, 2012

▲ Former Chief Rabbi Jonathan Sacks opposed the change in the law on same-sex marriages in the UK

▲ Two Jewish men getting married

Links

For more information about Jewish marriage and the ketubah, see Chapter 2, pages 50–51.

> ❝ The LORD God said, "It is not good for man to be alone: I will make a fitting helper for him." ❞
>
> *Genesis* 2:18

Activities

1 Explain what you think is meant by a 'soulmate'.

2 What is the nature of marriage, according to Jews?

3 Explain three Jewish beliefs about the purpose of marriage.

4 Explain why some Jews disagree with cohabitation.

5 Explain contrasting views about same-sex marriage within Judaism.

Research activity

Find out which Jewish movements perform same-sex marriages or bless same-sex partnerships.

★ Study tip

Try to support your explanation of Jewish beliefs about the nature and purpose of marriage with quotations from the Tenakh, statements by Jewish authorities or words from the marriage ceremony.

Summary

You should now be able to explain Jewish beliefs about the nature and purpose of marriage, and religious and non-religious responses to same-sex marriage and cohabitation.

3.5   Divorce and remarriage

■ Divorce in Britain

In England and Wales in 2012 an estimated 42 per cent of all marriages ended in **divorce**. Divorce is allowed after one year of marriage if the marriage cannot be saved. A legally recognised civil divorce must be obtained through a court. **Remarriage** is allowed as many times as people wish, to a different partner or to their original spouse.

■ Reasons for divorce

There are many reasons why a marriage can fail. One of the most common causes of divorce is adultery. People can change, grow apart and fall out of love. Illness, addiction, work or money pressures and domestic violence or abuse can cause the complete breakdown of a relationship.

▲ *The Jewish court (Bet Din) grants religious divorces*

■ Jewish teachings about divorce

The Torah says a man could divorce his wife 'if he finds something indecent about her', which means finding her guilty of shameful conduct (Deuteronomy 24:1). However, Jewish marriage is a voluntary contract, so a divorce ('get') is allowed if both people agree. There do not have to be grounds (reasons) for divorce. The couple must try **reconciliation** first, but if they no longer love each other 'as one flesh', they can part. In Britain, Jewish couples must obtain a civil divorce, but this is not enough because they would still be considered married under Jewish law. The husband, with his wife's consent, must apply to the Jewish court (Bet Din) for a religious divorce ('get') to break the marriage contract (ketubah). This is particularly important for the woman because without a get her next marriage would be considered adulterous and her children religiously illegitimate.

Jewish teachings about remarriage

Unlike some religious people who believe it is wrong to remarry because the promises couples make before God should last until death, Jews think divorce is sad but not a disgrace. Young couples who divorce when still young are encouraged to remarry to have children because family life is seen as very important. In fact, some feel that it is a special mitzvah to remarry a divorced spouse.

However there are restrictions on remarriage:

- For Orthodox Jews, a couple who have been divorced cannot remarry each other if the ex-wife has married another man between times, even if her second husband has divorced her or died. However, the couple are allowed to marry other people.
- A man who is a kohen (descended from the priestly family) cannot marry a divorcee, even his own ex-wife.
- For both Orthodox and Reform Jews, a woman cannot remarry without a get. Liberal Jews do not require a get.

▲ Jewish couples are encouraged to make an effort to resolve their differences

Non-religious attitudes towards divorce

Most non-religious people accept divorce and remarriage from a practical point of view. They may take the view that if divorce causes the least harm in the situation, then it is morally right. Atheists do not believe that marriage promises are made before God so it is up to the couple to decide on the future of their relationship. The main priority for religious and non-religious people is the wellbeing of any children involved.

> ❝ whenever anyone divorces his first wife even the altar [God] in the Temple sheds tears. ❞
>
> *Babylonian Talmud, Sanhedrin* 22a

Discussion activity

Read the traditional story. With a partner or in a small group, discuss what it teaches about Jewish marriage and divorce.

⭐ Study tip

Look carefully at the scriptures and sacred writings that are the basis for Jewish beliefs about divorce and remarriage, so that you can refer to them if you need to.

Stories from Jewish tradition

A joyous divorce

A woman was married for many years to her husband, but had not had children. Her husband decided to divorce her, so he went to the rabbi. The rabbi said that just as they had celebrated their marriage with joy, so should they celebrate their divorce. Therefore the husband held a great feast. He told his wife to choose whatever possessions of his she wanted and that he would not refuse her anything.

His wife served him so much wine that he got drunk and fell asleep on his bed. She told her servant to take him on his bed to her bedroom in her father's house. Next morning, he asked why he had been brought there – wasn't it clear that he intended to divorce her?

She replied, 'Didn't you tell me that I could take whatever I wanted? I desire not gold, nor silver, nor precious gems, nor pearls. All I want is you.'

When the husband heard this, his love for his wife was rekindled and he took her back. God blessed his decision by granting them children.

Midrash Rabbah, Shir HaShirim 1

Summary

You should now understand some reasons for divorce and religious and non-religious attitudes to divorce and remarriage in contemporary British society. You should be able to explain Jewish beliefs about divorce and remarriage.

Religious teachings about the nature of families

The nature of families in Britain today

In contemporary Britain, the types of families may have changed but the **family** is still considered the best environment for bringing up children and keeping society stable. The basic unit of mother, father and children (a **nuclear family**) is still most common in the UK, although now approximately 25 per cent of children live in single-parent families. There are more 'blended families' or 'step families', where divorced people with children have married new partners with children of their own. **Same-sex parents** may have children from previous relationships, legally adopt children, conceive through in vitro fertilisation, or use surrogates. In the past, families were larger, often including grandparents and other relatives (an **extended family**) all living together. For many non-Western cultures, the extended family unit is still very common.

Jewish beliefs about the family

In Judaism, the family is very important. It is in the family that religious practices such as welcoming Shabbat and keeping kosher are learned and where many festival activities take place. It is also where children learn the values of charity, respect, kindness, hospitality and peace.

The Jewish people view themselves as an extended family. Jews address God as the God of Abraham, Isaac and Jacob, and Reform Jews add Sarah, Rebecca, Rachel and Leah. Jews are referred to as the Children of Israel. It is through the Jewish family that Jewish culture and identity is preserved.

There are examples in the Tenakh of people who practised **polygamy**, and there was a law that protected inheritance rights of the firstborn child (Deuteronomy 21:15–16). However, Jews believe that at the beginning God created the ideal marriage of one man and one woman for life. For over a thousand years in Europe, rabbis have forbidden polygamy. Polygamous marriages cannot be performed in Britain because **bigamy** is illegal.

The role of parents and children

Jewish men and women are equal but have different, complementary roles within the family. Traditionally, men were expected to work, provide for their wife and children, and take responsibility for decisions in the family. Women were expected to look after the home and raise children. Some Jews still follow this pattern but in contemporary Britain it is not unusual for both parents to work and share domestic responsibilities.

Jewish parents are expected to love and care for their children, set a good example for them, teach them right from wrong, and bring them up in their faith. Parents are increasingly sending their children to schools with a Jewish faith basis, or may send their children to classes to learn how to read Hebrew and to study the Torah and Talmud, particularly to prepare for Bar or Bat Mitzvah. Some Orthodox parents will try to help find a suitable marriage partner for their children.

Objectives

- Explore the nature of families in the twenty-first century.
- Understand Jewish beliefs and teachings about the nature of families and the role of parents and children, including the issues of polygamy and same-sex parents.

Key terms

- **family:** a group of people who are related by blood, marriage or adoption
- **nuclear family:** a couple and their dependent children regarded as a basic social unit
- **same-sex parents:** people of the same sex who are raising children together
- **extended family:** a family that extends beyond the nuclear family to include grandparents and other relatives as well
- **polygamy:** the practice or custom of having more than one wife at the same time
- **bigamy:** the offence in the UK of marrying someone while already married to another person

Links

For information on family life and festivals, look back to Chapter 2, pages 46 and 56–59.

Links

For more information about gender equality, see pages 78–79 in this chapter.

Grown-up children honour their parents as commanded in the Torah, and care for them in old age.

> ❝ Honour your father and your mother. ❞
>
> *Exodus* 20:12

The Talmud explains that honouring parents involves giving them food, drink, clothes and shoes. If they wish to meet people, they should be able to go out and get home safely. Jewish families may ask elderly parents to live with them when they are no longer able to live on their own, or make provision for them in appropriate care homes. Increasingly, grandparents are taking a greater part in helping in the family, sometimes almost reverting to the traditional extended family.

> ❝ Grandchildren are the crown of their elders, And the glory of children is their parents. ❞
>
> *Proverbs* 17:6

Orthodox Jews disapprove of same-sex parents because male homosexual relationships are forbidden in the Torah. They may also feel that it is best for children to grow up with a male and female role model as parents, just as the biblical role model is Adam and Eve. Reform Jews who do not object to homosexual relationships think the most important thing is for children to be raised in a secure and loving family, regardless of the gender of their parents.

▲ *Judaism teaches respect for older members of the family*

▲ *A Jewish mother has a special and significant role in passing down the faith to her children*

3.7 Religious teachings about the purpose of families

■ The purpose of families

The basic social unit in all societies is the family. It serves a number of purposes:

- It controls sexual behaviour because it is where **procreation** mainly takes place.
- It creates **stability** for family members and also for society itself.
- It provides for the **protection of children**, supplying their basic needs and keeping them safe.
- It is where children learn how to relate to others so they can grow up and contribute positively to society.
- It helps provide safety and security for the sick, elderly and disabled.
- For religious parents, it involves **educating children in a faith**.

■ The purpose of the family in Judaism

The family gives Jews the security and stability they need to practise their faith and pass it on. The family gives children a secure sense of identity and, with other families, a chance to have friends who share their beliefs and religious practices. Within the family, there is safety and security for the sick, disabled or elderly.

For centuries, Jews have been persecuted for being Jewish. At times it has been difficult for them to worship and keep Jewish traditions in public, but within the family they have been able to educate their children in the faith. Jewish parents hope their children will marry Jews and believe that parents have a duty to have children and bring them up as Jews.

■ Educating children in the Jewish faith

Many religious parents choose to raise their children in their faith, but for Jews it is a duty placed on them by God. The Shema, the important Jewish prayer, includes an instruction to teach children God's commandments:

> ❝ Take to heart these instructions with which I charge you this day. Impress them upon your children. Recite them when you stay at home and when you are away, when you lie down and when you get up. ❞
>
> *Deuteronomy 6:6–7*

A child learns how to be a Jew from family life, and by listening to family stories and teachings from Jewish scripture and traditions.

Objectives

- Explore the purpose of families in contemporary British society.
- Understand Jewish beliefs and teachings about the purpose of families, including procreation, stability, the protection of children and educating children in a faith.

Key terms

- **procreation:** bringing babies into the world; producing offspring
- **stability:** safety and security; a stable society is one in which people's rights are protected and they are able to live peaceful, productive lives without continuous and rapid change
- **protection of children:** keeping children safe from harm
- **educating children in a faith:** bringing up children according to the religious beliefs of the parents

Activities

1 Explain three purposes that the family serves in society today.

2 Explain two ways in which Jewish families might differ from non-religious families in contemporary Britain.

3 Explain contrasting beliefs in contemporary Britain about caring for the elderly.

> 66 The parent who instructs by personal example rather than mere words, his/her audience will take his/her advice to heart. The parent who does not practise what he/she so eloquently preaches, his/her advice is rejected. 99
>
> *Commentary to Ethics of Our Fathers*

Jewish parents try to teach their children how to observe the Sabbath and festivals, and how to keep Jewish dietary laws. They encourage them to take part in study and activities related to their faith. They take them to the synagogue and involve the children in preparing for Shabbat. They are also encouraged to take part in customs linked to festivals, such as clearing the house of leaven before Passover and asking about the meaning of the festival during the traditional seder service.

▲ *A young boy learns about the Passover as the family celebrate, following the ceremony in a special book, the Haggadah*

Judaism recognises that the wellbeing of society is determined by how children are treated. Just as parents were treated with love and care by their own parents, so they must show the same kindness and love to their children and grandchildren. This concern for future generations is shown in a story from the Talmud.

Stories from Jewish tradition

A story from the Talmud

One day when Honi [the righteous man] was out walking, he came upon a man planting a carob tree. "How long will it be before this tree bears fruit?" Honi asked.

"Seventy years," the man replied.

"How do you know you'll be alive in seventy years?"

"Just as I found carob trees when I came into the world," answered the man, "so I am now planting carob trees for my grandchildren."

Babylonian Talmud, Ta'anit, 23

▲ *Esther Rantzen, a well-known Jewish woman, founded ChildLine, which works for the protection of children*

Links

For more information about Jewish practices and festivals, look back at Chapter 2, pages 46 and 56–59.

Discussion activity

Discuss this statement: 'It is never right to disrespect one's parents.' Try to think of two points of view.

⭐ Study tip

Remember that the 'nature' of families can refer both to the different types of families in Britain and to what they should ideally be like. The 'purpose' of families refers to what families are for.

Summary

You should now understand Jewish beliefs and teachings about the purpose of families, including procreation, stability, protection of children and educating children in a faith.

Gender equality in contemporary Britain

Many people in Britain today agree with the idea of **gender equality** but there are also many examples where it does not happen. Something that prevents it is **gender prejudice**, which is often based on **sexual stereotyping**. An example of this is the idea that women are more naturally caring or are the weaker sex, so should look after the home while men go out to work. Sexual stereotyping can lead to **gender discrimination**, perhaps by not giving a man a job that involves looking after young children or not employing a woman on a building site.

The Sex Discrimination Act (1975) made gender discrimination illegal in the UK. Despite this, women generally earn lower pay than men. Some are paid less than men who are doing the same jobs. Women make up roughly half of the workforce, but men hold a higher proportion of senior positions.

Discussion activity

Look at a list of staff in your school. Count the number of male and female staff. Are they about equal? Put a mark next to the teachers who hold positions of responsibility and a different colour mark next to those who do not. What conclusions might you draw from your findings?

Jewish beliefs about gender equality

Jews regard men and women as equals. Everyone is created in the image of God and therefore equal in God's sight.

The Tenakh tells stories of many important women who are greatly respected: Deborah, Abigail and Huldah are considered prophets. In traditional Judaism, women had the right to buy, sell and own property, make their own contracts and be consulted about their marriage long before these rights were given to women in other cultures. There is

▲ *Jewish women are expected to dress modestly but some might see this as gender discrimination*

Objectives

- Understand Jewish beliefs and teachings about the roles of men and women, gender equality, and gender prejudice and discrimination.
- Consider examples of gender prejudice and discrimination in contemporary British society.

Key terms

- **gender equality:** the idea that people should be given the same rights and opportunities regardless of whether they are male or female
- **gender prejudice:** unfairly judging someone before the facts are known; holding biased opinions about an individual or group based on their gender
- **sexual stereotyping:** having a fixed general idea or image of how men and women will behave
- **gender discrimination:** to act against someone on the basis of their gender; discrimination is usually seen as wrong and may be against the law

❝ And God created man in His image, in the image of God He created him; male and female He created them. ❞

Genesis 1:27

nothing in the Torah that says women should not work outside the home. In fact, Proverbs 31:10–31, which is often read at every Shabbat evening before the meal and at Jewish weddings, praises women's business skills as well as their homemaking abilities. Traditionally, Judaism has given men and women different roles in the family and within religion.

The roles of men and women

In Orthodox Judaism, the roles of men and women can be seen as 'separate but equal'. Men are expected to work to support the family, and women to care for the children and the home. Although her responsibilities are different, the mother's role in bringing up children in the faith is so important that Orthodox Jews excuse women from some religious duties. Although Orthodox women cannot be rabbis or sit with men in the synagogue, they can have careers. However, they always try to fulfil their role as wife and mother. Some Jewish women choose to remain at home to raise children because they see it as a greater opportunity for spiritual growth.

In Reform and Liberal Judaism, women are entitled to be rabbis, sit with men in the synagogue and handle the Torah scrolls. In all other areas of life, such as working outside the home and raising a family, Reform Jews are committed to equality of opportunity for women and men, and for equal sharing of duties within the home and within the religion. Israel had a woman Prime Minister (Golda Meir) long before the UK did.

Gender prejudice and discrimination

Some modern Jewish women are pressing for change. They feel that because they have different roles within Judaism, they do not enjoy equal opportunities. One example is the Jewish divorce law which says that only a man can initiate divorce and can refuse to grant a get to his wife, making it impossible for her to remarry within Judaism. Others have to do with rules about modesty, family purity and being able to be a witness in the Jewish law court (Bet Din).

▲ *Israelis, both men and women, must serve in the Israeli army and have equal rights to serve in any role. Jewish women are allowed to carry out national service (e.g. work as a paramedic or with the elderly) if they believe serving with the army will conflict with their religious observance, or if they are married, pregnant or a mother*

Links

For information on other types of prejudice and discrimination, see Chapter 8, pages 160–161.

For more information about gender equality within religion see Chapter 8, pages 162–163.

Discussion activity

Do you think men and women are equal in contemporary British society? Does either gender experience prejudice or discrimination in their roles as parents?

Activities

1 Explain contrasting Jewish beliefs about the roles of men and women.

2 'Jewish women have equal rights to Jewish men.' Evaluate this statement.

Links

For more about divorce, see Chapter 3, pages 72–73.

⭐ Study tip

It is important to remember that 'equal' does not mean 'the same'. Just because women have different roles does not always mean that they are seen to have less value than men.

Summary

You should now be able to explain Jewish and non-religious attitudes to the roles of men and women, gender equality and gender prejudice and discrimination, including examples.

Sex, marriage and divorce – summary

You should now be able to:

✔ explain Jewish teachings about human sexuality, including heterosexual and homosexual relationships

✔ explain Jewish beliefs and teachings about sexual relationships before and outside marriage

✔ explain Jewish attitudes to family planning and the use of different forms of contraception

✔ explain Jewish understandings of the nature and purpose of marriage

✔ explain Jewish and non-religious responses to same-sex marriage and cohabitation

✔ explain reasons for divorce in Britain today

✔ explain Jewish teachings about divorce and remarriage

✔ explain contrasting beliefs in contemporary British society about the three issues of homosexuality, sex before marriage and contraception, with reference to the main religious tradition in Britain (Christianity) and one or more other religious traditions.

Families and gender equality – summary

You should now be able to:

✔ explain Jewish beliefs and teachings about the nature of families and the role of parents and children, including the issues of polygamy and same-sex parents

✔ explain Jewish beliefs and teachings about the purpose of families, including procreation, stability, the protection of children and educating children in a faith

✔ explain religious beliefs, teachings and moral arguments about the roles of men and women, gender equality, and gender prejudice and discrimination

✔ describe examples of gender prejudice and discrimination in contemporary British society

✔ explain contemporary British attitudes (both religious and non-religious) towards all of the above issues.

Sample student answer – the 4 mark question

1. Write an answer to the following practice question:

   Explain two contrasting beliefs in contemporary British society about homosexuality. In your answer you should refer to the main religious tradition of Great Britain and one or more other religious traditions.   **[4 marks]**

2. Read the following student sample answer:

   "Orthodox Jews disapprove of homosexuality because the Torah says that men should not have sex with men. Reform or Liberal Jews think that sex is a private matter and they accept homosexuals in their synagogues and some will conduct same-sex marriages.
   Christian opinions are also divided. Some Christians think that the prime purpose of sexual relationships is to have children and therefore should only be conducted within marriage. Other Christians think that the most important thing is for people to love each other, so homosexuals in committed relationships are welcome in church."

3. With a partner, discuss the sample answer. Is the focus of the answer correct? Is anything missing from the answer? How do you think it could be improved?

4. What mark (out of 4) would you give this answer? Look at the mark scheme in the Introduction (AO1). What are the reasons for the mark you have given?

5. Now swap your answer with your partner's and mark each other's responses. What mark (out of 4) would you give the response? Refer to the mark scheme and give reasons for the mark you award.

Sample student answer – the 5 mark question

1. Write an answer to the following practice question:

   Explain two religious beliefs about divorce.
   Refer to scripture or sacred writings in your answer. **[5 marks]**

2. Read the following student sample answer:

   "Jews are not in favour of divorce. In fact it says in the Tenakh, 'Do not break faith with the wife of your youth. "I hate divorce," says the Lord.' But Jews accept that sometimes marriages break down and it is in the couple's interest to part. The Torah says that a man can divorce his wife if he finds something indecent about her. Since a Jewish marriage contract (ketubah) is voluntary, the couple can divorce as long as they both agree.
   Jews have to go to the Bet Din to obtain a 'get' (divorce) so that they can marry someone else. They are usually advised to try to reconcile their differences before taking such a serious step, but if they no longer love each other 'as one flesh' they can go ahead and obtain a get."

3. With a partner, discuss the sample answer. What does the answer contain that is particularly important? How do you think the answer could be improved?

4. What mark (out of 5) would you give this answer? Look at the mark scheme in the Introduction (AO1). What are the reasons for the mark you have given?

5. Now swap your answer with your partner's and mark each other's responses. What mark (out of 5) would you give the response? Refer to the mark scheme and give reasons for the mark you award.

Practice questions

1. Which one of the following is the name given to the practice in some religions of having more than one wife?

   A) Procreation   B) Contraception   C) Stability   D) Polygamy   **[1 mark]**

2. Give two religious beliefs about the purpose of families.   **[2 marks]**

3. Explain two contrasting beliefs in contemporary British society about sex before marriage.

   In your answer you should refer to the main religious tradition of Great Britain and one or more other religious traditions.   **[4 marks]**

4. Explain two religious beliefs about the nature of marriage.

   Refer to scripture or sacred writings in your answer.   **[5 marks]**

5. 'Same-sex parents are just as good at bringing up children as other parents.'

   Evaluate this statement. In your answer you:
   - should give reasoned arguments in support of this statement
   - should give reasoned arguments to support a different point of view
   - should refer to religious arguments
   - may refer to non-religious arguments
   - should reach a justified conclusion.   **[12 marks]**

How big is our universe?

We can imagine just by seeing the sky on a cloudless night that the **universe** is enormous. Our galaxy, the Milky Way, is one of billions of galaxies in the universe. If a rocket could travel at the speed of light, it would take around 100,000 years to cross the Milky Way. Light travels at a speed of 186,000 miles per second, which is equal to 671 million miles an hour or about 6 trillion miles a year. Travelling to the next galaxy would take about 2.5 million light years. Scientists claim that the currently observable universe is about 93 billion light years in diameter. No one knows if the universe goes on forever or if it's the only one that exists. Was there a time when nothing existed? Did the universe come about by accident or was it designed and created?

The creation of the universe

Christians and Jews share the same creation stories. They are found in Genesis, the first book of the Torah. Genesis 1 and 2 tell of how, by speaking, God created everything that exists. It is difficult to say what was there 'before' since there was no time.

> " When God began to create heaven and earth – the earth being un-formed and void … "
>
> *Genesis* 1:1

Creation took six days (Genesis 1) and God was pleased with his work and on the seventh day God rested and made it holy. During the first four days, the earth, the sky, the seas and plants were created. Then, on the fifth day, came living creatures, birds and fish. On day six, the animals and humans were made.

> " And God created man in His image, in the image of God He created him; male and female He created them. "
>
> *Genesis* 1:27

Some Orthodox Jews take this account literally and believe that this is exactly how the world was created. The Jewish calendar was designed to start with the day when Adam and Eve were created (the sixth day of creation). The calendar suggests that the world is less than 6000 years old and that we currently live in the 5770s. Historically, this was the

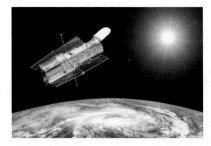

▲ *The Hubble Space Telescope has looked further into space than any other telescope*

view held by many famous rabbis but most modern rabbis accept that the world is much older than this.

Many Jews have, for hundreds of years, interpreted the creation stories not in a literal way, but as expressing spiritual ideas through symbols. Today, Reform Jews and others continue to understand these stories to be important, not as scientific accounts, but as ways of emphasising the special place human beings have in the creation, the belief that they are made in the image of God, and their responsibility for the world.

Today, many Jews believe that it is impossible to know the length of each of the 'days' of creation. They argue that time itself is one of God's creations and the 'days' referred to in Genesis may be just an indication of the stages of creation, and each day could represent millions of years. For example, within Orthodox Judaism, there is a wide range of views about the age of the universe and the age of the earth.

■ The Big Bang theory

Scientists have held several theories about how the universe was formed. Currently the leading scientific explanation is the **Big Bang** theory, which suggests that about 13.8 billion years ago, the universe began as an incredibly hot and very dense point that started to expand. The expanding material cooled and became grouped together, forming the stars and galaxies we know of today. Some scientists are puzzled that the rate of expansion appears to be accelerating and not slowing as they would have expected.

> ❝ in Your sight a thousand years are like yesterday that has past, like a watch in the night ❞
>
> *Psalm* 90:4

Many Jews believe that the Big Bang theory suggests that the universe started at a particular moment, so it does not conflict with the Genesis account. They argue that the cause of the Big Bang was God and that the universe came about by design, not by accident. This interpretation is possible if each of the 'days' of creation in the Genesis story stands for a long period of time and not just 24 hours.

▲ *Deep space*

Discussion activity

In pairs or small groups discuss the following statement:

'God must have created the universe; no other idea makes sense.'

Activities

1 How does Genesis explain the formation of the universe?
2 What happened during the 'days' of creation?
3 What religious values do Jews believe are to be found in the creation stories?

⭐ Study tip

Make sure you know the Genesis creation stories and the different ways Jews interpret them.

Summary

Jews believe that God created the universe and was pleased with his creation. You should now know about the scientific theory of the Big Bang, and how different Jews interpret this theory.

Activities

1 Explain why many modern Jews believe that the world is much older than the Jewish calendar suggests.
2 Explain Jewish views about the scientific theory of the Big Bang.

4.2 The value of the world

■ Stewardship

The Jewish scriptures say that the world belongs to God ('The earth is the Lord's and all that it holds', Psalm 24:1) and that humans have the **responsibility** of looking after his creation. Failure to look after the environment is, therefore, neglecting what God has given to humankind to protect. According to Genesis 2:15, the first man, Adam, was put in the Garden of Eden 'to till it and tend to it'. When Adam and Eve disobeyed God by eating the forbidden fruit, they were thrown out of Eden, and Adam was told: 'By the sweat of your brow shall you get bread to eat, until you return to the ground' (Genesis 3:19).

> ❝ When God created the first human beings, God led them around all the trees of the Garden of Eden and said: "Look at My works! See how beautiful they are – how excellent! For your sake I created them all. See to it that you do not spoil and destroy My world; for if you do, there will be no one else to repair it. ❞
>
> *Ecclesiastes Rabbah* 7:13

In return for the privilege of living on earth, Jews believe that humans, as the pinnacle of God's creation, have the duty to manage the world so that it is not damaged or destroyed. This special responsibility to protect and care for the Earth is known as **stewardship**. The Jewish concept of *bal tashchit*, 'do not destroy', forbids any unnecessary destruction. In return for looking after the world, God has given people permission to use, in a sustainable and unselfish way, the resources he has provided.

■ Dominion

Jews believe that humans have been given the power and authority to rule over the world in order to manage it well. This is known as having **dominion**. In the Garden of Eden, God said to Adam and Eve:

> ❝ Be fruitful and increase, fill the earth and master it; and rule the fish of the sea, the birds of the sky, and all the living things that creep on earth. ❞
>
> *Genesis* 1:28

Although humans rule over the world, they should not do so in a selfish way because people are only tenants of God's property.

■ The value of the world – awe and wonder

It is impossible to put a value on our world because it seems to be unique and irreplaceable. Scientists are unaware of anywhere else in the solar system, or even the universe, that has the right conditions for human life. To destroy the earth would mean the destruction of life. Astronauts, looking at the world from space, are filled with **awe** and **wonder** at

Objective

- Understand Jewish beliefs about the value of the world and the duty of human beings to protect the world.

Key terms

- **responsibility:** a duty to care for, or having control over, something or someone
- **stewardship:** the idea that believers have a duty to look after the environment on behalf of God
- **dominion:** having control or mastery over something
- **awe:** a feeling of respect, mixed feelings of fear and wonder
- **wonder:** marvelling at the complexity and beauty of the universe

▲ *Many people go to visit the vast and amazing Grand Canyon in Arizona, USA*

Activities

1 Explain why the creation stories encourage Jews to care for the world.

2 What is the difference between stewardship and dominion?

3 Explain why the world is so valuable.

the beauty of the planet. The beauty of nature is breathtaking in features such as the Great Barrier Reef, Grand Canyon, Niagara Falls and the Himalayan mountains, and sights like mist in the valley, dew on a cobweb or a golden sunset. The world has the 'wow' factor and Jews believe that this must be cherished.

■ Pollution

Pollution is damaging the world. Air pollution is caused by emissions from factories and vehicles. It leads to acid rain, global warming, and smog in cities like Beijing and Athens. Land pollution, resulting from toxic waste, pesticides and the use of chemicals, can cause contamination, which gets into food production. Water pollution results from oil spills and materials dumped at sea, and chemicals leaking into rivers. Stagnant water on land can become breeding grounds for disease-carrying insects such as mosquitoes. Much of this pollution has been caused by humans.

Jews see pollution control as important because God has given humans the responsibility, as trustees or stewards, to care for the world. At a meeting of leaders of five of the world's major religions in 1986, Rabbi Arthur Hertzberg summed up the Jewish response:

▲ *The beautiful Great Barrier Reef is under attack from pollution and rising sea temperatures*

❝ And not only regarding trees, but even one who destructively breaks vessels or rips up clothing or tears down a building or seals up a spring or wastes food violates the Negative Commandment of 'Do not destroy'. **❞**

Maimonides – Mishneh Torah, Laws of Kings and Wars 6:14

❝ Now, when the whole world is in peril, when the environment is in danger of being poisoned and various species, both plant and animal, are becoming extinct, it is our Jewish responsibility to put the defence of the whole of nature at the very centre of our concern. **❞**

Assisi Declarations on Nature

Activities

1 Describe three ways in which humans are polluting the world.
2 What does the Jewish statement in the Assisi Declarations say about the environment?

Discussion activity

In small groups or pairs, discuss the following statement: 'Caring for the environment is the most important thing a Jew can do.'

Do you agree? Consider other duties which Jews should carry out.

★ Study tip

When considering Jewish attitudes to the world and the environment, it is important to be able to explain the teaching of stewardship and human responsibility.

Summary

You should now know that Jews believe that they have been given the responsibility by God to look after and protect his world. Jews believe that the world is valuable because God created it.

▲ *Material dumped at sea often washes ashore to pollute coastlines*

4.3 The use and abuse of the environment

■ Use but not abuse

As the population of the world increases, there is a greater demand on the planet's **natural resources**. Future generations could be deprived of many important resources because natural resources take many years, in some cases millions of years, to form. Once fossil fuels and minerals are used up they are as good as gone forever. Realising the problem of the current **abuse** of **non-renewable resources**, representatives from governments and religious leaders have met at Earth Summits to try and encourage **sustainable development**. Since the first meeting in Rio de Janeiro in 1992, there have been several other conferences to discuss problems like **deforestation**, greenhouse gas emissions, climate change, pollution, poverty and scarcity of water. The Rio summit resulted in a plan to promote sustainable development called Agenda 21, in which people were encouraged to think globally and act locally. In 2015, this plan was further developed by Agenda 2030, and was supported by many Jews. This Agenda, promoted by the United Nations, is said to be a 'plan of action for people, planet and prosperity'.

■ Renewable resources

Scientists are trying to develop non-polluting forms of energy that produce electricity without using up valuable natural resources. In the right climate and conditions, wind, sunshine and water can be used to generate power without burning fossil fuels. However, many people think large wind turbines spoil the landscape. They argue that solar farms use up large areas of land that could be used for food production. Israel has become a world leader in the use of solar power. Almost every home has a solar-powered hot water system. As it is such a precious commodity, Israel reuses almost all of its waste water for agricultural irrigation rather than letting it run into the sea.

▲ *Many wind turbines have been built in the UK in recent years*

Activities

1 How have Earth Summits tried to address some of these problems?
2 Give three examples of renewable resources that can be used to produce energy.

Objective

- Understand Jewish beliefs about the use and abuse of the environment, including the use of natural resources.

Key terms

- **natural resources:** the various materials found in nature – such as oil and trees – that can be used by people to make more complex products
- **abuse:** misuse, of the world and the environment
- **non-renewable resources:** things the earth provides that will eventually run out as there is a limited amount of them; examples include oil, coal, gas and other minerals
- **sustainable development:** building and progress that tries to reduce the impact on the natural world for future generations
- **recycling:** reusing old products to make new ones
- **deforestation:** the cutting down of large amounts of forests, usually for business needs
- **environment:** the natural world; the surroundings in which someone lives

Activity

Explain briefly the problems caused by the abuse of natural resources.

Research activity

Use the Internet to find out more about the Earth Summits and what they are trying to achieve.

◼ Judaism and the environment

Jews believe that God put human beings in charge to look after the **environment** and they are, therefore, accountable for their actions.

> 66 You have made him master over Your handiwork, laying the world at his feet 99
>
> *Psalm 8:7*

This means that it is important not to abuse the world but to treat it with respect. In the Torah, the Jews were instructed to rest the land once every seven years (Leviticus 25:4–5) and every 50 years, called the Jubilee Year (Leviticus 25:11). This would help the land regain some of its fertility. The destruction of the tropical rainforests is of particular concern for Jews. Deuteronomy 20:19 gives the instruction not to destroy fruit trees when laying siege to a city. Respect for trees is shown at the annual festival of Tu B'Shevat (New Year for Trees), which is held on the fifteenth day of the month of Shevat. Jewish children are encouraged to plant saplings or shrubs on this day, teaching them the importance of preserving the environment.

▲ *Around 7.3 million hectares of forest, an area a little larger than the country of Ireland, are lost each year according to the United Nations' Food and Agriculture Organization*

Coalition on the Environment and Jewish Life

The Jewish Council for Public Affairs set up the Coalition on the Environment and Jewish Life (COEJL). The COEJL works with other faith groups through the National Religious Partnership on the Environment to promote action to care for God's creation. This includes encouraging the use of renewable energy, reducing greenhouse gas emissions and educating people to use natural resources responsibly. It supports Jewish values, such as tikkun olam (healing the world) and promotes the idea of sustainable development. This includes encouraging people to reduce waste, recycle things like glass, paper and cans, and reuse materials where possible. COEJL has highlighted the dangers of mercury emissions as these may cause serious health problems, including damage to the lungs, kidneys, skin and eyes and harm to the nervous and digestive systems.

Discussion activity

In small groups or in pairs, discuss the following statements:

a 'The needs of people are more important than worrying about the use of natural resources.'

b 'Deforestation must be stopped immediately because its impact on the climate is enormous.'

Activity

Explain Jewish beliefs about looking after the land and trees.

Extension activity

Use the Internet to find out more about the work of COEJL.

⭐ Study tip

It would be helpful to know what the Torah says about the environment and be able to give examples of what Jews are doing to protect the world.

Summary

You should now understand Jewish beliefs about the use and abuse of the world's natural resources and the need to live sustainably.

The use and abuse of animals

■ The treatment of animals

Judaism teaches that animals are part of God's creation and that people have a responsibility to treat them with respect and compassion. Jews believe that humans have been made in the image of God and, therefore, are more valuable than animals. However, this does not mean that they believe animals can be treated cruelly or should be exploited for human greed.

The story of Noah and the Ark illustrates how valuable animals are to God, because Noah was instructed to save every species from the flood (Genesis 7:2–3). The teaching of *tza'ar ba'alei chayim* (compassion for the suffering of living creatures) means that causing pain to any living animal must be avoided because they are God's creations. The Talmud interprets the words of God in Deuteronomy 11:15 ('I will provide grass in the fields for your cattle – and thus you shall eat your fill') to mean that Jews should feed their animals before feeding themselves. The Torah contains many teachings about how animals should be treated. For example, in the Ten Commandments, the instruction is given that they should not be worked on the Sabbath day (Exodus 20:10). When they are used for work, they should be treated kindly. For example, they should not be stopped from eating when working.

Objectives

- Understand Jewish beliefs about the use and abuse of animals.
- Explain Jewish attitudes towards animal experimentation and the use of animals for food.

▲ These two oxen have been muzzled to stop them eating while working – forbidden in Deuteronomy

> 66 You shall not muzzle an ox while it is threshing. 99
>
> *Deuteronomy* 25:4
>
> 66 A righteous man knows the needs of his beast 99
>
> *Proverbs* 12:10

Key terms

- **vegetarian:** a person who does not eat meat or fish
- **vegan:** a person who does not eat animals or food produced by animals (such as eggs); a vegan tries not to use any products (such as leather) that have caused harm to animals

■ Animal experimentation

Experiments on animals are widely used to develop new medicines and to test the safety of other products. The animals are usually specifically bred for this purpose. The experiments and tests are controversial because they often cause pain to the animals involved and affect their quality of life.

Because animals are not regarded as equal to humans, Jewish and Christian teaching does not forbid animal testing, providing the reason for the tests is a good one. Research to test potential new medicines that might alleviate human suffering is permitted if there is no alternative way of finding out if it works, and if it is safe for human use. Suffering must be kept to a minimum and the unnecessary repetition of

Contrasting beliefs

Research Christian beliefs about animal experimentation and record any similarities and differences that you find to Jewish beliefs.

experiments should be avoided. Testing products such as make-up and perfume on animals is seen as wrong. In 2007, Israel banned animal experimentation for all cosmetics and cleaning products.

Some Jews oppose animal testing because they think it unacceptable to make animals suffer. Some argue that animals and humans might react differently to medicines, making the animal tests pointless. Another argument is that many of the experiments could be done using computers or cell culture instead.

■ Use of animals for food

In the Genesis creation stories, human beings were at first only given permission to be vegetarians. It was after the flood that God gave Noah permission to eat meat. Jews have strict rules of slaughter (called shechita) in order to keep the animal's suffering to a minimum. This involves cutting the throat with a single stroke using a sharp instrument known as a chalaf. Other rules forbid a cow or sheep from being slaughtered on the same day as its young (Leviticus 22:28). This mitzvah suggests that to kill both mother and offspring on the same day is cruel and shows a lack of mercy, and so it teaches Jews to act with mercy. It is forbidden to eat meat from some animals, for example, pigs. Hunting to provide food is allowed, but not hunting purely for sport. The rules in the Torah allow Jews to eat any animal that has a completely split hoof, and that chews the cud. They may also eat fish which have fins and scales. Many Jews in Britain eat meat and keep the Jewish food laws, including not mixing dairy and meat foods and following kosher (dietary) laws. Some choose to be vegetarians or vegans but this is a matter of personal choice.

▲ *A shop sign in Manchester advertising kosher food*

Extension activity

Use the Internet or the library to find out more about the rules concerning Jewish food, including how animals are slaughtered for meat.

★ Study tip

When you are answering an evaluation question on a controversial issue such as animal experimentation, try to make sure that you can give arguments for more than one point of view.

Activities

1 Explain three examples of the teachings that encourage Jews to treat animals with respect.
2 In what circumstances would some Jews support animal experimentation?
3 Give three reasons why some Jews might oppose all animal testing.
4 When does the Torah say that people were first given permission to eat meat?
5 Explain the Jewish rules about which animals may be eaten and how they should be slaughtered.

Summary

You should now know and understand Jewish beliefs and attitudes to the use and abuse of animals, animal experimentation, and the use of animals for food.

The origins of human life

Adam and Eve

Genesis chapter 1 says that God created the humans on the sixth day of creation, after creating everything else, such as plants and animals.

> ❝ And God created man in His image, in the image of God He created him; male and female He created them. ❞
>
> *Genesis* 1:27

In the second chapter a different explanation is given.

> ❝ the LORD God formed man from the dust of the earth. He blew into his nostrils the breath of life, and man became a living being. ❞
>
> *Genesis* 2:7

Next, God created the Garden of Eden, and to provide Adam with a companion, God created Eve. While Adam was sleeping, God took part of the man's side and formed Eve, the first woman. Both were in the Garden of Eden and had a close relationship with God until they were persuaded by a serpent to eat fruit from the forbidden tree. As a result of their disobedience, Adam and Eve were removed from the Garden. They were not allowed to eat from the tree of life and become immortal.

▲ *'Thorns and thistles shall it sprout …'* (Genesis 3:18)

Women would now face pain in childbirth (Genesis 3:16) and man would need to work hard because the ground would produce thorns and thistles (Genesis 3:17–18).

The Theory of Evolution

During the nineteenth century, an English naturalist, Charles Darwin, went on a five-year voyage around the world to study plants and animals. In Australasia, he saw that many of the plants and animals were different to those found in other parts of the world. As a result of his studies, in 1859 he published a book called *The Origin of Species by Means of Natural Selection*. In it he explained the Theory of **Evolution**.

Put simply, the Theory of Evolution includes the idea that over millions of years, all life developed from simple single-celled organisms. Single cells divided and became two cells and so on. Through random **mutations**, along with natural selection, different species developed,

Objectives

- Understand Jewish beliefs about the origins of human life.
- Explore the relationship between evolution and creation.

Key terms

- **evolution:** the process by which living organisms are thought to have developed and diversified from earlier forms of life during the history of the earth
- **mutation:** the changing of the structure of a gene or chromosome that gives the life-form a different feature to that of the parents'; this difference may be transmitted to following generations
- **adaptation:** a process of change, in which an organism or species becomes better suited to its environment

Activities

1 What do Genesis chapters 1 and 2 say about the creation of human life?

2 Why were Adam and Eve turned out of the Garden of Eden?

such as different sorts of fish. Fish eventually gave rise to amphibians, amphibians to reptiles, reptiles to birds and mammals, and then finally human beings. If a random mutation is an advantage to a creature, it survives and is more likely to breed. Some, like the dinosaurs, die out because they are unable to compete or adapt to changes in the environment. This is called the 'survival of the fittest'; the fittest and most suited to their environment are the creatures that survive.

Many scientists suggest that humans may have started evolving from apes about 2.5 million years ago. They believe that the apes developed into humans with the same anatomy about 200,000 years ago.

▲ *Charles Darwin has appeared on stamps in many countries*

■ Judaism and evolution

Many argue that the Theory of Evolution suggests that creatures change by accident, by chance or because of **adaptation**. The Torah, on the other hand, suggests that a single, deliberate and intelligent force is found in all things and all events because God designed everything. For this reason, some Jews do not accept the Theory of Evolution. Some Jews oppose the theory because they think that scientists' dating of the world is wrong, and the world is much younger. Others believe that the Theory of Evolution does not fit with the belief of a divine creator or with the first two chapters of Genesis.

However, others believe that the Theory of Evolution can be accepted together with the belief in a divine creation. They suggest that the days in Genesis are not meant to be taken as 24-hour days but as much longer periods of time. Many Jews, who accept that the Genesis stories demonstrate spiritual truth and are not to be taken literally, accept evolutionary explanations about life. They believe that God designed nature so that there would be the survival of the fittest and the evolution of species, until eventually human beings existed. Others argue that science and religion are attempting to answer different questions. Science seeks to find out how it happened; Judaism asks the question, 'Why did human life begin?'

> ❝ Lots are cast into the lap; The decision depends on the LORD. ❞
>
> *Proverbs* 16:33

Activities

1 Explain the Theory of Evolution and the idea of the survival of the fittest.

2 Explain Jewish responses to the Theory of Evolution.

3 'Everything has come about by accident, not design.' Evaluate this statement. Give arguments for and against, and reach a conclusion.

Discussion activity

With a partner or in a small group, discuss the following: 'It is not possible to believe in both evolution and Jewish beliefs about the origins of human life based on the Torah.'

⭐ **Study tip**

It is a good idea to be aware of the range of Jewish beliefs about how life developed on earth.

Summary

You should now be able to explain Jewish and scientific beliefs about the origins of life on earth and consider how they relate to each other.

Abortion

■ The sanctity of life and abortion

Judaism teaches that human life is sacred and God-given. Jews believe in the sanctity of life and that humans are made in the image of God (Genesis 1:26–27). Life is precious and a God-given blessing.

> ❝ It was You who created my conscience;
> You fashioned me in my mother's womb. I praise You,
> for I am awesomely, wondrously made; ❞
>
> *Psalm* 139:13–14

Therefore, **abortion** on demand is forbidden in Judaism because it would only be considered for serious reasons.

Pro-life groups, such as the Society for the Protection of the Unborn Child (SPUC), use the concept of the sanctity of life as one of their main arguments against abortion.

Links

To remind yourself of the meaning of the sanctity of life, return to Chapter 1, pages 24–25.

■ The quality of life

A good quality of life means a person can enjoy happiness, health, freedom, dignity and a good standard of living. If an unborn baby looks as if it will have a life of misery and suffering, then its **quality of life** is likely to be very poor. There are several reasons why a poor quality of life might be predicted. For example, if a family is struggling to survive because of extreme poverty, another baby might be difficult to feed. It could face a life of hunger and suffering. Likewise, if tests show that the child is going to be born with severe disabilities, the future for that child is going to be bleak.

Pro-choice groups, such as Abortion Rights, focus many of their arguments in favour of the woman having the right to choose an abortion on quality of life issues.

Objectives

- Understand what is meant by the sanctity of life and the quality of life.
- Consider Jewish beliefs about whether or not it is right to have an abortion.

Key terms

- **abortion:** the removal of a foetus from the womb to end a pregnancy, usually before the foetus is 24 weeks old
- **quality of life:** the general wellbeing of a person, in relation to their health and happiness; also, the theory that the value of life depends upon how good or how satisfying it is

Extension activity

Consider the legal position in the UK and Jewish beliefs on when an abortion might be allowed. Record any similarities and differences.

▲ *Is it possible to decide on the quality of a new life before the baby is born?*

■ UK law on abortion

The 1990 Human Fertilisation and Embryology Act allows
an abortion up to the 24th week in a licensed clinic if two
doctors agree that any of the following conditions apply:

1 the mother's life is at risk as a result of the pregnancy

2 the pregnancy may risk the mother's mental or physical
  health

3 another child will damage the mental or physical health
  of existing children

4 there is a significant risk that the baby will be born with
  severe physical or mental disabilities.

For conditions 1 and 4, the 24th week limit does not apply.

■ Judaism and abortion

Although Jewish teaching does not forbid abortion outright,
it is viewed as something to be avoided if possible because
killing a foetus challenges the sanctity of life and because
Jews are mindful of their duty to save and preserve life
whenever possible.

In Judaism, a foetus is not considered to be a person until it
is halfway down the birth canal, so most Jews do not consider abortion
to be murder. However, the foetus should have some protection because
it is growing towards being a person, and should not be harmed without
a very good reason. The further the pregnancy progresses, the more
characteristics the foetus gains, so if an abortion is to take place,
the earlier it is done, the better.

When the pregnancy is the result of rape or incest, or if the baby would
be born disabled, an abortion may be allowed if there is evidence that
the mother will suffer distress or ill health. The mother's life always
takes precedence over the life of the foetus, so an abortion is carried out
if the mother's life is at risk. There are different views within Judaism
about when an abortion should be allowed, and some Jewish women
may consult a rabbi before making a decision.

▲ *Some believe that it should be the woman's choice
whether or not to have an abortion*

Activities

1 Explain what is meant by the
  sanctity of life.

2 Explain briefly the meaning of
  quality of life.

Contrasting beliefs

Research Christian beliefs that
contrast with Jewish beliefs
about abortion. For example,
find out Roman Catholic and
Methodist views about when life
begins and when an abortion
might be allowed.

★ Study tip

Jews are divided on the issue of abortion.
It would be useful to be prepared to
explain their different responses.

Summary

You should now
understand what is meant
by the sanctity of life and
quality of life, and Jewish
beliefs about abortion.

Discussion activity

Discuss in pairs different circumstances where an abortion might be
considered. One person should argue the case of the sanctity of life and the
other the importance of quality of life.

Activities

1 Under what circumstances does UK law allow an abortion to take place?

2 Explain Jewish attitudes to abortion.

3 'The wellbeing of the mother should be the main reason for an abortion.'
  Evaluate this statement. Give arguments for and against, and reach a
  conclusion.

▪ What is euthanasia?

The word **euthanasia** comes from two Greek words: *eu* which means 'good' and *thanatos* which means 'death', so euthanasia means 'a good or gentle death'. Some people believe that if a person has a terminal illness and is suffering pain and has no hope of recovery, they should be allowed to choose to die.

Euthanasia has been debated several times in Parliament, but is still illegal in Britain. In some European countries, such as Belgium, Holland and Switzerland, euthanasia may be allowed under certain conditions.

▪ Types of euthanasia

- **Voluntary euthanasia** is when the person asks a doctor to end their life.
- **Non-voluntary euthanasia** is when the person is too ill to ask to die but a doctor will end their life for them if it is thought to be in the best interests of the person.
- **Involuntary euthanasia** is the killing of sick and disabled people without considering what is best for them, and without consultation.

▪ Forms of euthanasia

There are two forms: **active euthanasia** and **passive euthanasia**. Active euthanasia is when steps are taken to end a person's life, for example, giving a lethal injection. Passive euthanasia is when the patient dies because the medical professionals either do not take the action necessary to keep the patient alive or they stop treatment that is keeping the patient alive, such as switching off a life support machine.

▪ Judaism and euthanasia

Both Judaism and Christianity teach that active euthanasia is murder. It makes no difference if the person concerned wants to die. Judaism teaches that human life is sacred and

▲ *British grandmother, Jackie Baker, who suffered from a degenerative disease, chose to end her life through assisted suicide at a euthanasia clinic in Switzerland*

of great value. People are regarded as fully human throughout the last stages of life and are entitled to receive good medical care and attention. Jews believe that doctors have a duty to preserve life, and a doctor must do everything he or she can to save a patient's life. That does not mean that Jews believe that if a patient is dying doctors should artificially

> ### Objectives
>
> - Investigate what is meant by euthanasia.
> - Understand Jewish beliefs about euthanasia.

> ### Key terms
>
> - **euthanasia:** killing someone painlessly and with compassion, to end their suffering
> - **active euthanasia:** ending a life by deliberate action, such as by giving a patient a lethal injection
> - **passive euthanasia:** allowing a terminally ill or incurably ill person to die by withdrawing or withholding medical treatment

extend their suffering. Although doctors should not hasten death, in the case of someone who is terminally ill, they are allowed to remove whatever is preventing the person from dying. So if a patient is certain to die, and is only being kept alive by a life support machine, medical professionals would be allowed to switch off the life support machine because it is preventing the natural process of death. Also, it is not forbidden to give pain relief medicine even if it may hasten death, as long as the dose is not certain to kill, and the intention is not to kill, but to relieve pain.

> ❝ A season is set for everything, a time for every experience under heaven: A time for being born and a time for dying ❞
>
> *Ecclesiastes* 3:1–2

▲ *Euthanasia is a complex topic and people's views on it vary greatly*

Stories from Jewish tradition

Rabbi (Judah the Prince) lived in the second century CE. He was a great teacher and his students honoured him. When he was dying, they came and prayed at his house. There was a belief that if the psalms were recited, it would prevent the soul from departing. The story is told in the Talmud, Ketubot 104a:

The Rabbi's maid went up on the roof. She said, "Those on high are seeking Rabbi and those below are seeking Rabbi. May it be God's will that those below conquer those on high!" But when she saw how many times he would take off and put on his tefillin as he went to the toilet, and how he was suffering, she said, "Would that those on high would win against those below." But his students did not cease from begging for God's mercy so that Rabbi would live, so she went up to the roof and took a pot and threw it down hard from the roof. They were interrupted in their prayers and went silent momentarily, and in that moment the soul of Rabbi was able to depart.

Contrasting beliefs

Find out what Christianity says about euthanasia. Learn any similarities or differences between Christian and Jewish beliefs.

★ Study tip

If you are evaluating whether people should support euthanasia, remember to include the fact that there are different forms of euthanasia.

Activities

1. Explain briefly the different types of euthanasia.
2. Briefly describe two situations where people may wish to have euthanasia.
3. Explain Jewish attitudes towards euthanasia.
4. Explain what can be learned from the story of Rabbi (Judah the Prince).
5. 'For those suffering, life should only be prolonged if there is a chance that the patient will fully recover.' Evaluate this statement. Give arguments for and against, and reach a conclusion.

Summary

You should now be able to explain what is meant by euthanasia and Jewish attitudes to it.

Is death the end?

Many people have asked questions about what, if anything, happens after they die. Some claim to have had 'near-death experiences' (NDEs), where they have gone along a tunnel towards a light and in some cases appear to have met deceased members of their families or a divine figure. Some people say that they are able to talk to the dead or that they have seen ghosts. However, there is no scientific proof that such claims provide a glimpse into a possible afterlife. Atheists believe that when the heart stops beating and the brain is dead, the person has stopped living and there is nothing beyond this life.

Judaism does not focus much attention on the afterlife. For Jews, it is this life which is of immediate concern. Jews believe that death is not the end, but have different views on what happens in the afterlife. Many say that although they do not know what happens, they have trust in God.

Life comes from God who is in control of everything. God created humans in his own image (Genesis 1:27) and he breathed life into Adam:

> ❝ the Lord God formed man from the dust of the earth. He blew into his nostrils the breath of life, and man became a living being. ❞
>
> *Genesis 2:7*

Many interpret this as breathing the soul (nefesh) into the body but the Jewish scriptures do not give any clear teaching about the relationship between the body and soul. Jews do not consider this to be important because they believe that God decides the length of a person's life and what happens after death. Ecclesiastes 3:1–2 says there is a time for everything, including 'A time for being born and a time for dying'. So death comes to everyone but exactly what happens when a person dies is not fully understood.

The uncertainty about the afterlife helps Jews to focus on the value and importance of life and to ensure that they obey the command to love God, keep God's laws and remain a holy nation. It is seen as important to follow God and do God's work in the world. If life is respected and valued, and lived according to God's laws, Jews believe that the future can be safely left in God's hands.

The afterlife

Unlike in many other religions, there is little teaching in the Jewish holy books about what happens in the afterlife. The Torah describes death as

▲ *When a Jew visits a loved one's grave, they place a stone there as a sign of memories which are firm and solid*

Objective

● Understand Jewish beliefs about death and an afterlife.

Key term

● **resurrection:** the belief that after death the body remains in the grave until the end of the world, before rising again when God will come to judge

Discussion activity

In pairs, discuss what you believe about life after death. How does this compare with Jewish beliefs?

Contrasting beliefs

Find out what Christianity says about life after death. Learn any similarities or differences between Christian and Jewish beliefs.

a time to re-join one's ancestors (for example, see Genesis 25:8, 17). The phrase used each time to describe this is 'gathered to his people'. A place called Sheol is referred to several times in the Tenakh. It is described as a place of silence (Psalm 115:17) and darkness:

> 66 Before I depart – never to return – For the land of deepest gloom; A land whose light is darkness, All gloom and disarray, Whose light is like darkness. 99
>
> *Job* 10:21–22

Activities

1 Give three examples of why some people believe in life after death.

2 Explain why many Jews are not concerned about what happens after death.

3 What do Jews believe about Sheol?

■ Resurrection

A belief in **resurrection** is held mainly by Orthodox Jews. The prophet Daniel wrote about a time of resurrection when the soul will reunite with the body.

> 66 Many of those that sleep in the dust of the earth will awake, some to eternal life, others to reproaches, to everlasting abhorrence. 99
>
> *Daniel* 12:2

The Talmud also contains some ideas about resurrection. There are references to the idea that the Messiah will come at some time in the future and at that time the righteous dead will resurrect and live in peace in a restored Israel.

There are many different views within Judaism about the afterlife. Reform and Liberal Jews reject the idea of the resurrection of the dead.

■ Judgement

The Jewish afterlife is called Olam Ha-Ba (the World to Come). Many Orthodox Jews believe in heaven (Gan Eden) but not in a place of permanent punishment. A soul-cleansing process, which is temporary, is part of traditional Jewish belief. Judaism does not include the concept of eternal (everlasting) punishment.

Links

For more information about Jewish beliefs about life after death and judgement, look back to Chapter 1, pages 14–15.

★ Study tip

When discussing Jewish beliefs concerning the afterlife, it would be helpful to include the differences between Orthodox and Reform Jews, using examples.

▲ *A funeral procession on the Mount of Olives, Jerusalem; many Jews like to be buried there and hope for a resurrection when the Messiah comes*

Activities

1 Explain what Jews believe about the resurrection of the dead.

2 What do Jews say about heaven, hell and judgement?

Summary

You should now know and understand different opinions in Judaism about death and the afterlife.

The origins and value of the universe – summary

You should now be able to:

✔ explain Jewish teachings, beliefs and attitudes about the origins of the universe, including different interpretations of these

✔ explain the scientific views, such as the Big Bang theory and its relationship with religious views

✔ explain Jewish teachings about the value of the world and the duty of humans to protect it, including the ideas of stewardship, dominion, responsibility, awe and wonder

✔ explain teachings and beliefs about the use and abuse of the environment

✔ explain beliefs about the use of natural resources

✔ explain the problems caused by pollution and Jewish responses to the issue

✔ explain teachings, beliefs and attitudes about the use and abuse of animals

✔ explain religious beliefs about animal experimentation

✔ explain Jewish responses to the use of animals for food.

The origins and value of human life – summary

You should now be able to:

✔ explain Jewish teachings about the origins of human life, including different interpretations of these

✔ explain the relationship between scientific views, such as evolution, and religious views

✔ explain the concepts of the sanctity of life and quality of life

✔ explain religious views concerning the issue of abortion, including situations when the mother's life is at risk

✔ explain religious beliefs about euthanasia

✔ explain Jewish beliefs about death and an afterlife, and their impact on beliefs about the value of human life

✔ explain similar and contrasting beliefs in contemporary British society to the three issues of abortion, euthanasia and animal experimentation, with reference to the main religious tradition in Britain (Christianity) and one or more other religious traditions

✔ explain contemporary British attitudes (both religious and non-religious) towards all of the above issues.

Sample student answer – the 12 mark question

1. Write an answer to the following practice question:

   'There must be life after death.'
   Evaluate this statement. In your answer you:
   - should give reasoned arguments in support of this statement
   - should give reasoned arguments to support a different point of view
   - should refer to religious arguments
   - may refer to non-religious arguments
   - should reach a justified conclusion. **[12 marks]**

2. Read the following student sample answer:

   "Many people claim to have had near death experiences. Many of them follow a similar pattern. For example, when undergoing a heart operation or something similar they experience going along a tunnel towards a bright light at the end. As a result they may believe that there is definitely life after death. Others believe that there are ghosts of those who have died.

Jews believe that there is an afterlife. The Tenakh speaks of a place called Sheol, where the dead go. There, cleansing takes place before it is possible to enter into God's presence. Most Jews hope that there is a resurrection of the dead when the Messiah comes and reigns.

Is this wishful thinking? Atheists believe that death is the end. When the heart stops beating and the brain stops functioning then life finishes. There is no proper evidence to suggest that each person has a soul which lives on forever. No one can prove that there is life after death.

I am not sure what to believe. No one will know for sure if there is life after death until they die. If there is, then they will know. If there isn't then death will be the end. We can't really say that there must be life after death because no one knows for absolute certain."

3. With a partner, discuss the sample answer. Is the focus of the answer correct? Is anything missing from the answer? How do you think it could be improved?

4. What mark (out of 12) would you give this answer? Look at the mark scheme in the Introduction (AO2). What are the reasons for the mark you have given?

5. Now swap your answer with your partner's and mark each other's responses. What mark (out of 12) would you give the response? Refer to the mark scheme and give reasons for the mark you award.

Practice questions

1 | Which one of the following is the number of days the Genesis story says it took God to create the universe?

A) Four   B) Forty   C) Six   D) Sixty   **[1 mark]**

2 | Give two reasons why religious believers might oppose animal experimentation.   **[2 marks]**

3 | Explain two similar beliefs in contemporary British society about euthanasia.
In your answer you should refer to the main religious tradition of Great Britain and one or more other religious traditions.   **[4 marks]**

4 | Explain two religious beliefs about what happens when a person dies.
Refer to scripture or sacred writings in your answer.   **[5 marks]**

> **Study tip**
>
> Limit your answer to two religious beliefs but be sure to explain them. It is important to include references to scripture and sacred writings. These may be quoted or paraphrased and may form part of the explanation.

5 | 'Religious believers should not eat meat.'
Evaluate this statement. In your answer you:

- should give reasoned arguments in support of this statement
- should give reasoned arguments to support a different point of view
- should refer to religious arguments
- may refer to non-religious arguments
- should reach a justified conclusion.   **[12 marks]**

5 The existence of God and revelation

5.1 The Design argument

■ Belief in God

A **theist** believes that God created the universe and life on earth for a purpose. Some theists argue that nature is so complex that God must have designed it. It could not have happened by random chance. An **atheist** believes that there is no God and that there is no evidence that the universe or life on earth was created by God. Atheists argue that the universe just happened and life evolved. An **agnostic** believes that it is impossible to know for certain whether or not God exists. After all, no one can see God or produce God as proof.

■ A Jewish Design argument

The Torah teaches that God's creation was perfect and good. God created order in the world and put humans in charge of creation (see Genesis 1 and 2).

Many Jews believe that Planet Earth, our world, is so well ordered and balanced for life to exist, so complex and beautiful, that it must have been designed. A design needs a designer, and the only one powerful enough to design the universe is God, therefore God exists. Maimonides, a twelfth-century Jewish philosopher, argued for God's design of the universe by quoting this text about how God created a universe of masses of stars, each with a name and purpose:

> ❝ Lift high your eyes and see: Who created these? He who sends out their host by count, Who calls them each by name: Because of His great might and vast power, Not one fails to appear. ❞
>
> *Isaiah 40:26*

Stories from Jewish tradition

A story based on a legend about Rabbi Meir, a second-century rabbi:

A philosopher told a rabbi that he did not believe the world was created by God. The rabbi showed him a beautiful poem and told him it had come into being when a cat accidentally knocked a pot of ink over the paper. The philosopher said it would be impossible: 'There must be an author. There must be a scribe.' The rabbi responded, 'How could the universe … come into being by itself? There must be an Author. There must be a Creator.'

Objectives

- Consider the Design argument, including its strengths and weaknesses.

Key terms

- **theist:** a person who believes in God
- **atheist:** a person who believes that there is no God
- **agnostic:** someone who thinks there is not enough evidence for belief in God
- **Design argument:** the argument that God designed the universe because everything is so intricately made in its detail that it could not have happened by chance

Links

For more information on the creation, look back at Chapter 4, pages 82–83.

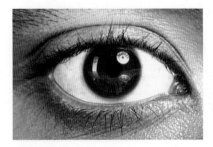

▲ *The eye is more complex than a telescope. Does this prove that God designed it?*

Design arguments

Over the years, Christian philosophers have put forward several versions of the **Design argument** (sometimes called the teleological argument).

Thomas Aquinas (1225–1274)	Only an intelligent being could keep things in the universe in regular order. The planets, sun, moon and stars rotate in a set pattern in the solar system because God holds them in place.
Isaac Newton (1642–1727)	The human thumb's design is so clever, and unique to every individual, that it alone convinced Newton that there was a designer of the world, God.
William Paley (1743–1805)	The intricate workings of a watch show it was designed deliberately for a purpose. Its pieces could not have come together by themselves. Similarly, nature shows evidence of design, for example the eye for sight, birds' wings for flight, etc. The universe is more complicated than a watch and must have had a designer, God.
F. R. Tennant (1866–1957)	If the strength of gravity, the power and speed of the expansion caused by the Big Bang, or the difference in size between a proton and a neutron had been just a tiny bit different, then life would not exist. Therefore the world must have had a designer, God.

■ Strengths and weaknesses of the Design argument

Everyone can see nature is beautiful, complex and follows orderly laws. Most Jews welcome scientific discoveries and see no contradiction between their faith in God as designer of the universe and scientific theories like the Big Bang and evolution.

▲ *The intricate workings of a watch show that it has been designed*

Atheists argue that the process of natural selection (in which the fittest survive and the rest die out) happens by chance. The thumb, the eye and birds' wings are all the result of evolution, not a designer God. Any order in the universe is a natural necessity for life to exist but has not been designed. Humans make up ideas about order just to explain nature.

Atheists also ask why there is so much suffering in the world if God designed it. Cruelty in nature, diseases, earthquakes and wars all suggest any design is faulty. Would a designer God create evil and suffering?

Activities

1 Explain Jewish beliefs about the design of the universe.
2 Explain the Design argument of William Paley.
3 'Natural disasters prove that the world is not designed.' Evaluate this statement.

Research activity 🔍

Try to find out more about the Design arguments of the philosophers mentioned above. Which argument, if any, do you think is the most convincing for the existence of a designer God?

Links

For more details on the problem of suffering and evil, see pages 106–107.

⭐ Study tip

Try to learn one of the more detailed Design arguments, such as William Paley's argument.

Summary

You should now be able to explain and discuss the Design argument, including its strengths and weaknesses.

The First Cause argument

People naturally try to find causes for events that take place, including what caused the universe. If you traced your life back, as suggested in the discussion activity, you would probably find that there are only two possibilities, either there is a starting point when the universe began, or there is no starting point or beginning: the universe goes back into infinity.

The **First Cause argument**, also called the cosmological argument, relies on the belief that the universe had a beginning and a cause like all other things that exist. The argument goes:

- Everything that exists must have a cause – something that starts it off.
- The universe exists so something must have caused its beginning.
- There had to be something eternal that was not caused by anything.
- The **eternal** first cause is God.
- Therefore God exists.

It would be difficult to explain the existence of the universe if it did not have a beginning. Theists claim that God started the chain of events that led to the present.

Over the last 50 years, most scientists have come to accept that the universe began as a result of the Big Bang. But where did the material that was created at the Big Bang come from? What existed before the Big Bang? There must have been a cause for the Big Bang and the start of the universe. Modern theists, including many Jews, would argue that God was the eternal, uncaused cause of the Big Bang.

Thomas Aquinas First Cause argument

Thomas Aquinas, a thirteenth-century Christian philosopher, argued that nothing can become something by itself. Things cannot cause themselves to come into existence; therefore the universe must have been caused by something outside it. Everyone accepts that the universe exists, so, Aquinas argued, it must have had a creator to begin with, an uncaused cause, the eternal, almighty God.

A Jewish First Cause argument

In the eleventh century, Rabbi Bachya ben Joseph ibn Paquda argued that nothing creates itself, so there must be a first cause that is self-existent and eternal.

Objectives

- Examine the First Cause argument for the existence of God, including its strengths and weaknesses.

Discussion activity

With a partner, trace the events of your life back to the moment of your birth, back to when your parents met, back to when they were born, and so on. How far can you go?

Key terms

- **First Cause argument:** also called the cosmological argument, the argument that there has to be an uncaused cause that made everything else happen, otherwise there would be nothing now
- **eternal:** without beginning or end
- **creation:** the act by which God brought the universe into being

▲ *Did God set the universe in motion?*

> ❝ … since it is impossible for a thing to have made itself, it must be that the world has a Maker Who started it and brought it into existence. ❞
>
> Rabbi Bachya ben Joseph ibn Paquda

Maimonides, in the twelfth century, had a similar view:

> ❝ The World is either eternal or created in time. If it is created in time, it undoubtedly has a Creator who created it in time. ❞
>
> Maimonides

■ Objections to the First Cause argument

- Atheists say the argument contradicts itself: if everything that exists has a cause, what caused God?
- If you say that God is eternal and has always existed, why can't the universe always have existed too?
- Just because events have causes, it does not mean the universe itself has a cause.
- The Big Bang was a random, spontaneous event, not an action by God.
- Religious **creation** stories are just myths (stories which tell a spiritual, rather than actual, truth).

Theists would argue back that only God is eternal, beyond time and space. The cause of the Big Bang is not yet known, so why could it not be God?

▲ *Scientists are still trying to discover more about the origins of the universe*

Activities

1 Explain two strengths and two weaknesses of the First Cause argument.

2 Why do dominoes fall in a domino rally? How could this idea link to the First Cause argument?

3 'The First Cause argument is a stronger argument for the existence of God than the Design argument.' Evaluate this statement.

Research activity

Find out about Thomas Aquinas' 'first way' of proving the existence of God. God has been described as the Prime Mover because of this argument.

★ Study tip

Try to remember that Jews believe God created the world, but they do not all agree with the First Cause argument or the Design argument. Some think that God's revelation in the Torah is enough proof of God's existence.

Summary
You should now be able to explain the First Cause argument and discuss its strengths and weaknesses.

■ What is a miracle?

For theists, a **miracle** is an event performed by God that seems to break the laws of nature. The event should have no other explanation. It may be a recovery from a fatal illness that doctors cannot explain or people being saved from almost certain death by a freak occurrence.

For Jews, a miracle is a wonder that shows God's loving power. It can be supernatural, but it does not have to be. The Tenakh speaks of 'signs' and 'wonders' rather than 'miracles' but when extraordinary events happen, they are seen as clear signs of God's power and will. When the prophet Elijah challenged the priests of Ba'al to a contest, God performed a miracle:

> ❝ Then fire from the LORD descended and consumed the burnt offering, the wood, the stones, and the earth; and it licked up the water that was in the trench. When they saw this, all the people flung themselves on their faces and cried out: "The LORD alone is God, The LORD alone is God!" ❞
>
> *I Kings* 18:38–39

Objectives

- Examine the argument from miracles for the existence of God, including its strengths and weaknesses.
- Consider one example of a miracle.

Key term

- **miracle:** a seemingly impossible event, usually good, that cannot be explained by natural or scientific laws, and is thought to be the action of God

God has the power to go against the laws of nature that God created, but God often acts in accordance with those laws; for example, when the Israelites were hungry, while wandering in the desert, God blew quails from the sea for them to eat (Numbers 11:31).

Some people may call a wonderful event like the birth of a baby a 'miracle', but this is not really a miracle in the same way. Babies are born every day and science can explain the process. If a woman was unable to conceive and then did so after praying to God, she might be justified in describing her pregnancy as a miracle. Whether something is a miracle often depends on interpretation and the faith of the witnesses. Jews would regard many wonderful acts of God as miracles, but in relation to arguments about the existence of God, 'miracles' are events which cannot be explained by science.

▲ *'Moses led the people across the Red Sea on dry land' (Exodus 14: 21–22). This miracle is remembered by Jews each year at the festival of Passover*

Argument from miracles

Theists argue that if there is no scientific explanation for an event, then it must be supernatural, in other words, caused by something outside nature. Since only God is outside nature, then it must be the result of God's intervention in the world. Therefore God exists.

Theists believe that miracles show God's love and care for people. They argue that there are too many accounts of miracles for them not to happen, and some happen to non-believers who become believers as a result of them. Many miracles are investigated thoroughly before they are accepted, so that there is sound medical or scientific proof that they are genuine.

There is a traditional Jewish saying that anyone who believes that all the miracles said to have been performed by miracle workers actually happened is a fool, but anyone who believes that they could not have happened is an unbeliever.

Objections to the argument from miracles

Atheists might argue that miracles cannot prove God's existence because:

- miracles are no more than lucky coincidences
- they may have scientific explanations which have not yet been discovered
- miracle healings may be the result of mind over matter on the part of the sufferer, or a misdiagnosis by doctors
- some 'miracles' are fakes, made up by people who want fame or money.

David Hume, an eighteenth-century philosopher, argued against miracles. He said that there can never be enough evidence to deny the laws of nature, and that witnesses to miracles are unreliable because most of them are primitive, uneducated people. Religions depend on miracles to prove they are true, but all the religions cannot be right.

Some theists object to miracles because they seem to show God as unfair by picking and choosing who is helped. For example, why save someone from cancer and allow thousands to die in a natural disaster? They argue that as God is all-just and all-loving, miracles do not happen.

 Does God choose to save only some people?

Extension activity

Interview two people, one from a religious background and one from a non-religious background to find out their views about miracles. Have they known anyone who has experienced a miracle? Do they think miracles are possible?

⭐ **Study tip**

It would be useful to know how Jews and non-believers would explain a 'miracle'.

It is helpful to know contrasting beliefs about miracles with reference to the main religious tradition in Britain (Christianity) and non-religious beliefs such as atheism or humanism.

Activities

1 **a** Choose one example of a miracle from the Tenakh and record what took place. (You could choose one of the events described on these pages or, for example, Exodus 14:15–31, 2 Kings 4:1–7 or 2 Kings 5:1–19.)

   b Explain whether you think God was working within the laws of nature or outside of the laws of nature as the miracle.

2 Explain in detail the reasons why atheists disagree with miracles as evidence for God.

3 'Miracles make God appear unfair.' Evaluate this statement.

Summary

You should now be able to discuss and evaluate the argument from miracles and describe one example of a miracle.

Further arguments against the existence of God

Faith and proof

We have considered three arguments for God's existence: Design, First Cause, and the argument from miracles. None of these offer conclusive **proof** that God exists. Theists already have **faith** in God. These arguments may serve to strengthen their faith. If a belief were proved to be a fact, then it would no longer be a matter of faith.

How science is used to challenge belief in God

Some atheists argue that we do not need to invent a God to make sense of what we do not know at the moment (sometimes called a 'God of the gaps'). Science will eventually discover all the facts about how the universe began. God is not needed.

For most atheists, evolution has shown that there is no specific design in the universe and that living species have naturally adapted to survive. Again, there is no need for God to explain the development of human life. It is just nature. Also, science is now closer to creating human life, and some atheists say this is further evidence that God does not exist.

The question of evil and suffering

We live in a world full of **evil** and **suffering**. The news is full of examples of crimes committed against innocent people and natural disasters that destroy lives. Some atheists use the fact that there is evil and suffering in the world to argue that God does not exist:

- God is believed to be all-knowing, all-powerful and all-loving.
- God therefore should be aware of evil, should be able to prevent it, and would want to do so.
- God does not do this, so God does not exist.

There is cruelty within nature (cats naturally kill mice, for example). Natural disasters are also evidence of 'poor design'. Why would a good God create a world that contains suffering or create humans that choose evil over good?

Jewish responses

Jewish scriptures and science are both seen as showing the same divine truth. The rabbis of the Talmud used astronomical calculations to create the Jewish calendar and referred to many scientific theories of their day. Maimonides, in the thirteenth century, tried to bring together Judaism and science. He said that the Torah must be grounded in reason, so if scientific findings contradicted the Torah, the Torah should be

▲ *Will science replace belief in God?*

interpreted in the light of the new science. Today many Jews, including some Orthodox rabbis, reject a literal reading of Genesis 1 and 2 and accept current scientific explanations for creation. Some Orthodox Jews reject evolution; they believe the creation in Genesis should be taken literally rather than as a religious story.

> ❝ Science takes things apart to see how they work. Religion puts things together to see what they mean. ❞
>
> Rabbi Jonathan Sacks

> ❝ Evolutionary theory, properly understood, is not incompatible with belief in a Divine Creator, nor with the first 2 chapters of Genesis. ❞
>
> Rabbinical Council of America

According to the Torah, God gave Adam free will to choose between right (following God's guidance) and wrong (giving in to temptation):

> ❝ And the LORD God commanded the man, saying, "Of every tree of the garden you are free to eat; but as for the tree of knowledge of good and bad, you must not eat of it; for as soon as you eat of it, you shall die." ❞
>
> *Genesis* 2:16–17

People's faith and character are tested through suffering. Evil arises because humans have freedom of choice over moral issues. While God allows evil, God does not will it. Whatever happens is God's will, so God has reasons for allowing evil that humans cannot know. If God constantly intervened to stop evil, humans would not be free.

> ❝ "We are, first, commanded to survive as Jews, lest the Jewish people perish. We are commanded, secondly, to remember in our very guts and bones the martyrs of the Holocaust, lest their memory perish. We are forbidden, thirdly, to deny or despair of God, however much we may have to contend with him or with belief in him, lest Judaism perish. We are forbidden, finally, to despair of the world as the place which is to become the kingdom of God, lest we help make it a meaningless place in which God is dead or irrelevant and everything is permitted. To abandon any of these imperatives, in response to Hitler's victory at Auschwitz, would be to hand him yet other, posthumous victories." ❞
>
> Emil Fackenheim

Activity

Explain what you think Fackenheim is saying about what the Jews may learn from the evil of the Holocaust.

Activities

1 Explain two ways in which atheists use science to argue that God does not exist.

2 Explain two Jewish responses to these arguments.

3 Explain Jewish beliefs about evil and suffering in the world.

4 'When science discovers all the answers, there will be no need for God.' Evaluate this statement.

Links

For more on creation, see Chapter 4, pages 82–83.

▲ *God created free will so that people have the freedom to choose between right and wrong*

⭐ Study tip

It would be a good idea to learn arguments both for and against the existence of God and use these to form your own conclusion.

Summary
> You should now be able to discuss the arguments against the existence of God based on science and on the problem of suffering and evil.

Special revelation and enlightenment

■ What is meant by the divine?

Every religion accepts that there is an **ultimate reality** that is eternal and unchanging. Ideas about **the divine** include God, gods or ultimate reality. Buddhists, for example, think of ultimate reality as an eternal truth or principle that governs the universe. Hindus worship one God (Brahman) through different gods and goddesses that reveal different aspects of God. Jews emphasise the oneness of God, the source of all life and of all morality and values, in the prayer they say twice a day, the Shema:

> ❝ Hear, O Israel, the Lord is our God, the Lord is One. ❞
>
> *Opening line of the Shema*

Links

For more information on Jewish beliefs about God, see Chapter 1, pages 8–13.

■ How may God be known?

Some theists say that God cannot be known because God is pure mystery and beyond human understanding. Human language limits God, so God cannot be described. Jews accept that God is beyond our limited understanding, but believe that it is possible to know something of God's nature and purposes through **revelation**. Humans can only know God if God chooses to reveal himself to people, not through any efforts of their own. There are two main kinds of revelation: **special revelation** and general revelation.

■ Special revelation

Special revelation is when people experience God directly in a particular event. It might be a dream, a **vision**, a prophecy, a miracle, or hearing 'God's call', either alone or with a group of people. These experiences usually have a huge impact on people and can change their lives.

Jewish scriptures describe God's self-revelation to the Jewish people through the law, the prophets and the covenant. There are many examples of prophets hearing God's call or being asked to give the people God's message. A famous example is the story of Moses and the burning bush.

Visions

A vision is a form of special revelation that comes as a picture or image. People see holy people, angels or hear messages from God. A vision holds a deep meaning for the person receiving it and makes them aware of reality in a new way or with a new intensity. In Isaiah 6:1–6, the prophet Isaiah received a vision of the Lord seated on a throne,

Objectives

- Examine special revelation as a source of knowledge about the divine.
- Consider enlightenment as a source of knowledge about the divine.
- Consider one example of a vision.

Key terms

- **ultimate reality:** the supreme, final, fundamental power in all reality
- **the divine:** God, gods or ultimate reality
- **revelation:** an enlightening experience; a divine or supernatural experience in which God shows himself to believers
- **special revelation:** God making himself known through direct personal experience or an unusual specific event
- **vision:** seeing something, especially in a dream or trance, that shows something about the nature of God or the afterlife
- **enlightenment:** the gaining of true knowledge, particularly in the Buddhist tradition, that frees a person from the cycle of rebirth by seeing what the truth about life really is

Links

For more information about general revelation, see pages 110–111.

Contrasting beliefs

Use the Internet or library to find out about contrasting understandings of the divine in two religions.

Hearing God's call

The Lord's angel appeared to Moses as a flame coming from the middle of a bush. Moses saw that the bush was on fire but was not burning up. When he went to look, God called his name and said: 'Do not come any closer. Remove your sandals from your feet, for the place on which you stand is holy ground […] I am the God of your father, the God of Abraham, the God of Isaac, and the God of Jacob.' (Exodus 3:5–6). Moses covered his face because he was afraid to look at God. God told Moses to return to Egypt and demand the release of the Jewish slaves. Moses was reluctant at first, and he asked God his name. God told Moses to tell the people 'I Shall Be' sent him to their aid. This experience convinced him that he must risk his life and confront the king of Egypt to let God's people go.

▲ *Moses received a special revelation of God (Exodus 3:1–4:17)*

surrounded by winged heavenly beings (seraphim) singing praise to God. Isaiah's lips were touched with a hot coal to show his sins were taken away. Isaiah then heard the voice of the Lord ask: 'Whom shall I send?' and Isaiah replied, 'Here am I! Send me!'.

Enlightenment

Buddhists do not believe in God or gods. Buddhists seek understanding of what is true and what is not, that is, ultimate reality. Through meditation and practising the Buddhist way of life, they hope to achieve **enlightenment** – to end suffering and achieve happiness by escaping the cycle of birth, death and rebirth. Enlightenment is also a goal of Sikhs and Hindus who believe in God. They seek enlightenment through prayer, meditation and following a religious way of life.

▲ *Siddattha Gotama reached enlightenment when he meditated under the bodhi tree*

Research activity

Try to find out the circumstances surrounding the enlightenment of Siddattha Gotama, the Buddha ('the enlightened one').

Activities

1 Read the case study. What did Moses learn about God from his special revelation?

2 Explain, using an example, the effect a vision might have on the person who receives it.

3 What might an atheist say about visions?

4 'God cannot be known.' Evaluate this statement.

⭐ Study tip

Even if you are not studying Buddhism, it is helpful to learn the meaning of 'enlightenment'. It is a form of special revelation, but, in Buddhism, not a revelation from God.

Summary
You should now be able to discuss what is meant by special revelation, including enlightenment and visions.

General revelation

■ General revelation

Unlike special revelation, which is direct and sometimes dramatic, **general revelation** comes through ordinary, everyday experiences that are open to everyone. Some people feel God's presence in **nature** or when they read religious **scriptures** or take part in worship. Some feel sure of God's existence through their reason, conscience or sense of right and wrong. For others, the lives and work of religious leaders who seem particularly close to God reveal something of God's purposes for humans. General revelation is available to anyone, but these experiences do not convince everyone that God is real because they depend on people's interpretation.

Some examples of revelation can be both general and special, depending on the circumstances. For example, reading scripture is open to anyone (general) but it may be the means of a direct personal experience of God for an individual (special).

▲ *Can scriptures light the way to an understanding of God?*

■ Nature as a way of understanding the divine

The beauty of nature, the power of storms and the sea, the wonder of a newborn baby, the complexity of the human body and the order and design in nature reveal God as present within the creation to many people. The Tenakh has many verses which speak of the natural world as a sign of God's power, wisdom and love for his creation:

> **❝** How many are the things You have made, O Lᴏʀᴅ; You have made them all with wisdom; the earth is full of Your creations. There is the sea, vast and wide, with its creatures beyond number, living things, small and great. **❞**
>
> *Psalm* 104:24–25

Objective

- Examine general revelation, including nature and scriptures, as a way of understanding the divine.

Key terms

- **general revelation:** God making himself known through ordinary, common human experiences
- **nature:** the physical world, including plants, animals and landscape; the environment or natural world
- **scriptures:** the sacred writings of a religion

Links

Remind yourself of the Design argument on pages 100–101.

Activities

1 Explain, giving an example, the meaning of general revelation.

2 How is a general revelation different from a special revelation?

3 Explain what nature reveals to Jews about God.

> ❝ Give ear to this, Job; stop to consider the marvels of God. Do you know what charge God lays upon them when His lightning-clouds shine? Do you know the marvels worked upon the expanse of clouds by Him whose understanding is perfect … ❞
>
> *Job* 37:14–16

Just as a sculpture or piece of music gives an insight into the artist, so nature gives believers an insight into God. When Jews look at the world around them, they think God is shown as creative, artistic, clever, powerful and awesome. This leads to feelings of awe and wonder at the power of God to create and to destroy. There are many blessings that Jews may say on seeing oceans, magnificent mountains, rainbows or other natural wonders.

■ Scripture as a way of understanding the divine

One of the main ways in which the divine is revealed is through the scriptures (sacred writings) of a religion. For Jews, the Tenakh (the Torah, the prophets and the writings) reveals God's commands and saving actions on behalf of the Jewish people. Just as there are differences of opinion within Christianity about the interpretation of scriptures, so too the Tenakh is interpreted differently by different groups of Jews. Orthodox Jews regard the Torah as the word of God revealed through Moses to the people of Israel at Mount Sinai around 1280 BCE. The word of the Torah is considered divine and timeless, and therefore cannot be altered. Reform and Liberal Jews think the Torah was inspired by God, but that God's will was revealed to human beings gradually, over a period of time. They think scriptures need to be interpreted in the context of society today.

Some people, such as atheists or humanists, believe that scriptures cannot reveal anything about God because they are merely their authors' opinions. Atheists might admire scriptures as ancient historical documents, but they would not regard them as evidence for God's existence.

▲ *Does nature reveal the majesty of God?*

Research activity 🔍

Read Psalm 8. What does nature reveal about God, according to the psalmist? Explain how an atheist would respond to this psalm.

Discussion activity 💬

'Scriptures are the words of human beings, not the words of God.' With a partner or in a small group, discuss this statement. Share your ideas with the class.

⭐ Study tip

It is helpful to know contrasting beliefs about nature as a way of understanding the divine with reference to the main religious tradition in Britain (Christianity) and non-religious beliefs such as atheism or humanism.

Contrasting beliefs

Use the Internet or library to find out more about contrasting religious beliefs about nature and revelation.

Links

To remind yourself of the Jewish scriptures, see Chapter 2, pages 44–45.

⭐ Study tip

It would be helpful to be able to identify the differences between special and general revelation. Try to remember that scriptures can be an example of both, depending on the circumstances.

Summary

You should now be able to discuss what is meant by a general revelation and how nature and scripture reveal the divine to some people.

■ Different ideas about the divine

Religions may describe the nature of God, gods or ultimate reality in different ways. As we have already noted, it is difficult to describe the unseen, infinite God within the limits of human language. Yet there are many similarities in the way different religions understand the divine or describe God's nature.

All major religions apart from Buddhism agree that there is only one God who is creator, controller and maintainer of the universe. God is seen as omnipotent and capable of doing anything, such as creating the universe. God is omniscient because God is aware of everything that happens, past, present and future. God is seen as **benevolent** in providing everything people need for survival on earth.

▲ *What does this picture suggest about God as transcendent?*

Religious thinkers use the words immanent, transcendent, personal and impersonal to describe the differences between ideas about God.

- An **immanent** God is present in the universe and involved with life on earth. People are able to experience God in their lives. God acts in history and influences events.

- A **transcendent** God is beyond and outside life on earth and the universe. God is not limited by the world, time or space. God existed before the universe he created so is separate from it. A transcendent God does not intervene in people's lives.

- People who believe God is **personal** think of God as having human characteristics, such as being merciful or compassionate. They believe God loves and cares about every individual and that they can have a relationship with God through prayer.

Objectives

- Investigate the different ideas about the divine that come from revelation.
- Know and understand qualities of God such as omnipotent, omniscient, benevolent, personal, impersonal, immanent and transcendent.

Key terms

- **benevolent:** all-loving, all-good; a quality of God
- **immanent:** the idea that God is present in and involved with life on earth and in the universe; a quality of God
- **transcendent:** the idea that God is beyond and outside life on earth and the universe; a quality of God
- **personal nature (of God):** the idea that God is an individual or person with whom people are able to have a relationship or feel close to
- **impersonal nature (of God):** the idea that God has no 'human' characteristics, is unknowable and mysterious, more like an idea or force

Links

To remind yourself of why the existence of suffering and evil makes some people question these qualities of God, see page 106–107.

Links

To remind yourself of Jewish beliefs about God, see Chapter 1, pages 8–13.

- An **impersonal** God is the opposite and does not have human characteristics. God is more like a force or an idea, like a prime number (a number that can only be divided by itself and 1). This God is an absolute being, which is only understood in terms of itself.

Can God be immanent and transcendent, personal and impersonal?

Many religious people, including Jews, believe they can experience God and have a personal relationship with him (immanent and personal) but also that God is the eternal, unlimited creator of the universe (transcendent and impersonal). Some religions emphasise one description more than another, but others say that all these aspects of God's nature are true even though they seem contradictory. God is a mystery, beyond human understanding.

Jews believe they have a special relationship with God because God made a covenant with them through Abraham and Moses. God will protect the Jews as long as they obey his laws. In the Torah, God is described as both merciful and just. His punishments are tempered by his love and compassion for his people.

▲ *Many Jews feel the personal presence of God with them wherever they are*

For Jews, God is beyond human knowledge and understanding, omniscient and omnipotent. He is awesome, the Lord of creation:

> ❝ So that they know, from east to west, that there is none but Me. I am the Lᴏʀᴅ and there is none else, I form light and create darkness, I make weal and create woe – I the Lᴏʀᴅ do all these things. ❞
>
> *Isaiah 45:6–7*

Research activity 🔍

Look up Exodus 34:5–7 and write down all the descriptions of God given in these verses. Explain what these descriptions add to your understanding of Jewish beliefs about God.

⭐ Study tip

Try to use the key terms listed here in your answers to show your knowledge of technical vocabulary.

Activities

1 Explain what religious believers mean when they say God is:

   a immanent

   b personal.

2 Explain why religions have different ways of describing God.

3 'It is easier to think of God as personal rather than impersonal.' Evaluate this statement.

Summary

You should now be able to explain and discuss different ideas about the divine that come from revelation and understand some of the qualities that are used to describe what God is like.

The value of revelation and enlightenment

■ The value of revelation and enlightenment

As we have seen, all forms of revelation (special or general) and enlightenment have great value to believers. Revelation or enlightenment can:

- provide theists with proof of God's existence
- help start a religion
- enable believers to have a relationship with the divine or to understand the truth about life (enlightenment)
- help people to know what they must do to live as God wishes.

Individual revelations can have a huge impact on those who receive them, often changing not only their religion but their entire way of life.

All of these factors apply to Judaism. God's revelation to Abraham persuaded him to abandon the worship of idols and believe in the one God, travel to Canaan and establish the Jewish nation. The revelation of the Torah to Moses on Mount Sinai, witnessed by the entire community and totally accepted by the people, enables Jews to fulfil the conditions of their covenant relationship with God; the Torah helps them to live as God wishes by following his commandments. The patriarchs and prophets often received direct revelations from God that required a complete change of life or resulted in persecution and threats of death. An example is the prophet Jeremiah. He was attacked by his own brothers, beaten and put into the stocks by a priest, imprisoned by the king, threatened with death, thrown into a pit by Judah's officials, and opposed by a false prophet.

Objectives

- Investigate the value of revelation and enlightenment as sources of knowledge about the divine.
- Understand difficulties in accepting the reality of some examples of revelation.

▲ Jeremiah's life was threatened because of his revelations from God

> So they took Jeremiah and put him down in the pit […] which was in the prison compound; they let Jeremiah down by ropes. There was no water in the pit, only mud; and Jeremiah sank into the mud.
>
> *Jeremiah* 38:6

All these stories of people who received revelations from God can be read in the Tenakh to inspire faith and courage in people today.

■ Revelation – reality or illusion?

Atheists would say that God does not exist, so all revelations are illusions. Some revelations may be difficult to prove, even to religious

Links

To remind yourself of the covenant, see Chapter 1, pages 18–21.

believers, because they are subjective, cannot be tested scientifically, and can be interpreted in different ways.

To determine whether a revelation is real, religious people might consider whether the revelation:

- matches the real world, for example the claim that people can fly is less likely to be real than the claim that water in a place can, and does, cure people

- supports the beliefs of a religion or contradicts them

- has an impact, for example changes an atheist or agnostic into a believer, or converts someone from one religion to another.

▲ *Mirages show how the mind can play tricks.*

Different ideas arising from revelations

Atheists argue that religions have conflicting revelations which show that they cannot be true. Buddhists do not believe in God, and within other faiths there are different understandings of God.

There are conflicting ideas between religions about how God wants people to live, for example drinking alcohol is forbidden in the Qur'an, but the drinking of wine forms part of many Jewish religious festivals. Even within a religion, there may be different interpretations of the meaning of particular revelations. For example, Orthodox and Reform or Liberal Jews do not always agree on the interpretation of scriptures or how these should be applied to moral issues.

Alternative explanations of revelations

Atheists put forward other explanations for these experiences. For example, a special revelation, such as a vision, could be brought about by alcohol or drugs, or the person could be so desperate to have a revelation that it is just wishful thinking. The person may be suffering from a physical or mental illness that makes them hear voices or makes their mind play tricks. There is also the possibility that the people who claim to have revelations are lying in order to achieve fame or money, or are merely mistaken.

Atheists would say that general revelations depend on a person's religious beliefs in the first place, so they cannot reveal anything about God, especially to an unbeliever. For example, when an atheist and a theist look at a beautiful landscape, one just sees nature and the other sees God's creation.

Activities

1 Explain why revelation is important to the Jewish community.

2 Explain three reasons why atheists reject revelations.

3 'It is impossible to prove whether or not a revelation is true.' Evaluate this statement.

⭐ Study tip

In this theme you may also be asked about enlightenment. This term is more commonly used in Buddhism.

Summary

You should now be able to explain the value of revelation and enlightenment for religious believers and discuss the difficulties in accepting the reality of some examples of revelation.

💬 Discussion activity

Remind yourselves of what you found out about the Buddha's enlightenment in the Research activity on page 109. In pairs, imagine you lived at the time of the Buddha. How would you know whether he had truly become enlightened? Write down three questions you would want to ask him, and get your partner to write down what he might reply.

Philosophical arguments for and against the existence of God – summary

You should now be able to:

✔ explain and evaluate the Design argument, including its strengths and weaknesses

✔ explain and evaluate the First Cause argument, including its strengths and weaknesses

✔ explain and evaluate the argument from miracles, including its strengths and weaknesses

✔ describe one example of a miracle

✔ explain and evaluate the arguments against the existence of God based on science and on the problem of suffering and evil.

The nature of the divine and revelation – summary

You should now be able to:

✔ explain what is meant by special revelation and enlightenment as sources of knowledge about the divine (God, gods or ultimate reality)

✔ describe one example of a vision

✔ explain what is meant by general revelation, including nature and scripture as a way of understanding the divine

✔ explain the different ideas about the divine that come from revelation

✔ explain the meaning of qualities of God such as omnipotent, omniscient, benevolent, personal, impersonal, immanent and transcendent

✔ explain the value of revelation and enlightenment as sources of knowledge about the divine

✔ explain and evaluate the difficulties in accepting the reality of some examples of revelation

✔ explain and evaluate the problem of different ideas about the divine arising from these experiences

✔ explain and evaluate alternative explanations for the experiences and the possibility that the people who claimed to have them were lying or mistaken

✔ explain contrasting perspectives in contemporary British society to all the above issues

✔ explain contrasting beliefs in contemporary British society to the three issues of miracles, visions, and nature as a source of revelation, with reference to the main religious tradition in Britain (Christianity) and non-religious beliefs such as atheism or humanism.

Sample student answer – the 4 mark question

1. Write an answer to the following practice question:

   Explain two contrasting beliefs in contemporary British society about nature as a source of knowledge about the divine.

   In your answer you should refer to the main religious tradition of Great Britain and non-religious beliefs. **[4 marks]**

2. Read the following student sample answer:

   "Christians believe that nature is so complex and suited to its purposes that there must have been a divine being who created all that there is. When a Christian looks at a beautiful natural scene, he or she may feel God's presence, majesty and power.
   Atheists may find nature beautiful but they do not think it is evidence for God. They think the world started with the Big Bang and just evolved without any need for a creator."

3. With a partner, discuss the sample answer. Is the focus of the answer correct? Is anything missing from the answer? How do you think it could be improved?

4. What mark (out of 4) would you give this answer? Look at the mark scheme in the Introduction (AO1). What are the reasons for the mark you have given?

5. Now swap your answer with your partner's and mark each other's responses. What mark (out of 4) would you give the response? Refer to the mark scheme and give reasons for the mark you award.

Sample student answer – the 5 mark question

1. Write an answer to the following practice question:

   Explain two religious beliefs about what God is like.

   Refer to scripture or sacred writings in your answer. **[5 marks]**

2. Read the following student sample answer:

   "Jews believe in the oneness of God. God has no equal and only God should be worshipped. This belief in the unity of God affects every aspect of life including the way Jews behave. This belief in one God is called monotheism, whereas belief in many gods is called polytheism.
   Jews also believe that God is immanent. An immanent God is one who is involved in human life and in events on earth. Jews think that people can experience God by praying to God and that God acts in history to save people."

3. With a partner, discuss the sample answer. It fails to do something which is important. How do you think the answer could be improved?

4. What mark (out of 5) would you give this answer? Look at the mark scheme in the Introduction (AO1). What are the reasons for the mark you have given?

5. Now swap your answer with your partner's and mark each other's responses. What mark (out of 5) would you give the response? Refer to the mark scheme and give reasons for the mark you award.

Practice questions

1. Which one of the following best expresses the idea that the divine (God, gods or ultimate reality) is all-knowing?

   A) Omnipotent   B) Omniscient   C) Transcendent   D) Immanent   **[1 mark]**

2. Give two types of special revelation. **[2 marks]**

3. Explain two contrasting beliefs in contemporary British society about the Design argument for God's existence.

   In your answer you should refer to the main religious tradition of Great Britain and non-religious beliefs. **[4 marks]**

4. Explain two religious beliefs about visions.

   Refer to scripture or sacred writings in your answer. **[5 marks]**

5. 'The First Cause argument proves that God exists.'

   Evaluate this statement.

   In your answer you:

   - should give reasoned arguments in support of this statement
   - should give reasoned arguments to support a different point of view
   - should refer to religious arguments
   - may refer to non-religious arguments
   - should reach a justified conclusion. **[12 marks]**

6 Religion, peace and conflict

6.1 Introduction to religion, peace and conflict

Throughout history, human beings have chosen to fight battles or **wars** to gain territory and to settle disputes. There are several examples in the Torah, such as the conquest of Canaan (the Promised Land) at the time of Moses and Joshua, which was achieved by fighting.

▲ *Mt Nebo, from where Moses viewed the Promised Land before his death*

It is likely that, at any time, somewhere in the world, people are being deliberately killed in a war. Many will have been fighting but some, such as women and children, will not have fought. While all countries have laws against murder, the rules of war are different. In war, killing is considered to be acceptable. Some Jews may speak out against any kind of killing, but others will be prepared to fight for their country and their faith, even if they believe that war is fundamentally wrong.

There are four key concepts you need to know to understand Jewish attitudes to war.

■ Peace

Throughout the scriptures, there are laws and guidance to help Jews establish a peaceful society. The intention of those fighting a war should be to create **peace** once the war is over. Jews living outside Israel may take part in wars declared by the country they live in, if the intention is to create peace. However, instability and resentment after a war can often lead to fighting breaking out again.

When Jews greet and bid farewell to each other, they often use the Hebrew word 'Shalom'. This is usually interpreted to mean peace. However, it means more than this. It is complete peace, which brings feelings of contentment, completeness, wellbeing and harmony.

In the Tenakh (Isaiah 2:4), the prophet Isaiah looked forward to a time when God would bring real and lasting peace.

Objectives

- Be aware of war as a way of resolving differences.
- Know and understand the key concepts of peace, justice, forgiveness and reconciliation.

Key terms

- **war:** fighting between nations to resolve issues between them
- **peace:** an absence of conflict, which leads to happiness and harmony
- **justice:** bringing about what is right and fair, according to the law or making up for a wrong that has been committed
- **forgiveness:** showing grace and mercy and pardoning someone for what they have done wrong
- **reconciliation:** the restoring of harmony after relationships have broken down

> ❝ nation shall not take up sword against nation; they shall never again know war. ❞
>
> *Isaiah 2:4*

Justice

Many wars are fought to achieve **justice**. The above quote from Isaiah looks forward to a time when God, as the ultimate judge, will establish justice between nations and settle their disputes.

The Jewish prophets constantly warned the Jewish people about the importance of justice, especially for the vulnerable and poor in society. The importance of loving God and obeying his law is a major theme in their teachings.

> " He has told you, O man, what is good,
> And what the LORD requires of you:
> Only to do justice
> And to love goodness,
> And to walk modestly with your God; "
>
> *Micah* 6:8

Justice is often linked with equality. If nations do not have the same opportunities for their people to thrive, resentment may build at what people see as unfair. This could lead to conflict especially if more privileged parts of the world are seen to be the cause.

Forgiveness

Jews believe that **forgiveness** is an important element in living peacefully. It does not always mean that no action should be taken to right a wrong, possibly through conflict or punishment, but forgiveness should always follow. After forgiveness, action to establish peace and justice should take place or problems are likely to reoccur. Jews believe that God sets the example regarding forgiveness by offering forgiveness to all who repent in faith. This belief is best shown in the festival of Yom Kippur. In the days leading to Yom Kippur, Jews are expected to atone for any harm they have done, and to restore any personal relationships that may have broken down. Yom Kippur gives them the opportunity to express sorrow for sin and to seek God's forgiveness.

Reconciliation

Reconciliation follows conflict. In the twenty-first century, there has been sporadic conflict between Israelis and Palestinians. Organisations run by ordinary Jews and Palestinians are working to build peace. For example, the Parents Circle – Families Forum (PCFF) has brought together more than 600 Palestinian and Israeli families who have lost an immediate family member in the conflict. Together, they call for peace and reconciliation. They believe that their own joint activities show how reconciliation between individuals and nations is possible. They hope to persuade both sides of the conflict to act similarly, having reached the conclusion that the process of reconciliation between nations is necessary to achieve lasting peace.

Research activity

Using the Internet, find out more about PCFF.

Discussion activity

Look back to the information about Moses and the conquest of Canaan on pages 20–21. Do you think the conquest should have been achieved by force or should the Jews have tried to find an alternative way of settling in Canaan 3000 years ago? Discuss this in a small group. Each group should prepare a short report to be read to the rest of the class.

Activities

1 Write a short paragraph about each: peace, justice, forgiveness and reconciliation.

2 'Peace, justice, forgiveness and reconciliation should be taken together when considering war and what happens once a war has been fought.' Do you agree with this statement? Give your reasons why.

3 Do you agree that organisations such as the PCFF do more good than those fighting in a conflict? Explain your reasons.

Links

Find out more about Yom Kippur in Chapter 2, pages 56–57.

★ Study tip

These four concepts are linked. When writing about one of them, it is likely that you may need to refer to at least one other.

Summary
You should now be aware that war is a way of resolving differences and that concepts of peace, justice, forgiveness and reconciliation are important in the aftermath of war and in preventing future conflict.

■ Violence and protest

The right to protest is considered to be a fundamental democratic freedom. The law in the UK allows individuals and groups to protest in public to demonstrate their point of view. If the **protest** involves a procession or a march, the police must be told at least six days before it takes place. The police can request alterations to the route or even apply to a court for an order to ban the march. They may do this if they feel that the march might intimidate other people or if they predict that **violence** will be involved.

Some Jews believe that protest is important to bring about change, especially when vulnerable groups need support. Many believe it is important to protest about injustice and that to remain silent is a sin. Some believe that not to protest is seen as agreeing with something that is wrong. When accepting the Nobel Peace Prize in 1986, the Jewish writer Elie Wiesel, a survivor of the Holocaust, said:

▲ *Demonstrators protesting peacefully in Israel in 2011*

> ❝ We must always take sides. Neutrality helps the oppressor, never the victim. Silence encourages the tormentor, never the tormented. Sometimes we must interfere. When human lives are endangered, when human dignity is in jeopardy, national borders and sensitivities become irrelevant. Wherever men or women are persecuted because of their race, religion, or political views, that place must – at that moment – become the centre of the universe. ❞
>
> Elie Wiesel

Peaceful protest

In October 2015, around 70 pro-Israel supporters gathered outside the Palestinian Mission in London. Their protest was linked to the conflict between Israel and Palestine. They paid respect to victims of the conflict by holding a minute's silence and also chanted slogans such as 'Yes to peace, no to terror'. Even though there was a pro-Palestine counter-demonstration, there was no violence and the police made no arrests.

▲ *Elie Wiesel*

■ Terrorism

A much more serious form of violent protest is **terrorism**. This is where an individual, or a group who share certain beliefs, use terror as part of their campaign to further their cause. Their violence is usually committed against innocent civilians and takes place in public. Suicide bombers, car bombs, and gunmen shooting into crowds of people are all tactics of terrorism. Terrorists believe that by killing people in this way, the rest of society will become more aware of their cause, will be scared of them and will push the authorities into giving way to their demands.

Gay Pride March

In July 2015, an ultra-Orthodox Jewish man pulled out a knife during an otherwise peaceful Gay Pride parade in Jerusalem. Before he was tackled by a police officer and arrested, he stabbed six people including sixteen-year-old Shira Banki who later died in hospital. The attacker, Yishai Schlissel, had been released from prison just three weeks earlier for a similar offence in 2005. The parade continued once the wounded had been taken to hospital with protesters chanting 'end the violence'.

Both the President and Prime Minister of Israel strongly condemned the attack, with the President referring to it as 'a terrible hate crime'. Other Jewish religious, political and community leaders spoke of their horror and sadness that such a thing should happen. Ultra-Orthodox Jews generally oppose same-sex sexual relationships, which were made legal in Israel in 1988, although very few would support the actions of the attacker.

▲ *Hundreds gathered to pay tribute to Shira Banki, an innocent victim of violence*

Most Jews consider terrorist acts of violence to be wrong, especially as the victims are usually innocent people going about their normal daily business. They prefer more peaceful ways of resolving issues.

6.3 Reasons for war

Some people find it very difficult to understand why anyone is prepared to fight in a war or why their country wants to go to war. However, it is a fact that people are willing to fight in wars in great numbers. Whenever the UK is involved in war, both full-time and volunteer personnel are called upon to fight. During the First and Second World Wars, the need for fighters was so great and casualties were so high that people in the UK were ordered to fight for their country.

Throughout history, war has been used as a way to gain more land or territory, or even to regain land lost in a previous war. An example in ancient Jewish history is the conquest of Canaan, commanded and directed by God at the time of Joshua. However, since then, Jews have also lost their land on many occasions, and been forced to live under occupying powers such as the Babylonians and Romans.

Greed as a reason for war

Greed can be one of the reasons why countries invade others. In modern times, this is often in order to control important resources, such as oil. In this way, rich and powerful countries can get richer and more powerful, perhaps causing poverty in the defeated country because their main source of income is taken away.

In the Tenakh, there are many references to the effects of greed and to God's disapproval of greed. The tenth commandment is 'You shall not covet' (Exodus 14:17) in order to guard against jealousy because jealousy is closely connected with greed. The prophet Amos criticised the people for cheating the poor in order to increase their own wealth and power (see Amos 2:6–7 and 4:1). In Proverbs, it is written:

> **"** A greedy man provokes quarrels,
> But he who trusts the LORD shall enjoy prosperity. **"**
>
> *Proverbs* 28:25

When explaining what God would do to punish Israel in the early sixth century BCE, the prophet Jeremiah wrote:

> **"** For among My people are found wicked men, […] their houses are full of guile; That is why they have grown so wealthy. They have become fat and sleek; They pass beyond the bounds of wickedness, […] Should I not punish such deeds **"**
>
> *Jeremiah* 5:26–29

Self-defence as a reason for war

Whenever one country attacks another, it expects to meet some resistance from the invaded country. Most people consider fighting in **self-defence**

Objectives

- Understand why wars are fought.
- Understand Jewish attitudes about reasons for war.

Key terms

- **greed:** a selfish desire for something
- **self-defence:** acting to prevent harm to yourself or others
- **retaliation:** deliberately harming someone as a response to them harming you

▲ *Greed to control the supply and price of oil is believed to have been a factor in some recent wars*

to be morally acceptable, and believe they have a right to defend the values, beliefs and ways of life that their country lives by. During the Second World War the UK fought to defend itself against Nazi invasion and help defeat what it saw as an evil threat to the whole of Europe.

Many people believe it is acceptable to fight to defend other nations under threat. In 1948, after the Holocaust, the present-day nation of Israel was set up and Israel has been keen to safeguard its territory, and protect its citizens from attack. Since 1948, Israel has been in conflict with its neighbouring countries, Egypt, Jordan, Syria, Lebanon, Iraq and Iran, which Israelis have seen to be threatening their security. Israel gained some land as a result of these defensive wars, much of which has been returned through a process of negotiation.

■ Retaliation as a reason for war

Wars are sometimes fought in **retaliation** against a country that is seen to have done something very wrong.

Links

For more information about situations when it is argued that war can be justified, see pages 126–127.

Activities

1 'Greed, self-defence and retaliation are all causes of war.' Do you agree with this? Explain why.

2 'There are no causes of war that should be used to justify war.' Do you agree with this statement? Give reasons, including some based on Jewish teaching.

Terrorist attack

On 11 September 2001, terrorists from al-Qaeda hijacked four passenger aircraft in the US. Two were flown into the twin towers of the World Trade Center in New York, and one into the Pentagon (the headquarters of the US Department of Defence). The fourth crashed in a field in Pennsylvania after the passengers tried to overcome the hijackers. The total death toll was 2996, with many survivors suffering great trauma that has affected their lives ever since. Around 15 per cent of those killed were Jewish.

The US government ordered military action against Afghanistan because they believed that the country was providing shelter for the al-Qaeda terrorist group and its leader Osama Bin Laden. The UK provided military personnel to support the US action. In all, 454 British military personnel died in the Afghanistan campaign. Bin Laden was eventually killed by US forces in May 2011.

Although many people believed that al-Qaeda needed to be prevented from undertaking such terrorist activity, invading Afghanistan was seen by some to be an act of retaliation.

▲ *The second of the twin towers is attacked and destroyed*

In his code of Jewish Law, Maimonides referred to revenge as an extremely bad and unworthy action in everyday life. He believed spiritual matters are more important than revenge based on material or worldly things.

In the Torah, it says:

> ❝ You shall not take vengeance or bear a grudge against your countrymen. Love your neighbour as yourself ❞
>
> *Leviticus* 19:18

Although many Jews are able to follow this advice in much of their daily interaction with other people, when it comes to situations of war, they may find it much more difficult.

⭐ Study tip

If you cannot fully remember a quote you wish to use, you could paraphrase it but do not use quotation marks around it.

Summary

You should now understand three different causes of war and Jewish attitudes towards them.

6.4 Nuclear war and weapons of mass destruction

■ The use of nuclear weapons

This picture was taken just after around 60,000 people in the city of Hiroshima died as a result of an atom bomb (an early form of **nuclear weapon**) being dropped on it by US forces fighting in Second World War. The death toll rose to around 140,000 in the months that followed as many more died as a result of radiation. Three days later, a second Japanese city, Nagasaki, was also destroyed by

▲ The Japanese city of Hiroshima shortly after an atom bomb was dropped on it on 6 August 1945

an atom bomb. Six days after that Japan surrendered and ceased fighting against the allied forces. This effectively marked the end of the Second World War, which for some people justified the use of these weapons.

Discussion activity

'Dropping atom bombs on Japan brought an end to the Second World War; so it was the right thing to do.' With a partner, discuss this statement. Decide whether you agree with it and think of reasons to support your opinion.

Since the end of the Second World War, many of the wealthier countries in the world, including the UK, have researched and developed considerably more powerful nuclear weapons. Despite some countries agreeing to reduce the number of nuclear weapons they possess, there are now enough to completely destroy the world we live in several times over.

Einstein and Oppenheimer

Albert Einstein and J. Robert Oppenheimer were Jewish scientists who were actively involved with others in the development of the atom bombs that were dropped on Hiroshima and Nagasaki. They both saw it as necessary to develop such a weapon before the Nazis did. Indeed in 1939, Einstein urged the President of the USA, Theodore Roosevelt, to set up the Manhattan Project in order to develop the technology needed to create the atom bomb. Oppenheimer was appointed as Director of the project in 1942 and three years later, the atom bombs were first used. However, three months later Oppenheimer resigned his position and was strongly opposed to developing the H-bomb, a development of the atom bomb and forerunner of the nuclear weapons that exist today. Einstein also strongly opposed nuclear weapons in his later life.

Objectives

- Be aware of the issues of nuclear war and weapons of mass destruction.
- Understand the possible implications of using nuclear or other weapons of mass destruction.
- Consider whether the use of such weapons is justified.

Key terms

- **nuclear weapons:** weapons that work by a nuclear reaction, devastate huge areas, and kill large numbers of people
- **weapons of mass destruction:** weapons that can kill large numbers of people and/or cause great damage
- **chemical weapons:** weapons that use lethal chemicals to poison, burn or paralyse humans and destroy the natural environment
- **biological weapons:** weapons that contain living organisms or infective material that can lead to disease or death

Although it is thought that Israel has nuclear weapons, many Jews feel uneasy about living in a world where nuclear weapons exist. It is a fundamental belief held by Jews and Christians that, as the creator, only God has the authority to end the life that he created. One of the Ten Commandments states 'You shall not murder' (Exodus 20:13). Some Jews and Christians believe that although killing in war is not usually considered to be murder, the use of nuclear weapons, which would kill huge numbers of innocent civilians, can never be justified.

> ❝ At this crucial crossroads of history, we join to call on the world to recognise that violence begets violence; that nuclear proliferation benefits no one; that we can, we will, and we must find other ways to protect ourselves, our nations and our future: for it is not sufficient to have peace in our time, but, instead, we must leave a peaceful world to our children. ❞
>
> Rabbi David Saperstein, Director of the Religious Action Centre of Reform Judaism, 1974 to 2015

▪ Weapons of mass destruction

In addition to nuclear weapons, there are other **weapons of mass destruction** in existence.

A **chemical weapon** is a weapon containing lethal chemicals that, when released, cause numerous deaths. In 1993, the Chemical Weapons Convention (CWC) made the production, stockpiling and use of these chemicals illegal, worldwide. However, since then they are believed to have been used in countries such as Iraq and Syria.

Biological weapons introduce harmful bacteria and viruses into the atmosphere. When they enter the food chain or water supplies, they cause illness and death on a massive scale. As with chemical weapons, they are illegal but there are instances of their use and many countries still possess them.

As with nuclear weapons, chemical and biological weapons have the capacity to kill large numbers of people, including civilians. Although the life of a person in the military is worth the same as any other life, the rules of war allow military personnel to be valid targets. Civilians pose no threat and so they are supposed to be protected.

Activities

1 Nuclear weapons, chemical weapons and biological weapons are all weapons of mass destruction. Explain how they differ from each other.

2 Discuss whether those who make scientific and technological discoveries should only proceed with their research if they can guarantee that it will not be used to kill people. Give your reasons. Would your answer be different if the guarantee not to kill was limited to civilians?

3 Using any relevant Jewish beliefs and teachings, explain Jewish attitudes to weapons of mass destruction.

Contrasting beliefs

To find out more about Christian views on weapons of mass destruction to compare and contrast with Jewish views, use the Internet to read about Christian CND.

▲ Albert Einstein on an Israeli postcard and postage stamp

▲ J. Robert Oppenheimer (1946)

★ Study tip

When using a quote to support an idea, make sure it is relevant and that your interpretation of it is correct.

Summary

You should now be able to describe the effects of nuclear weapons and other weapons of mass destruction, and considered Jewish attitudes to these issues.

The just war theory

In the fourth century the Christian St Augustine wrote about the morality of war, and his thoughts were developed into a distinct set of criteria by Thomas Aquinas in the thirteenth century. Further adaptations have been made to the **just war** theory up until the present day. All the following conditions must apply for the war to be a 'just war':

- The war must have a *just cause*. This may include self-defence or defending someone else. It must not be to gain territory or resources, or in retaliation.
- The war must be declared by the *correct authority*. This should be the government or lawful rulers of the country.
- The *intention* of the war has to be to defeat wrongdoing and promote good. The good achieved by the war must outweigh the evil that led to it.
- Fighting must be a *last resort*. All other ways of resolving the issue, such as diplomacy, must have been attempted before war can be declared.
- There must be a reasonable *chance of success*. It is unjust to ask people to fight a war if it is probable that the war will be lost and they will be killed.
- The methods used to fight the war must be *proportional* to achieve success. Excessive force should not be used.

The way the war is fought must obey the following conditions:

- The war must be fought by *just means*. Innocent people and civilians must not be targeted or harmed.
- Only *appropriate force* may be used. This includes the type of force and how much is used.
- *Internationally agreed conventions* on the conduct of war must be obeyed. The Geneva Convention, accepted by the UK government in 1957, lays down the rules that must be obeyed in war.

Jewish teachings on types of war

There is no specific just war theory in Judaism, although many Jews are prepared to accept the above criteria. From very early times, Jewish rabbis have thought that there are three types of war:

Objectives

- Understand the just war theory.
- Understand Jewish criteria for fighting in wars.
- Apply Torah teachings to decisions about when and how to fight.

Key terms

- **just war:** a war which meets internationally accepted criteria for fairness
- **obligatory war:** a war that God commanded Jews to fight
- **defensive wars:** wars that Jews are obliged to fight if attacked
- **optional wars:** wars that Jews fight for a good reason, and where all peaceful ways to prevent conflict have been tried

Discussion activity

Look carefully at the six criteria for a just war. With a partner, try to rank them in order of importance with the most important first.

Activities

1 Explain the three types of war in Judaism.
2 'There should be no rules governing how a war is fought.' Do you agree with this statement? Give reasons for your opinion. How do you think a Jew would respond to this quote?

⭐ **Study tip**

Learning the words in italics may help you to remember the just war conditions.

Obligatory wars are wars that God commanded Jews to fight. The conquest of Canaan under Joshua could be seen as an obligatory war.

If the Jewish people are attacked, they are obliged to defend themselves (self-defence). These **defensive wars** include pre-emptive strikes against a potential enemy who is preparing an attack on them. Pre-emptive strikes are sometimes seen as a normal way of dealing with attackers, justified by a verse from Genesis:

> ❝ Whoever sheds the blood of man, by man shall his blood be shed; for in His image did God make man. ❞
>
> *Genesis 9:6*

▲ *This sculpture is outside the United Nations building in Manhattan, New York. What do you think it is saying about war?*

Optional wars are fought for a good reason, and when all peaceful ways to prevent conflict have been tried.

> ❝ When you approach a town to attack it, you shall offer it terms of peace […] If it does not surrender to you, but would join battle with you, you shall lay siege to it ❞
>
> *Deuteronomy 20:10–12*

Jews therefore believe it is important that before a war is declared, everything possible should be done to make peace.

There are certain rules that must be followed in conflict. Only military personnel should be targeted in battle, and before battle commences, wherever possible, civilians should be allowed the opportunity to get out of harm's way. Some Jews believe that if civilians do not take such an opportunity, they lose their civilian status and protection. The landscape should not be destroyed because it is a source of food, and civilians and prisoners should be treated well and with dignity. Wars should not be fought to build an empire, destroy another nation, steal resources or take revenge.

Activity

Explain reasons why civilians should be protected in war.

Summary

You should now know the criteria for a just war and Jewish attitudes and teachings about war.

> ❝ When in your war against a city you have to besiege it […] you must not destroy its trees […] You may eat of them, but you must not cut them down.
>
> *Deuteronomy 20:19*
>
> If your enemy is hungry, give him bread to eat; if he is thirsty, give him water to drink. ❞
>
> *Proverbs 25:21*

▲ *Jews are forbidden to destroy fruit trees in a time of conflict*

■ What is a holy war?

To many people the concept of a **holy war** seems to be a contradiction. They think that no activity that involves killing people in large numbers can possibly have any religious inspiration and justification. However, in the Tenakh, there are many references to God helping the Jews to establish themselves in the Promised Land by winning battles. These are usually regarded as obligatory wars, but some Jews believe that this category of war cannot be applied in this century.

The concept of 'war by commandment' was used to justify some conflicts in the Tenakh, sometimes against tribes such as the Amalekites who were seen to threaten the Jews and prevent peaceful settlement. These conflicts were seen to be based on or required by the Torah, usually as a defensive war. Of the 613 mitzvot, three make reference to the Amalekites.

▲ Graggers are often used during Purim to make a noise when Haman's name is mentioned

During the festival of Purim, Jews celebrate the saving of the Jews from Haman, a Persian political leader. Whilst the story from the Book of Esther is read, people make disapproving noises or shout when Haman's name is mentioned. This reminds Jews that they may need to protect their faith as Esther did, and may need to follow her resourcefulness and talents in order to do so.

For most Jews, the concept of a holy war no longer applies. However, a small minority of Orthodox Jews living in the West Bank region believe there is a divine obligation to reclaim the whole of the land of Israel. According to Rabbi Reuven Firestone, Professor of Medieval Jewish and Islamic Studies in Los Angeles, they believe God wants them to remove Palestinian settlers. They believe that the conquest and settlement of Israel is an obligatory war, or a 'war by commandment'. But the Israeli government and most Jews living throughout Israel reject this interpretation.

■ Religion and belief as a cause of war and violence

It is clear that religious beliefs have sometimes contributed to conflicts and wars. In some, religious beliefs have been mixed with political beliefs, and wars have resulted between people of different religions.

Objectives

- Understand the features of a holy war.
- Consider whether religion can be seen as a cause of war and violence.
- Understand Jewish approaches to war and violence.

Key terms

- **holy war:** fighting for a religious cause or God
- **anti-Semitism:** prejudice against Jews
- **terrorist:** someone engaged in the unlawful use of violence, usually against innocent civilians, to achieve a political or religious goal

Activities

1 Explain what a holy war is.
2 Explain the concept of 'war by commandment'.
3 Why do you think that in modern times most Jews do not agree with the idea of a holy war?

Discussion activity

With a partner, discuss how far believers should go to defend their faith.

At other times, religious groups who are in a minority have been persecuted simply because of their race or religion or both. The Jews were subjected to violence during the Second World War when six million Jews died at the hands of the Nazis, not because they threatened violence or war, but just because they were Jews and were made scapegoats. Most Jews in the UK do not see the need to respond violently to what they see to be religious offences or an attack on their faith. This does not mean they approve of such actions; they just believe that the teachings of their faith do not encourage a violent response from individuals. They also believe that they should keep within the law and rely on the police to take any appropriate action. An example of this is in their response to **anti-Semitism** in the UK.

Activities

1 What is anti-Semitism?

2 How do you think Jews should respond to anti-Semitism? Explain your reasons.

3 'Religious prejudice such as anti-Semitism is always wrong.' Give reasons why many believe this to be true.

Anti-Semitism in the UK

The Community Security Trust is a charity that works to protect Jews in the UK from anti-Semitism. It reported that in the first six months of 2015, the number of reported incidents of anti-Semitism rose by 53 per cent to 473. Of these, 44 were classed as violent attacks and 35 involved the damage or desecration of property, including synagogues and cemeteries. Part of the rise in incidents has been put down to an increase in reporting such crimes. There has been a similar increase in Europe. In France, in January 2015, four hostages taken in a Paris kosher grocery store were murdered.

The chief executive of the Community Security Trust David Delew said: 'The **terrorist** attacks on European Jews earlier this year, following the high levels of anti-Semitism in 2014, were a difficult and unsettling experience for our Jewish community.'

Jews in the UK rarely react with violence to anti-Semitism, in spite of the offence and sadness it causes.

Research activity

Use the Internet to find out more about the work of the Community Security Trust.

⭐ **Study tip**

When considering conflicts that involve people of a certain faith, make sure you remember that religion may not be the cause.

Summary

You should now know the features of a holy war and that many Jews do not believe it is relevant to their faith. You should have considered whether religion can be seen as a cause of war and violence, and understand Jewish attitudes to war, anti-Semitism and the use of violence.

▲ *Jewish groups protested peacefully against anti-Semitism in London, 31 August 2014*

6.7 Pacifism and peacemaking

■ What is pacifism?

A **pacifist** is a person who for some reason, religious or not, believes that war and violence can rarely or never be justified, and that conflicts should be settled in a peaceful way. Pacifists believe that it is always wrong to fight, even in self-defence. Judaism does not teach that it is always wrong to fight. Jews generally believe that under certain criteria, war is a necessary evil and a duty of their faith. Despite this, some Jews choose to become pacifists. However, all Jews strongly believe that the principles of justice and peace make avoiding war an ideal.

▲ A symbol of peace

Jews believe that although fighting a war under certain criteria is acceptable, it is much better if there is no war, whether just or not. Working together to avoid situations where war is a possible outcome is better than fighting. The United Nations, founded in 1945, encourages its nearly 200 member countries to resolve disputes peacefully.

■ Peace teachings from the Tenakh

There are several teachings in the Tenakh that show that a peaceful world is something to aim for. Psalm 34:15 advises people to 'Shun evil and do good, seek peace and pursue it.'

In describing the establishment of God's kingdom, the Prophet Micah predicted it would be a time when God would settle disputes and when weapons would be unnecessary. If the prediction were correct, it makes setting up such a situation on earth an ideal to work towards.

> ❝ He will judge among the many peoples, And arbitrate for the multitude of nations, [...] And they shall beat their swords into ploughshares And their spears into pruning hooks. ❞
>
> *Micah 4:3*

When the prophet Isaiah prophesied about the coming of the Messiah, he spoke of 'peace without limit':

> ❝ In token of abundant authority And of peace without limit Upon David's throne and kingdom, That it may be firmly established In justice and in equity Now and evermore. ❞
>
> *Isaiah 9:6–7*

Objectives

- Consider pacifism as an alternative to conflict.
- Understand why some Jews are pacifists.
- Know about the work of a Jewish pacifist organisation.

Key terms

- **pacifism:** the belief of people who refuse to take part in war and any other form of violence
- **peacemaking:** the action of trying to establish peace
- **peacemaker:** a person who works to establish peace in the world or in a certain part of it

Research activity

Find out about the work of the United Nations. Explain ways in which it tries to prevent war.

Contrasting beliefs

Use libraries or the Internet to find out about Christian attitudes to pacifism, and whether any contrast with Jewish beliefs.

Activities

1 Explain what pacifism is.
2 Explain how respecting human rights helps to bring about peace and justice.
3 'Wars are won by weapons, but peace is won by ideas.' Explain what this statement means. Do you agree with it?

■ Peacemaking

Pacifists strongly believe that it is best to work at preventing war from becoming a possibility. Promoting justice and human rights are an important part of this. If people are not denied basic freedoms and rights, they are less likely to fight. Peace is not just an absence of war; it is a sense of wellbeing and security. Jewish pacifists believe this can come through religious faith, supported by prayer and by following Jewish law. Being at peace with oneself helps people to avoid conflict with others.

Peacemaking is best when **peacemakers** are active. Developing good relationships with people and other nations and faiths, talking to each other and working together on specific joint projects all make conflict less likely. The former Chief Rabbi of the United Hebrew Congregations of the Commonwealth, Lord Jonathan Sacks wrote: 'wars are won by weapons, but peace is won by ideas.'

Links

For more information on peace, justice and reconciliation, see pages 118–119.

Research activity

Use the Internet to find out why a dove with an olive branch is used as a symbol of peace.

Dr Marshall Rosenberg

Dr Marshall Rosenberg, who died in 2015, was a psychologist and founder of the Centre for Nonviolent Communication. The Centre grew out of work he was doing with those in the USA who, in the 1960s, were working towards equal rights for all. He tried to make peace between rioting students and college administrators, and campaigned peacefully to ensure that students of all races could attend any school. Dr Rosenberg's work included offering courses on non-violent communication in over 60 countries, working with teachers, mental health and healthcare providers, prisoners, the military, police officers, faith leaders and individual families. Those with whom he worked believed that this training vastly strengthened their ability to resolve differences peacefully. In order to extend the work, he also trained others to run similar courses with similar results.

Although Dr Rosenberg was Jewish, the organisation he founded both employs and provides help for people of all faiths. His peacemaking beliefs and activities are easily shared by members of other faiths.

Discussion activity

Discuss with a partner whether you think promoting justice and human rights is the best way to prevent conflict. Share your conclusions with others.

★ Study tip

It is important to know about pacifism and peacemaking and understand why some Jews are pacifists while others are not.

Summary

You should now be able to explain the concept of pacifism, and understand why some Jews are pacifists. You should also know about a Jewish pacifist organisation which promotes peacemaking.

Providing help to victims of war

Casualties are an unavoidable part of war. In addition to the harm that is caused to those directly involved in the fighting, harm is also caused to their families and friends. For example, if the main wage earner dies in a war, their family may struggle financially without them. If a place of work is destroyed in a war, nobody can earn a wage there. If crops are destroyed or water supplies polluted, starvation could follow for those who live in the surrounding area.

In the UK, if a member of the military is killed or injured, financial systems are in place to look after those left behind. Injured military personnel receive free health care with some specialised care being provided by charities such as Help for Heroes. However, injury or death still have devastating effects on friends and families and can cause long-term emotional wounds.

There are many organisations that offer help and care for victims of war, wherever they live and whichever side of the conflict they were on. The work of some Jewish organisations is based on the Jewish principles of pikuach nefesh, saving a life, and tikkun olam, healing the world.

▲ *A soldier helps an injured colleague*

Objectives

- Understand what can be done to help victims of war.
- Understand the work of a present day Jewish organisation that helps victims of war.

Ziv Medical Centre

From around 2014, more than two thousand Syrians, wounded in war, were dumped on the Israeli–Syrian border and taken to Northern Israel for life-saving medical treatment. The Israeli government allowed four hospitals, including the Ziv Medical Centre in Zefat, to carry out this treatment with their patients being sent back home to Syria once they had recovered.

Many of the people whose lives were saved by the hospitals' medical teams had been taught as children to hate Israel, believing the country to be the biggest enemy to Syrians. Such caring actions on behalf of the Israel government and the reaction of most of the Syrians who were healed, together with their families, have been seen as 'planting seeds of peace'.

Links

For information about pikuach nefesh, see Chapter 1, pages 24–25, and for more about tikkun olam, see Chapter 4, page 87.

Magen David Adom UK

Magen David Adom (MDA) is a Jewish charity based in the UK that raised nearly £7 million in 2013. Their work involves helping to fund an emergency medical and ambulance service in Israel, which consists largely of volunteers. They also provide help wherever it is needed throughout the world. Their mission is to provide medical care and treatment for people of any nationality, race, religion, ethnic origin, age, disability, sexual orientation or political affiliation. This includes victims of conflict for whom they offer a vital life-saving service. Unlike the UK, Israel does not have a government-run medical emergency and ambulance service. Magen David Adom provides such a service. It is partly financed by donations, mainly from the Jewish community in 17 countries around the world. The charity also provides first aid training in Israel, and, in co-ordination with the Red Cross and Red Crescent, in many countries throughout the world.

▲ *A Magen David Adom ambulance*

Activities

1 Explain how war can have a negative effect on families.
2 Outline the work of Magen David Adom.
3 'Victims of war should not have to rely on support from voluntary organisations.' Write arguments both for and against this statement.

Research activity

Use the Internet to find out more about the work of MDA.

Sheku and Sierra Leone Poverty Relief

Sierra Leone, a country in West Africa that suffered from a civil war between 1991 and 2002, is still trying to build up its economy to provide even a basic standard of living for its citizens. Poverty is widespread and the effects of the civil war are still being felt. Most of the population are Muslims.

Sheku is a young boy who in 2007 faced the prospect of having both his lower legs amputated to save his life. The operation had a high risk of failure but thanks to generous support from a trustee who went on to form the Sierra Leone Poverty Relief charity, it was successful, even though Sheku remained in hospital for seven years before he was well enough to leave.

Sierra Leone Poverty Relief is headed by a teacher at Immanuel College in Hertfordshire and her husband. The college, a Jewish independent day school, is one of the main providers of funds that allows the charity to extend educational opportunities for young people in Sierra Leone and to fund medical care. The students at Immanuel College hold regular money raising events and base their support on a verse from the Psalms: 'How good and how pleasant it is that brothers dwell together.' (Psalm 133:1).

Activities

1 Explain how Sierra Leone Poverty Relief provides funds to assist the people of Sierra Leone.
2 How does the quote from Psalm 133 link to the work of Sierra Leone Poverty Relief?

⭐ Study tip

Making reference to case studies can be a good way of developing points that you have made.

Summary

You should now know about and understand support given to victims of war, including the work of Magen David Adom.

Religion, violence, terrorism and war – summary

You should now be able to:

✔ explain Jewish teachings, beliefs and attitudes about the meaning and significance of peace, justice, forgiveness and reconciliation

✔ explain Jewish teachings, beliefs and attitudes about violence, including violent protest, and terrorism

✔ explain Jewish teachings, beliefs and attitudes about the reasons for war, including greed, self-defence and retaliation

✔ explain Jewish teachings, beliefs and attitudes about pacifism and peacekeeping.

✔ explain beliefs and teaching about the just war theory, including the criteria for a just war

✔ explain ideas about holy war

✔ explain the meaning of pacifism and Jewish belief about war and peace.

Religion and belief in twenty-first-century conflict – summary

You should now be able to:

✔ examine religion and belief as a cause of war and violence in the contemporary world

✔ explain religious attitudes to nuclear weapons and the use of weapons of mass destruction

✔ explain religion and peacemaking in the contemporary world, including the work of individuals influenced by religious teaching

✔ explain religious responses to the victims of war, including the work of one present-day religious organisation

✔ explain contemporary British attitudes (both religious and non-religious) towards all the above issues

✔ explain contrasting beliefs in contemporary British society to the three issues of violence, weapons of mass destruction and pacifism with reference to the main religious tradition in Britain (Christianity) and one or more other religious traditions.

Sample student answer – the 12 mark question

1. Write an answer to the following practice question:

'The best way to bring about world peace is for more individuals to become pacifists.'
Evaluate this statement. In your answer you:
- should give reasoned arguments in support of this statement
- should give reasoned arguments to support a different point of view
- should refer to religious arguments
- may refer to non-religious arguments
- should reach a justified conclusion. **[12 marks]**

2. Read the following student sample answer:

I disagree with this statement because if people become pacifists, they will make themselves easy targets for their enemies. If you are fighting for a cause or for your country, it is safest to attack the easiest targets and pacifists are easy targets. Pacifism will achieve nothing. The best way to bring about world peace is to take on those who threaten peace and defeat them. Peace will follow once those who threaten war are removed from the scene. Jews mainly are not pacifists. They believe that there are certain reasons, mainly in self-defence and to defend Israel, that mean they have to fight. When they settled into the Promised Land, they fought against the people who were living there and killed thousands of them. If they had not done this, God would not have been able to keep the promise he made to Moses. Fighting is a natural part of what it means to be human and this is how humans have survived.

However some people think differently. Many Jews, whilst not necessarily being pacifists, believe that justice and peace make war something they want to avoid. There are quotes in the Tenakh such as 'Shun evil and do good, seek amity and pursue it' (Psalms) that tell Jews that they should be pacifists and that they should stop wars. The prophets looked forward to a time of peace and 2500 years later we should be closer to getting there. I don't really agree with this because pacifists trust that if you do not pose a threat to people, they will leave you alone. This may work but people like Hitler would probably just have seen it as a sign of weakness and taken advantage. Sometimes you have to defend yourself against evil people and Judaism allows this but pacifism doesn't.

Real pacifism is more than refusing to fight though. Pacifists actually work at establishing peace by getting on with everybody. If this is what a pacifist really does then maybe the statement could be true although it will have to be worked at.

3. With a partner, discuss the student answer. Can you identify two different points of view? Are they contrasting? Does it contain religious arguments? If so, are they simple or detailed? How accurate are they? Can it be improved? If so, how?

4. What mark (out of 12) would you give this answer? Look at the mark scheme in the Introduction (AO1). What are the reasons for the mark you have given?

5. Now swap your answer with your partner's and mark each other's responses. What mark (out of 12) would you give the response? Refer to the mark scheme and give reasons for the mark you award.

Practice questions

1. Which one of the following most accurately describes a violent protest?

   A) Demonstration   B) Riot   C) Strike   D) March   **[1 mark]**

2. Give two reasons for war.   **[2 marks]**

3. Explain two contrasting beliefs in contemporary British society about whether countries should possess weapons of mass destruction.
   In your answer you should refer to the main religious tradition of Great Britain and one or more other religious traditions.   **[4 marks]**

4. Explain two reasons why religious believers should help victims of war.
   Refer to scripture or sacred writings in your answer.   **[5 marks]**

5. 'The just war theory is the best way to limit the damage war can cause.'
   Evaluate this statement. In your answer you:

   • should give reasoned arguments in support of this statement
   • should give reasoned arguments to support a different point of view
   • should refer to religious arguments
   • may refer to non-religious arguments
   • should reach a justified conclusion.   **[12 marks]**

■ What are crime and punishment?

A **crime** is any action which is against the law that has been put in place by the proper rulers of any state. In the UK this is the government, which must get the approval of Parliament before any new crimes are written into law. The police arrest people who are suspected of having broken the law by committing crimes. If, after questioning, the police are confident that they have the right person, they charge them with having committed the offence.

Once charged of a serious crime in the UK, suspected offenders face a hearing in front of a local magistrate before being required to appear in a Crown Court before a judge and jury of twelve people, selected at random. Less serious cases are dealt with by a magistrates' court, while some more minor crimes result in the police giving the offender an official caution if they admit they are guilty.

▲ *The statue of Lady Justice stands on top of the Old Bailey Central Criminal Court in London*

Offenders who are found guilty by a court face a legal **punishment**. Most serious offences such as murder and rape carry a life sentence in prison, although this rarely means offenders spend the rest of their life in prison. Less serious offences are punished by a shorter spell in prison, or with non-custodial sentences such as community service or paying a fine. If a court decides that the person has committed no crime, they are released without any punishment. Under no circumstances can a British court impose a sentence intended to cause physical harm (corporal punishment) or death (capital punishment). However, in some countries, such as China, parts of the USA, Iran and Saudi Arabia, the death penalty is permitted.

Objectives

● Know the definitions of crime and punishment.

● Understand the legal position about crime and punishment.

● Understand concepts of good and evil intentions and actions.

Key terms

● **crime:** an offence which is punishable by law, for example stealing, murder

● **punishment:** something legally done to somebody as a result of being found guilty of breaking the law

● **evil:** the opposite of good, a force or the personification of a negative power that is seen in many traditions as destructive and against God

Discussion activities

1 What is the difference between a crime and a punishment?

2 With a partner suggest what punishment should be given for murder, assault, dropping litter, burglary, lying to a court and buying alcohol under age. You need to think of reasons and then discuss your list and suggestions with others.

In no instance is an individual victim of a crime allowed to punish the offender. Such action is also against the law and punishable by the law.

Civil law is different from criminal law. Civil law concerns disputes between private individuals or groups. This includes such matters as settlement of a divorce, disputes between landlords and tenants and disputed wills. Cases are usually dealt with in a small claims court, although more serious cases will be heard in the Crown Court.

■ Good and evil actions

Many people would say that any action that obeys the law is a good action. However, a good action also includes that which is good but not specified by the law, such as generosity and love. There is no law that says whether you have to support charities or not, but offering support in some way to a good cause is usually considered a good thing. Actions encouraged or required by genuine religious faith are usually considered to be good too.

Evil actions are those which cause suffering, injury or possibly death. These include murder, causing a terrorist explosion and child abuse, which are all illegal.

▲ *Taking a human life is usually considered to be an evil action*

Jews understand evil actions to be actions that go against the teaching and laws of God. Jews believe firmly in only one supreme God and so do not believe in a being who acts in opposition to God. They believe that there is an evil inclination in human beings, which tempts them to do the wrong thing. This is what makes free will a real challenge.

When Jews speak about evil or criminal actions, they mean that the offence is profoundly immoral and wicked and offends God.

Activities

1 Explain the meaning of 'evil actions'.
2 Explain what Jews mean by 'an evil inclination'.

Discussion activity

'Free will has nothing to do with God.' Discuss with a partner whether you think this statement is true.

★ Study tip

When writing about crime and justice you might find it simpler to restrict yourself to writing about the UK legal system.

Summary

You should now know more about the meaning of crime and punishment and understand why actions are described as evil.

■ Reasons why some people commit crime

While most people believe that all crime is wrong, sometimes how wrong it is may depend upon why it was committed. Sometimes it is due to selfishness, whereas at other times there may be circumstances that make it more understandable. In Jewish teaching, there is rarely any justification for committing crimes, especially as Jews treat the mitzvot in the Torah as of prime importance, and these inform the law in Jewish society. The law is important because it keeps order in society so that people can live in peace.

> ❝ Those who forsake instruction praise the wicked,
> But those who heed instruction fight them.
> Evil men cannot discern judgment,
> But those who seek the LORD discern all things. ❞
>
> *Proverbs 28:4–5*

Poverty

It is a fact that in the UK, some people live in **poverty** and cannot afford the necessities of life. Welfare payments should cover living expenses but sometimes, for whatever reason, they do not. This can lead some people to steal food and essentials that they cannot afford to buy. Even though this may seem to be a good reason, it is still against the law and people will still be arrested for stealing. Some punishments given by a magistrates' court, such as a fine, may make the situation worse rather than better, for example by making the person even poorer.

Jews discourage committing crimes out of need, preferring to help the poor to remove the need to commit crime. The Talmud places an obligation on Jews to ensure that other Jews have their basic needs of food, clothing, and shelter. By being a Jew, one is responsible for the wellbeing of other Jews (see Shevuot 39a). In addition, the Torah statement, 'Love your fellow as yourself' (Leviticus 19:18), applies to all of humanity, Jew or non-Jew.

poverty mental illness
Upbringing
Opposition to an unjust law
greed Hate **Addiction**

▲ *Reasons often given for committing crimes; people have different views on which are the most common reasons*

Objectives

- Know and understand reasons why some people commit crime.
- Know and understand Jewish responses to reasons why some people commit crime.

Key terms

- **poverty:** being without money, food or other basic needs of life (being poor)
- **mental illness:** a medical condition that affects a person's feelings, emotions or moods, and perhaps their ability to relate to others
- **addiction:** physical or mental dependency on a substance or activity which is very difficult to overcome
- **greed:** selfish desire for something

Extension activity

In 2014, thousands of ultra-Orthodox Jews took to the streets of Jerusalem and New York to protest against Israel's decision to extend compulsory military service to young men of the Orthodox Jewish religious communities. In particular, a 19-year-old ultra-Orthodox Jew, David Croise, was arrested after an incident in a synagogue.

Use the internet to investigate views about this protest and discuss the issues it raises about personal faith and the laws of a country.

Upbringing

Growing up in a household where crime is a way of life may encourage a young person to follow the example of people they live with and drift into crime themselves. Their parents may even encourage them to commit crimes. Once they have been drawn into a life of crime, it is difficult for them to stop, even though they know that what they are doing is wrong.

Jews emphasise the importance of the family in bringing up their children within the faith, which gives moral guidance to prevent wrongdoing.

▲ *People who drive after drinking alcohol are more likely to crash their car*

Mental illness

Some people suffer from various **mental illnesses** that cause them to commit a number of different crimes. Anger management problems may lead to assault or murder. In cases involving serious crimes and serious mental illnesses, the offender may be viewed as unfit to stand trial. Although they do not receive a trial, they are likely to be sentenced to be kept in a secure unit where they receive the medical or psychological help they need.

Addiction

The nature of **addiction** to drugs means that the human body cannot cope without them. Addicts may resort to stealing to purchase the drugs their body needs.

The drug that causes more crime than any other is alcohol. People who have drunk too much alcohol lose control of their thoughts and actions to such an extent that they may commit acts of violence and get into fights. If they drive while under the influence of alcohol, they are more likely to cause an accident than if sober. While Jews do not forbid drinking alcohol (and drinking wine is important in several Jewish ceremonies), they discourage drinking it in excess.

Greed

In the UK personal possessions and wealth are often seen as signs of status. **Greed** can lead to crime, especially theft or fraud.

In the Ten Commandments, Jews are taught not to covet, which means they should not be jealous of what somebody else has.

Hate

Hatred is a negative feeling or reaction that can lead to violence against whoever or whatever the offender hates.

Opposition to an unjust law

According to lawmakers, any breach of the law is wrong. However, there are occasions where some people have deliberately broken laws they consider to be unjust. Opposition to unfair laws based on racial or gender prejudice, and breaking them out of protest, brought about changes to unjust laws throughout the twentieth century in various countries.

Discussion activity

'Many people try to prevent what causes crime in order to stop people from offending.' Discuss this statement with a partner and explain why people believe this is important, and which Jewish principles would support this approach.

Activities

1 List and explain each of the reasons for committing crime given here.

2 Add any other reasons you can think of and briefly explain them.

3 'There are no good reasons for committing crimes.' How far do you agree with this quote? Explain your opinion.

★ Study tip

Although the reasons for crime given on these pages are listed in the specification, you can write about any others you can think of.

Summary

You should now know and understand some reasons why people may commit crimes and have considered Jewish responses to some of these issues.

7.3 Jewish attitudes to lawbreakers and different types of crime

■ Jewish attitudes to lawbreakers

Without laws, society would descend into disorder and chaos. The law in the UK is there to protect the rights and security of all citizens, although some may be uneasy with some laws. However, Jews believe that they should obey the laws of the country where they live, provided they do not contradict Torah law.

The way that offenders are dealt with is also governed by the law. In the UK, all suspected offenders are presumed to be innocent until they are proven guilty and the courts exist to decide whether there is any doubt as to whether somebody is guilty. If there is any reasonable doubt, they are found not guilty and allowed to carry on with their normal life without any need for punishment.

The Jewish approach to lawbreakers is a mixture of mercy and justice. Punishments should be given that reflect the severity of the crime. This will serve as a deterrent to others. This attitude is found in the Torah, with harsh punishments serving to warn others not to transgress. On the other hand, the Rabbis were always keen to practise the teachings on mercy. Punishments should not be excessive. The perpetrators should be helped so that they do not offend again. Jews believe that inhumane treatment of offenders is wrong.

Most Jews also believe that offenders should be helped to change their ways so they do not reoffend once the punishment is over. Individuals should take responsibility for their actions and accept their punishment as being a fair response to the offences they have committed.

> **Objective**
>
> - Understand and analyse Jewish attitudes to lawbreakers and different types of crime.

> **Key term**
>
> - **hate crimes:** crimes, often including violence, that are usually targeted at a person because of their race, religion, sexuality, disability or gender

> **Discussion activity**
>
> 'UK law protects the rights and security of all citizens.' Discuss with a partner whether you agree with this statement. Can you think of any examples to support or oppose the statement?

> **"** A child shall not share the burden of a parent's guilt, nor shall a parent share the burden of a child's guilt; the righteousness of the righteous shall be accounted to him alone, and the wickedness of the wicked shall be accounted to him alone. **"**
>
> *Ezekiel* 18:20

Lawbreakers should try to pay back for the wrongs they have committed, for example if they have stolen money they should make efforts to repay it. Repaying money was a common way of righting wrongs in biblical times.

▲ *The police uphold the law to protect the rights and security of UK citizens*

■ Different types of crime – hate crime, theft and murder

There are many different types of crime, ranging in severity from minor crimes to very serious crimes such as mass murder. More severe punishments are reserved for the more serious crimes. However, even crimes which are classed as less serious such as theft are wrong. Some crimes are considered to be **hate crimes**. These are often violent crimes against someone because of their race, religion, sexuality, disability or gender. Because they are targeted at a person rather than a property, as in the case of theft, they are considered to be more serious crimes. They may cause fear or anger, feelings of powerlessness and loss of self-esteem. They disrupt lives. Hate crimes make the idea of a society without prejudice or discrimination impossible to achieve.

▲ *The entrance to Auschwitz concentration camp where many thousands of Jews were murdered during the Holocaust*

An example of a very serious crime, which in some cases is also called a hate crime, is murder. It could well be argued that there is no greater harm that can be done than to take a person's life. During the Second World War, Jews, Slavs, gypsies, disabled people, people of colour, Jehovah's Witnesses and homosexuals were all murdered by the Nazis. These were probably the worst hate crimes ever experienced.

■ Jewish attitudes to different types of crime

Jews condemn both hate crimes and murder. God created all humans with equal value and no individuals or groups should be singled out for inferior treatment. Leviticus 19:18 instructs Jews to love their neighbour. In a modern context, 'neighbour' means everybody, regardless of their race, religion, sexuality, disability or gender. Crimes always have a victim, so are unloving acts. The sixth commandment forbids murder.

Theft, as with other crimes, is a crime with a victim. Someone gets hurt if property they own is stolen from them. The eighth commandment is 'Do not steal' so while it may be considered by some to be a less serious crime, it is still against the will of God and therefore must not be done. Jews would say that it is impossible to judge the 'value' of someone else's property and the crime may have a greater effect on the victim than the monetary value of what is stolen.

Research activity 🔍

Find out more about Nazi concentration camps such as Auschwitz where Jews were murdered as part of the greatest hate crime the world has seen.

Discussion activity 💬

Do you think offenders should take responsibility for their own actions?

⭐ Study tip

If comparing the seriousness of different crimes, don't forget that all crimes involve victims in some way.

Summary

You should now understand Jewish attitudes to lawbreakers and different types of crime, and have analysed these attitudes.

Activities

1 Explain different attitudes to lawbreakers.

2 Explain what Jews believe about lawbreakers and different types of crime. Do you agree with them? Explain why.

3 Explain what is meant by a hate crime and why it is regarded as a very serious crime.

4 Do you think there is ever a good reason to steal? Explain your opinion.

■ The aims of punishment

Whenever a punishment is imposed by a court, the judge has to consider what purpose the punishment will serve. There are three main aims of punishment: retribution, deterrence and reformation.

Retribution

Retribution is the least positive of the three aims of punishment. It means to get your own back. In other words, retribution means that society, on behalf of the victim, is getting its own back on the offender. An early form of retribution, introduced in the Torah, suggested that those who commit crime should receive the same injuries and damage that they caused to their victim. This was intended to ensure that the punishment given was in proportion to the crime and that, for example, a village was not attacked and several people killed because some sheep had been stolen. In fact, to prevent this, Jewish scholars indicated that in relation to such crimes, money should be given in compensation instead.

> 66 But if other damage ensues, the penalty shall be life for life, eye for eye, tooth for tooth, hand for hand, foot for foot, burn for burn, wound for wound, bruise for bruise. 99
>
> *Exodus* 21:23–25

Many Jews reject a literal interpretation of this passage and reject the idea of retribution. They point to quotes such as Leviticus 19:17–18 as more relevant:

> 66 Do not hate your brother in your heart. Rebuke your neighbour frankly so you do not share in his guilt. Do not seek revenge or bear a grudge against one of your people, but love your neighbour as yourself.' 99
>
> *Leviticus* 19:17–18

Deterrence

Many believe that if offenders are seen to be punished for wrongdoing, and in some cases punished severely, the threat of similar punishment might put off others from committing crimes. This is called **deterrence**. For example, the threat of a ban from driving may deter people from driving under the influence of alcohol.

The offender themselves might be deterred from reoffending if they do not like the punishment they receive.

Objectives

- Know and understand three aims of punishment.
- Understand religious attitudes to three aims of punishment.

Key terms

- **retribution:** an aim of punishment – to get your own back; 'an eye for an eye'
- **deterrence:** an aim of punishment – to put people off committing crimes
- **reformation:** an aim of punishment – to change someone's behaviour for the better

Links

For more information on retribution in the context of the death penalty, see pages 150–151.

▲ *The entrance to Gloucester Magistrates' Court*

Years ago in Britain, people were punished in public, for example with public floggings and executions, in order to deter others. Making such an extreme example of offenders in an effort to persuade others to obey the law is not acceptable to many Jews today, who believe that every human being should be treated with respect, regardless of what they have done. They prefer that people should learn from the consequences of what happened to offenders in the past, and not from their own experience of being punished. However, if it is necessary for an individual to be punished as a deterrent, then it is acceptable. People who deserve punishment must learn from it and not repeat the offence, and the punishment should always be humane.

▲ *The threat of punishment should deter people from committing offences*

Reformation

Reformation is an aim of punishment that many people approve of because it seeks to help offenders by working with them to help them to understand that their behaviour is harming society. It is hoped that offenders will change their attitude and become responsible, law-abiding members of the community. In order for this to work, the offender needs to realise that their behaviour is wrong before they can hope to be reformed. This may involve group therapy sessions, individual counselling and treatment (if required), meeting their victims so they realise the harm they may have caused or working in the community (community service).

The importance of reformation was reinforced by the prophet Ezekiel:

> ❝ As I live – declares the LORD God – it is not My desire that the wicked shall die, but that the wicked turn from his [evil] ways and live. Turn back, turn back from your evil ways … ❞
>
> *Ezekiel* 33:11

This encourages Jews to use punishment to attempt to stop people from offending in future by setting an example and showing compassion. Working with offenders to turn their life around by helping them understand the effect of their actions on others is a positive response. However, this is not a replacement for punishment; it should happen at the same time as the punishment and is likely to take place in a prison.

Activities

1 Which of the three aims of punishment do you think is most important when deciding on what punishment to give? Explain why.

2 Why do you think most Jews believe reformation is the most important aim?

Activities

1 Carefully explain the three aims of punishment.

2 Are there any other aims of punishment you think should be added?

Discussion activity

'Punishment should make offenders suffer because they have done wrong.' Discuss this with a partner and write down reasons why some agree with this and others do not.

⭐ Study tip

There are other aims of punishment, such as protecting others in society.

Summary

You should now know and understand three main aims of punishment.

■ Jewish attitudes to suffering

For many people, suffering is an unfortunate part of living. It may be caused by something natural, such as an illness, or it may be due to how they have behaved or how somebody else has behaved. Whatever the cause of suffering, Jews believe they should try to help others who are suffering.

Many people believe that the greatest crime the world has ever seen was aimed at the Jews during the Second World War and in the events leading up to it. The Nazis, led by Adolf Hitler, ruled Germany. In Germany, there were communities of Jews who had lived and worked there for generations. They suffered increasing discrimination and persecution, which then developed into the mass murder of Jews, alongside other minority groups within Germany and other countries that the Nazi regime took over, especially Poland. In what was termed the 'final solution', Jews were rounded up and taken to concentration camps and death camps, such as Auschwitz in Poland. Auschwitz has now become a memorial to the millions who were murdered there. Present day Jews still find it difficult to understand how these crimes can have happened to people whom God chose and with whom he made covenants throughout their history. However, they do accept that such suffering is the result of human evil and of the ability of humans to make choices, to exercise their free will.

There are many accounts of how Jews and members of other faiths or no faith risked their own lives during the Second World War to save the lives of Jews, including children. They were determined to help because they believed the Nazis' actions were deeply wrong and they could not sit back and let it happen.

Objectives

- Know and understand Jewish attitudes to suffering.
- Understand what Jews should do if they cause suffering.

Key term

- **free will:** belief that God gives people the opportunity to make decisions for themselves

Activity

What can people learn from the example of Rabbi Harry Jacobi?

Research activity

Use libraries and the Internet to find out about Irena Sendler, another person who saved Jewish children. Alternatively, find out about how the people of Denmark saved Jewish citizens during the Second World War. Share your findings with others in the class.

Rabbi Harry Jacobi

Rabbi Harry Jacobi was one of the thousands of Jewish children who were evacuated from Nazi Germany. He arrived in Holland in 1939 but when the Nazis invaded Holland he was helped to escape again, to Britain. He was ordained as a rabbi in 1961 and is currently Vice President of Liberal Judaism.

In 2016, a large camp housing refugees and migrants, including unaccompanied children, had been set up in Calais in Northern France. The people wanted to settle in Britain but had to stay in the camp where conditions were terrible. Rabbi Harry Jacobi visited the children to deliver them school books and dictionaries. More importantly, he was able to give sympathy and hope. He helped put pressure on the British government to allow many of the children to be allowed to settle in Britain.

▲ Rabbi Harry Jacobi

Many people question why a loving God, who cares about his people, allows them to suffer. However, it would be wrong to blame God for criminal actions that cause suffering. Jews believe that God gave humans the **free will** to behave as they choose. The story of Adam and Eve teaches that this free will was misused even in the earliest times. This is why God gave the Jews the Torah to guide them in how to use free will responsibly. If Jews choose to follow the mitzvot and stay close to God, they will want to make good choices which do not harm others. However, there are consequences, including legal punishments imposed by courts, when people choose to behave in a way which harms other people and does not please God.

▲ *Why does God allow people to suffer?*

■ Jewish attitudes to causing suffering to others

Jews are very much opposed to causing others to suffer. However, their strong belief in justice means that they believe those who have done wrong should face punishment, especially if the wrongdoing has caused others to suffer. The teachings of prophets, such as Amos and Hosea, describe in detail the nature of the punishment and the suffering God was going to put upon his people for straying from his path. However, both Amos and Hosea emphasise that God will also be willing to take them back.

> 66 I will restore My people Israel. They shall rebuild ruined cities and inhabit them; […] I will them upon their soil, Nevermore to be uprooted From the soil I have given them 99
>
> *Amos 9:14–15*

As no human is perfect, it is inevitable that people may cause suffering, often by accident or because their mind is not clear for some reason. Having caused suffering, Jews believe it is important that they are honest to themselves, to other people and to God, and work at repairing the damage they may have caused. Rabbi Hillel taught about a basic Jewish principle: 'Do not do to others that which you would not want them to do to you.' This way, relationships can be restored.

Activities

1 Explain how a Jew might answer the question, 'Why does God allow people to suffer?'

2 Explain why Jews try not to cause others to suffer.

3 According to Jewish teaching, what should Jews do if they cause somebody else to suffer?

4 Do you think it is right that punishment should cause suffering? Explain your reasons.

Activities

1 How do Jews, who believe in a good, just and powerful God, explain their suffering?

2 Explain why free will should not allow people to do exactly as they wish.

Links

For more about suffering and some of its causes, see Chapter 5, pages 106–107.

★ Study tip

When writing that free will means people can do whatever they like, also mention the consequences of making wrong choices.

Summary

You should now have increased your knowledge and understanding of Jewish attitudes to suffering and understand what Jews would try to do if they cause suffering to others.

7.6 Jewish attitudes to the treatment of criminals – prison, corporal punishment and community service

■ Punishment

In UK law, there are many ways that criminals can be legally punished and several ways that they cannot. How severe the punishment is depends on the seriousness of the crime. It can range from a long-term stay in **prison** for a serious crime, to payment of a fine for a lesser one.

Reformation is considered to be the most important criterion used in deciding punishment, because in the long term, if through punishment a criminal is changed, both the individual and society benefit.

■ Prison

Prison is reserved for those who have committed a serious crime. Those considered a high threat to society when released, or to themselves or other prisoners, are kept in a high security prison. It is considered important that prisoners in UK prisons are not be mistreated and are kept safe. The punishment a prison imposes is loss of liberty, not inhumane treatment. Prisoners have no choice to live as ordinary people do, are locked in cells for much of the day, are fed at set times and have to do manual work for little money.

Although the Torah makes no mention of imprisonment, preferring monetary compensation, most Jews agree that these days prison should be used as a punishment for serious crimes. They believe it provides an opportunity for offenders to reflect on their actions, realise they were wrong and be determined not to commit another crime when released. Both remorse for the past and resolutions for the future are required.

■ Corporal punishment

Corporal punishment means to punish an offender by causing them physical pain. This could be by whipping them, or hitting them repeatedly with a cane. Many consider this a breach of the Human Rights legislation. Corporal punishment is illegal in the UK, which reflects the belief of many Christians and Jews that corporal punishment is wrong. However, it is allowed in some other parts of the world. Corporal punishment was also permitted in schools in the UK but is now illegal.

Although the Torah and Talmud both allow for corporal punishment, up to 40 lashes in order to limit the harm caused, it does not happen in Jewish practice today.

Objectives

- Know and understand three forms of punishment.
- Consider ways in which criminals are treated, and Jewish beliefs and attitudes to their treatment.

Key terms

- **prison:** a secure building where offenders are kept for a period of time set by a judge
- **corporal punishment:** punishment of an offender by causing them physical pain – now illegal in the UK
- **community service:** a way of punishing offenders by making them do unpaid work in the community

Links

For more about the aims of punishment, see pages 142–143.

▲ Up until the nineteenth century, offenders in the UK were punished by being locked in the stocks

> ❝ He who spares the rod hates his son,
> But he who loves him disciplines him early. ❞
>
> *Proverbs* 13:24

Jews today, in disciplining their children, emphasise the importance of kindness and compassion, and many would not use physical punishment to teach children right from wrong.

Jews expect people to be responsible for their actions and to be punished if appropriate. In relation to criminals, they interpret Proverbs 13:24 as emphasising the need for positive discipline, using methods that cause no harm, with a focus on helping offenders to realise the error of their ways and assist them in reforming.

■ Community service

Some crimes are punishable by **community service**. This may include offences such as vandalism, benefit fraud or minor assaults. Community service offers the offender a chance to make up for what they have done and receive help in reforming their behaviour. Because the aims of community service are positive and offer the chance to reform, many Jews agree that it is a suitable punishment for fairly minor offences.

In the UK, community payback is one part of a community sentence. This involves doing between 40 and 300 hours of unpaid work in the community, such as removing graffiti, clearing wasteland or decorating public places or buildings. While working, those who are doing community payback wear a high visibility orange vest so everybody knows they have been convicted of an offence.

Other elements included in community service might be treatment programmes for medical conditions or for drug or alcohol abuse if required, plus counselling sessions and basic education services.

Offenders under the age of 18 may be required to complete a work programme, make up for the damage they have caused to property or complete a rehabilitation order which makes it clear what they must and must not do for a set period of time. It may also require them to listen to the victim's side of the story and possibly apologise in writing or face to face.

Research activity 🔍

Find out information about other forms of punishment that are legally used in the UK.

Contrasting beliefs

Use the Internet or library to find out more about Christian beliefs about corporal punishment, and try to compare and contrast with Jewish views.

Prison	Corporal	Community
Legal	Punishment	Service
		Legal

▲ *Three forms of punishment*

⭐ Study tip

Remember that human rights is an important issue when considering punishment.

Activities

1 Write a list and give details to explain three forms of punishment.

2 Explain Jewish attitudes towards these three forms of punishment.

3 Do you agree that prisoners should be treated with dignity whilst in prison? Give reasons.

4 Explain Jewish attitudes to corporal punishment.

Summary

You should now know and understand three forms of punishment. You will have considered the way criminals are treated, and Jewish beliefs and attitudes to their treatment.

■ Forgiveness

Forgiveness is a core belief in Judaism and in Christianity and is strongly linked to **repentance**. However, Jews believe forgiveness should not be the automatic response of a person who has been wronged, and the offender should not expect it to be. Instead, those who have wronged others should show remorse to their victims, and honestly and directly ask for their forgiveness before they can expect to be forgiven by God.

The Ten Days of Repentance between Rosh Hashanah and Yom Kippur are traditionally the time to ask forgiveness for an offence, if it has not been asked for already. On Yom Kippur, Jews traditionally believe that transgressions between people and God are forgiven. Any transgressions between two people can only be forgiven if the transgressor has sought forgiveness from the person they have hurt. The person who has been hurt has a duty to forgive if they are genuinely asked, and many Jews will actively seek out anyone they feel they may have upset, insulted or wronged.

The prophet Isaiah illustrated God's role in forgiveness:

> ❝ Come, let us reach an understanding,
>
> –says the LORD.
>
> Be your sins like crimson,
>
> They can turn snow-white;
>
> Be they red as dyed wool,
>
> They can become like fleece. ❞
>
> *Isaiah* 1:18

It is only when temptation to repeat the offence in the future is resisted, that repentance is seen to be genuine and effective.

However, forgiveness is not a replacement for punishment. It is possible both to forgive somebody who has committed murder and to believe that justice is done when they are sentenced to a long period of imprisonment. However, the intention of the imprisonment should be to reform the prisoner. This requires them to acknowledge what they have done wrong, honestly seek forgiveness and then repent. Part of repentance is also to accept their punishment.

The phrase 'forgive and forget' is not in the Tenakh and is not Jewish teaching. Although people may consider that forgiving and forgetting is

▲ In Jewish teaching, it takes more than a bunch of flowers to gain forgiveness

good advice on occasions, such as when someone has caused upset and apologised, there are times when it is clear that forgiving and forgetting are two different things. For example, a victim of rape might, with difficulty, find it possible to forgive the rapist, but it is unlikely that they will ever be able to forget the experience.

Links

For more information about Rosh Hashanah and Yom Kippur, see Chapter 2, pages 56–57.

Simon Wiesenthal

Simon Wiesenthal was a Jew who survived the Holocaust. While a prisoner in a work squad during the Second World War, he was summoned to the bedside of a dying Nazi officer, who was responsible for the deaths and inhuman treatment of thousands of Jews. After confessing his many horrific crimes, the Nazi officer asked Simon to grant him forgiveness. Silently, Simon walked away. He felt he could not grant the man his last wish because he felt he could not grant forgiveness on behalf of the many people he had murdered. However, his refusal to forgive haunted him for many years afterwards, and every time he entered a hospital, and saw a nurse or a man with a bandaged head, the image of the man returned into his mind.

In support of Simon Wiesenthal, Harold S. Kushner, (Rabbi Laureate of Temple Israel in Natick, Massachusetts) wrote:

'[the officer's] plea for forgiveness was addressed to someone who lacked the power (let alone the right) to grant it. If he wanted to die feeling forgiven, he should have said to himself: "What I did was terribly wrong and I am ashamed of myself for having done it. I reject that part of myself that could have done such a thing. I don't want to be a person who would do such a thing, I am still alive, though I don't know for how much longer, but the Nazi who killed that child is dead. He no longer lives inside me. I renounce him."'

▲ *A stamp issued in honour of Simon Wiesenthal after his death*

Activities

1 What is forgiveness?
2 Explain in detail what Jews believe about forgiveness.
3 Explain why forgiveness is not a replacement for punishment.

 Study tip

You can use case study information to develop your answers.

Discussion activity

Was Simon Wiesenthal right in refusing to forgive the Nazi officer, and was Harold S. Kushner right in supporting his decision? Discuss this with a partner.

Summary

You should now understand more about Jewish attitudes to forgiveness and have considered a case study related to forgiveness.

7.8 Religious attitudes to the death penalty

■ The death penalty

The **death penalty** was abolished in the UK in 1965 as a temporary experiment and then permanently abolished in 1969. The European Community has since made it illegal in all member countries. Several campaigns have been carried out in the UK to try to have it reintroduced but have failed.

Since its abolition, three people executed in the early 1950s have been pardoned because new evidence that emerged after they were put to death has shown that they were innocent. In addition, there have been several instances, since abolition, where people have been wrongly convicted of murder and released from prison. If the death penalty had been an option in the UK, it is likely that they would have been executed for crimes they did not commit. The chance of killing an innocent person is one of the arguments put forward by those who argue against bringing back the death penalty in the UK.

■ Jewish attitudes to the death penalty

The Torah identifies 36 offences, such as murder, improper sexual relations and idol worship, that should be punishable by death. However, the Talmud makes it quite clear that executing offenders should not happen too often. It provides alternative ways of punishing people, lays down very strict rules regarding evidence that, in reality, are unlikely to be met, and interprets texts in a very strict way, which makes it almost impossible for an offender to be put to death. The death penalty was abolished in Israel in 1954 for all offences other than those committed in the Holocaust by the Nazis, or for treason in time of war. Only one Nazi war criminal, Adolf Eichmann, has been executed since 1954 and that was in 1962.

Some Jews believe that the death penalty should be allowed. They use teachings from the Torah to support their views. Their main justification is taken from Genesis:

> ❝ Whoever sheds the blood of man,
>   By man shall his blood be shed; ❞
>
> *Genesis* 9:6

▲ *Would a jury be less willing to find someone guilty of murder if the death penalty was legal?*

Objectives

- Know and understand arguments for and against the death penalty.
- Understand different Jewish attitudes to the death penalty.
- Understand contrasting views about the death penalty in contemporary British society.

Key term

- **death penalty:** capital punishment; a form of punishment in which a prisoner is put to death for crimes committed

Contrasting beliefs

How do Jewish attitudes to the death penalty compare with Christian views?

They may support this by making reference to the teaching in Exodus:

> " life for life, eye for eye, tooth for tooth … "
>
> *Exodus* 21:23–24

In addition to being seen as retribution, the death penalty is sometimes said to deter other people from committing murder. However, there is little evidence to support the view that the death penalty does deter people from committing serious crimes. Countries such as the UK that do not permit the death penalty do not all have higher murder rates than countries that do. Most people who commit murder do not think about what may happen to them, although they may consider it afterwards. It is possible that they do not expect to be caught anyway and in some cases they may be so angry that they do not care.

When dealing with a killer, many believe that the commandment 'do not murder' only applies to the offender and not to the executioner. However, Jews who oppose the death penalty do not believe that taking another life is the right thing to do. They believe that only God has the right to take life; after all, it is he who gifted life to humanity.

In the sixth century BCE, speaking on behalf of God, the prophet Ezekiel said: 'it is not My desire that the wicked should die, but that the wicked turn from his [evil] ways and live.'(Ezekiel 33:11).

While it can be argued that the rest of society is protected if murderers are executed, protection is also achieved by imprisoning murderers. Imprisonment also gives murderers the chance to repent, be forgiven and be reformed so that if released, they can become useful members of society. This is what many Jews want to happen, and is why they oppose the death penalty.

■ Attitudes to the death penalty in Christianity

There are mixed views about the death penalty in Christianity. Some of the arguments for either side are similar to those put forward by Jews, partly because they are based on the Tenakh. Many Christians believe that people should have the opportunity to repent and reform. Their approach to the death penalty may be influenced by Jesus' teaching about loving one's enemies, as well as by texts from the Tenakh:

> " As I live – declares the Lord God – it is not My desire that the wicked shall die, but that the wicked turn from his [evil] ways and live. "
>
> *Ezekiel* 33:11

▲ *There are many reasons why people oppose the death penalty*

Activities

1 Make a list of three arguments for and against the death penalty.

2 Explain different Jewish attitudes to the death penalty.

3 Do you think Jews should oppose the death penalty? Give religious reasons for both sides of the argument.

⭐ Study tip

You may have come across the quote 'an eye for an eye and the whole world will be blind.' While many Jews (and Christians) agree with this, it was first said by Mahatma Gandhi, a Hindu. It is not in the Tenakh.

Summary

You should now have greater knowledge and understanding of the death penalty, and should understand different Jewish and Christian attitudes to the death penalty.

Religion, crime and the causes of crime – summary

You should now be able to:

✔ explain Jewish beliefs and teachings about good and evil intentions and actions, including whether it can ever be good to cause suffering

✔ explain reasons for crime, including poverty and upbringing, mental illness and addiction, greed and hate and opposition to an unjust law

✔ explain views about people who break the law for these reasons

✔ explain Jewish views about different types of crime, including hate crimes, theft and murder.

Religion and punishment – summary

You should now be able to:

✔ explain Jewish beliefs and teachings about the aims of punishment, including retribution, deterrence and reformation

✔ explain Jewish beliefs and teachings about the treatment of criminals, including prison, corporal punishment and community service

✔ explain Jewish beliefs and teachings about forgiveness

✔ explain Jewish beliefs and teachings about the death penalty

✔ explain contemporary British attitudes (both religious and non-religious) towards all of the above issues

✔ explain contrasting beliefs in contemporary British society to the three issues of corporal punishment, the death penalty and forgiveness, with reference to the main religious tradition in Britain (Christianity) and one or more other religious traditions.

Sample student answer – the 4 mark question

1. Write an answer to the following practice question:

   Explain two contrasting beliefs in contemporary British society about corporal punishment.
   In your answer you should refer to the main religious tradition of Great Britain and one or more other religious traditions. **[4 marks]**

2. Read the following student sample answer:

   "Although the Tenakh mentions corporal punishment, in Britain today it is not allowed and most Jews wouldn't want it to be allowed anyway. In contemporary British society, corporal punishment is not used. It is not a loving action because it harms people, some of whom may be innocent, and doesn't reform them. In Britain, Christians used to use corporal punishment and it was used in schools until recently, but now most Christians are glad it has been banned."

3. With a partner, discuss the student answer. Can you identify two contrasting points? Is there reference to the main religious tradition in Great Britain (Christianity) and at least one other religious tradition. Can it be improved? If so, how?

4. What mark (out of 4) would you give this answer? Look at the mark scheme in the introduction (AO1). What are the reasons for the mark you have given?

5. Now swap your answer with your partner's and mark each other's responses. What mark (out of 4) would you give the response? Refer to the mark scheme and give reasons for the mark you award.

Sample student answer – the 5 mark question

1. Write an answer to the following practice question:

   Explain two religious beliefs about the reasons why some people commit crimes. Refer to scripture or sacred writings in your answer. **[5 marks]**

2. Read the following student sample answer:

   "Some people commit crimes because they have a mental illness that makes it difficult for them to resist temptation. As it is an illness, they should be treated and helped but punished as well. Jews believe help and punishment go together. Others may commit crimes because they are greedy and want things that don't belong to them. This is because the Ten Commandments say 'Thou shalt not covet'. It could also lead them to steal which also breaks a commandment."

3. With a partner, discuss the student answer. Can you identify two religious beliefs connected with the reasons for crime? Are the beliefs detailed and is the teaching relevant and accurate? Can the answer be improved? If so, how?

4. What mark (out of 4) would you give this answer? Look at the mark scheme in the introduction (AO1). What are the reasons for the mark you have given?

5. Now swap your answer with your partner's and mark each other's responses. What mark (out of 4) would you give the response? Refer to the mark scheme and give reasons for the mark you award.

Practice questions

1. Which one of the following is an aim of punishment?

   A) Prison   B) Deterrence   C) Forgiveness   D) Murder   **[1 mark]**

2. Give two different causes of crime. **[2 marks]**

3. Explain two contrasting beliefs in contemporary British society about whether the death penalty should exist in the UK.

   In your answer you should refer to the main religious tradition of Great Britain and one or more other religious traditions. **[4 marks]**

4. Explain two reasons why religious believers believe reformation is the best aim of punishment.

   Refer to scripture or sacred writings in your answer. **[5 marks]**

5. 'It is right to forgive all offenders whoever they are and whatever they have done.'

   Evaluate this statement. In your answer you:
   - should give reasoned arguments in support of this statement
   - should give reasoned arguments to support a different point of view
   - should refer to religious arguments
   - may refer to non-religious arguments
   - should reach a justified conclusion. **[12 marks]**

■ Human rights

A human right is something that a human being is entitled to because they are human. So all humans are entitled to **human rights** – they are universal. Human rights are based on the belief that every person deserves respect and should be treated carefully and with dignity. In some communities, some people suffer from bullying, exploitation or are treated as second-class citizens. This unfair treatment is not the fault of the victims concerned. It might happen because of their race, colour, religion, age, class, gender or because they have a disability. They may be denied the rights and freedoms that many other people enjoy. Although people-trafficking and slavery are illegal, they still occur in the world. Human rights violations like these can vary from verbal bullying to persecution and death in extreme cases. Jews have particularly suffered from persecution, for example, in the Second World War when the Nazis murdered around six million Jews in the Holocaust.

■ The Universal Declaration of Human Rights (UDHR)

After the Second World War, the United Nations expressed the desire that every person should have basic human rights so that they could enjoy freedom, justice and peace. Jews, along with members of other faiths and politicians, played an active part in the development of what has become known as the Universal Declaration of Human Rights (UDHR). Consisting of 30 articles, it was adopted by the United Nations General Assembly in 1948. It recognises the value of each individual and includes the right to an education and a fair trial. Articles state that:

> **“** Everyone is entitled to all the rights and freedoms set forth in this Declaration, without distinction of any kind, such as race, colour, sex, language, religion, political or other opinion, national or social origin, property, birth or other status …’ **”**
>
> *UDHR*, Article 2

> **“** Everyone has the right to freedom of thought, conscience and religion …’ **”**
>
> *UDHR*, Article 18

In 1998, to commemorate the fiftieth anniversary of the UDHR, the Declaration of Human Duties and Responsibilities (DHDR) was

Objectives

- Understand the need for laws to protect human rights.
- Understand Jewish teachings, beliefs and attitudes about human rights and explore the responsibilities that come with human rights.

Key terms

- **human rights:** the basic rights and freedoms to which all human beings should be entitled
- **responsibility:** a duty to care for, or having control over, something or someone

▲ *United Nations flag*

> **“** By three things is the world sustained: law, truth and peace. **”**
>
> *Ethics of the Fathers* 1:18

154

produced by the UN to remind countries of their duty to protect individuals.

■ The Human Rights Act (HRA)

The UK Parliament's Human Rights Act mostly came into force in 2000. The basic rights set out in the HRA include the right to education, family life, free elections, marriage, privacy and security. It prohibits the use of forced labour, slavery and torture and allows people to express their views, providing they do not stir up hatred, or harm people.

■ Responsibilities

Jews believe that with human rights comes the **responsibility** not to abuse them. If people are allowed freedom of speech, then alongside that right is the moral responsibility not to stir up hatred or encourage violence by what is said.

There have been many examples in history of situations where hateful and false things have been said, and Jews in particular have suffered the consequences. Anti-Semitism has occurred in many countries, including the UK, France, Germany, Spain and Russia. In some countries, Jewish customs, religion and traditions make Jews very distinctive from the other inhabitants. This has been used as an excuse to blame them for the problems of society. For example, in the fourteenth century many Jews were killed after a rumour was spread that they were responsible for the plague (known as the black death). In fact this plague had started in Central Asia and had been carried through the Silk Road trading route into Europe through rat fleas on black rats on merchant ships. It had nothing to do with the Jews.

It is important to realise that everyone has responsibilities in order to uphold rights. For example, if young people expect to be protected from cruelty and neglect, then they should not bully or harm each other. This principle applies to all the human rights. Jewish attitudes to human rights are based on the belief that every life is precious and sacred to God and should be respected. The protection of human rights is an important part of the faith and tradition of Judaism. The beliefs that people are created in God's image, that the human family is one, and that every person should deal justly with each other, are central to Judaism.

▲ *The right to vote is a fundamental human right*

 Guard your tongue from evil, your lips from deceitful speech. 🟦

Psalm 34:14

 You must not carry false rumours; 🟦

Exodus 23:1

Discussion activity 💬

In pairs or small groups discuss the following statement:

'Laws can be made but they will never stop human rights abuses.'

Extension activity 💡

Use the Internet or a library to find out more about the UDHR and the 30 articles. Choose three that you find interesting and write them down.

Activities

1 Explain some of the reasons why it is necessary to have human rights.
2 Explain why the United Nations adopted the Universal Declaration of Human Rights.
3 Give two examples of the 30 Articles of the UDHR.
4 What basic rights does the Human Rights Act include?
5 Explain why Jews believe that everyone has the responsibility not to abuse their human rights.
6 What is meant by anti-Semitism?

⭐ Study tip

It would be helpful to know some specific examples of rights given by the UDHR and be able to explain their importance.

Summary

You should now be able to explain the need for laws to protect people's rights and Jewish attitudes towards human rights.

Judaism and equality

Judaism teaches that God created humans in his image and therefore all people are of equal value (see Genesis 1:27). People may not look the same or have the same abilities, but all are precious to God. People should not be treated as if they are of less value because that is not respecting them or treating them fairly.

What is social justice?

Social justice occurs when people are treated as equals, have a fair allocation of community resources, and have their human rights protected. When something is unjust, people challenge it. The least advantaged members of society are cared for so that no one is exploited. This does not happen in some countries. If law and order breaks down, or if the rulers do not support treating everyone as equals, there is no social justice. In some countries, there is a great difference between the very rich and those who live in poverty, struggling to survive. People who believe in social justice want to see everyone being treated more equally, and want to get rid of extreme poverty. This applies to all, whatever their age, disability, gender, race, religion or sexuality.

▲ *World Day of Social Justice is 20 February*

Jews and justice

Jews believe that if they follow the laws of the Torah they will help to create harmony in society. Every individual needs to contribute to creating just and fair societies. The Children of Israel were told: '**justice** shall you pursue, that you may thrive and occupy the land that the LORD your God is giving you.' (Deuteronomy 16:20). This instruction was not always followed, and the prophet Amos who lived c750BCE challenged the people of Israel for ignoring justice and oppressing the poor. He warned them that their period of prosperity would soon come to an end because they lacked integrity, justice and compassion, and God would not ignore their wrongdoings. According to Amos, they were 'tilting a dishonest scale, and selling grain […] We will buy the poor for silver, the needy for a pair of sandals.' (Amos 8:5–6). This was breaking the law as given in Leviticus 19:35–36 ('You shall not falsify measures …'). Amos says that God will not accept their offerings unless justice is restored: 'But let justice well up like water, Righteousness like an unfailing stream.' (Amos 5:24).

Jewish ethical teaching is based on the principle found in Leviticus 19:18.

This is one of the key commands of the Torah which underpins Jewish belief about social justice and the way to treat people, whether Jew or Gentile. People should not be exploited, but treated with fairness, honesty and kindness. The Talmud contains a story of Rabbi Hillel who lived in the first century BCE. He was challenged by a non-Jew to summarise the teaching of the Torah in the length of time that he could stand on one foot. The Rabbi replied, 'What is hateful to yourself, do not do to your fellow man. That is the whole Torah, the rest is just commentary. Go and study it.' Jews believe that it is important to work for the good of the community, and have made significant contributions to improving life in the UK, for example, Dame Gail Ronson became the president of the Royal National Institute of Blind People and raised funds for many charities including Norwood Orphanage and Jewish Care.

There are a number of Jewish groups working for social justice. Tzedek, meaning justice, is one such charity. The aim of this organisation is to reduce poverty caused by humans by seeking to increase justice. Members fundraise for projects in Africa and Asia and send volunteers abroad to help in the developing world.

▲ Like Dame Gail Ronson, many Jews have been very prominent in charity work

> ❝ Love your fellow as yourself ❞
>
> *Leviticus* 19:18

Links

For more about Judaism and charity, see pages 168–169.

⭐ Study tip

When studying other parts of this chapter, such as the responsibilities and use of wealth, consider how they relate to social justice.

Summary

You should now be able to explain Jewish beliefs about equality and social justice.

Activities

1 Explain why the prophet Amos challenged the people of his day concerning fairness.

2 Explain what Rabbi Hillel meant when he summarised the teaching of the Torah. How do his words help Jews today?

Religious freedom in the UK

UK law now supports everyone having the freedom to follow the religion of their choice, but in the past this was not always the case. In the twelfth century and for the next 350 years, there were occasions when Jews were persecuted and even expelled from England. In Christianity too, in the past, there were bitter conflicts between different branches of the faith, resulting in people being unable to worship freely and being put to death for their religious views. During part of the sixteenth and seventeenth centuries, and more recently in Northern Ireland, there were hostilities between Roman Catholics and Protestants.

Nowadays, the adoption of the Human Rights Act 1998, and the Universal Declaration of Human Rights gives protection to the individual regarding **freedom of religion**. The law promotes tolerance and respect for those who hold different beliefs, and allows **freedom of religious expression**, providing it does not stir up hatred against others of different beliefs. People are free to choose to belong to any religion of their choice, or to have no religious belief at all. For example, Buddhists, Christians, Hindus, Jews, Muslims and Sikhs are free to construct places of worship (providing they keep to the planning laws) and follow their religion. Organisations like the Inter Faith Network for the UK work to promote good relations, understanding and cooperation between people of different faiths.

▲ *A Jewish synagogue in Birmingham; religious freedom includes being allowed to build places of worship, within planning laws*

Religious freedom

Judaism is essentially a non-missionary religion, because Jews do not try to convert people to their faith. Sincere converts can join Judaism, but that is unusual; nearly all Jews are born into the faith. Some may convert to the faith because they marry a Jewish person.

Objective

- Explore issues of freedom of religion and belief, including religious expression.

Key terms

- **freedom of religion:** the right to believe or practise whatever religion one chooses
- **freedom of religious expression:** the right to worship, preach and practise one's faith in whatever way one chooses

Activities

1 What laws have been adopted in the UK that give people freedom of choice regarding religious belief and religious expression?

2 Explain briefly what it means to be a non-missionary religion.

Discussion activity

With a partner, in a small group or as a class, discuss whether you agree with the following:

'Wherever they live, people should be free to express their religious beliefs however they wish.'

Jews believe that the seven Noachide commandments, which are basic moral laws, were given to all humankind after the great flood. God made a covenant with Noah, which included commandments such as not to kill human beings. Later, on Mount Sinai, Moses received the Torah laws. These apply only to the Jews, although many Gentiles (non-Jews) follow them as well. Some Jews believe that only when the Messiah comes to rule will the law go out from Jerusalem for all people. Until that time, Gentiles who follow the Noachide commandments are regarded as the 'righteous among the nations' and are assured of a place in the world to come.

Within Judaism, there are different branches of the faith, for example Orthodox, Reform and Liberal, but Jews are not expected to change their religion. After entering the Promised Land, the Jews were given the choice by their leader Joshua of choosing to follow the Lord or the local gods. He said, 'Or, if you are loath to serve the LORD, choose this day which ones you are going to serve – the gods that your forefathers served beyond the Euphrates, or those of the Amorites in whose land you are settled; but I and my household will serve the Lord.' (Joshua 24:15). The people responded that they would follow the Lord.

In the first century CE, the Romans ruthlessly crushed a revolt of the Jews in Judea who wanted to follow their own religion. As a result, the majority of survivors fled from Israel. Although they were scattered throughout the world, Jews have maintained their traditions, customs and beliefs, and the faith has survived. Since then, the Jews have faced much persecution and have settled in many countries amongst people of many different religions. Those Jews who do not wish to practise or follow their faith are known as secular Jews, although they remain Jewish by birth.

In Britain today, Jews are free to build synagogues, observe their festivals, worship and keep the Sabbath in whatever way their tradition dictates. They are able to dress in appropriate clothes for their branch of Judaism, which may distinguish them from the rest of society. For example, some strict Orthodox Jews called Hasidic Jews have beards and wear long side locks as an outward sign of their Jewish faith. They follow the teaching of Leviticus 19:27, 'You shall not round off the side-growth on your head, or destroy the side-growth of your beard.' The men wear dark suits and white shirts and married women cover their heads with a scarf, hat or wig. Unfortunately, while Jews have the freedom to dress traditionally, at times they are still the subject of anti-Semitic attacks by those who are prejudiced and do not understand the importance of religious freedom.

Links

For more information on worship in synagogues, see Chapter 2, pages 32–41.

Contrasting beliefs

Use the Internet to find out more about Christian beliefs about freedom of religious expression, and about inter-faith organisations and the work they do, such as the Inter Faith Network.

▲ *A Hasidic Jew*

⭐ Study tip

If you are asked to express an opinion about religious freedom and freedom of religious expression, include your own personal view and the reasons why you have arrived at your conclusion.

Summary

You should now be able to explain Jewish views concerning freedom of religion and freedom of religious expression.

Activities

1 What commandments do Jews believe are intended for all humans to keep?

2 Explain briefly the choice given by Joshua to the Jewish people.

3 Give three examples which show that Jews are free to express their religion in the UK in the way they choose.

159

8.4 Prejudice and discrimination

Prejudice means thinking less of a person because, for example, of his or her race, religion, gender, colour or age. It is an opinion that has been formed without good reason, knowledge or experience. Prejudice can lead to discrimination. This is when the thought leads to action. **Discrimination** means treating someone differently, usually badly or unfairly. For example, prejudice is when a person may dislike someone because they are of a different race or have a different religion. If, as a result, they refuse to give them a job because they are against their race or religion, that would be discrimination.

Sometimes, people are treated more favourably because of who or what they are. For example, wheelchair users might be given the front row at a football match so that they are able to get a good view of the game. This is known as **positive discrimination**. Sometimes it is used to help those who have not been given equal opportunities in the past. This might include employing more women in senior roles or people from minority ethnic groups.

■ Homosexuality

The Torah forbids a sexual relationship between two people of the same sex. Leviticus 18 gives instructions about unlawful sexual relations, which told the Israelites not to copy the Egyptians and the Canaanites. A reference to **homosexuality** is included in the list of instructions:

> ❝ Do not lie with a male as one lies with a woman; it is an abhorrence. ❞
>
> *Leviticus* 18:22

The Torah forbids a sexual relationship between two males. Genesis 19 describes how the men of Sodom wanted to have sex with the messengers who visited Lot's house (Genesis 19:4–5). Following these teachings, Orthodox Judaism considers homosexual physical relationships to be wrong although individuals should be treated with respect.

Reform and Liberal Jews emphasise the principles behind such stories, such as the Jews' disapproval of casual sex. They believe in social justice and believe that scriptural passages have to be interpreted in the light of Jewish history and development in the time following the writing of the Torah. Many take the view that what matters is whether or not two people love each other. They believe that what happens in private is up to the people involved. Some will accept civil marriages between gay couples and some will marry gay couples in a religious service.

Objectives

- Understand the difference between prejudice and discrimination.
- Investigate Jewish beliefs about homosexuality, racial prejudice and discrimination.

Key terms

- **prejudice:** unfairly judging someone before the facts are known; holding biased opinions about an individual or group
- **discrimination:** actions or behaviour that result from prejudice
- **positive discrimination:** treating people more favourably because they have been discriminated against in the past or have disabilities
- **homosexuality:** sexual attraction to members of the same sex
- **racism:** showing prejudice against someone because of their ethnic group or nationality

▲ *A gay couple*

■ Racial prejudice

The Torah teaches that all humans have been made in the image of God and so everyone should be treated with respect. This includes people of other races, for example, 'You shall not wrong a stranger or oppress him, for you were strangers in the land of Egypt.' (Exodus 22:20). Jews are expected to treat everyone fairly. They should not be prejudiced or discriminate against people of a different nationality.

The Jewish Council for Racial Equality (JCORE) was set up in Britain in 1976 to work with others to combat discrimination and promote racial harmony in this country. They provide resources and education which helps to promote racial and religious equality. Jews have suffered from a great deal of hatred, persecution and terrorism during their history, so they recognise how wrong **racism** is.

Research activity

Use the Internet or a library to find out about the diary of Anne Frank or the story of Corrie ten Boom.

Discussion activity

In pairs or small groups, discuss the following statement:

'There should be no gender prejudice or discrimination within religion.'

The Holocaust

The worst period of persecution of the Jews took place during the Second World War. Hitler and the Nazi regime stirred up anti-Semitism, and around six million Jews were murdered in Europe. The Nazis promoted the belief that some races were superior to others and this view led to racist behaviour and racist laws. Hitler began the persecution by making laws preventing Jews from working in many jobs, including the legal profession, schools and universities. Then, in 1938, he ordered an attack by military forces on Jews, their businesses and synagogues. Jews were forced to wear a Star of David so they could be identified, and their rights of citizenship were removed. Once the war started, the attacks on Jews grew worse, and they were forced to live in overcrowded ghettos. Hundreds

▲ *The entrance to the Yad Vashem Children's Memorial, Israel's official memorial to the Jewish victims of the Holocaust*

of thousands were transported to concentration camps like Auschwitz, as well as some non-Jewish people. Some were put to work, but those who were unable to do so were murdered. Deadly Zyklon B gas was released inside the communal shower rooms, and then the bodies were incinerated. All their belongings were taken for reuse. Those who were not killed immediately quickly became weak from lack of food and the appalling conditions. When they became too weak to work, they were murdered too.

★ Study tip

Learn some examples from the Torah so that you can use them when discussing Jewish teachings and attitudes to homosexuality and racism.

Activities

1 Explain the difference between prejudice and discrimination.

2 What is positive discrimination?

3 Explain Jewish attitudes to homosexuality.

4 What does the Torah say about racism?

5 Describe how Jews have suffered from racial discrimination.

Summary

You should now know the difference between prejudice and discrimination, and be able to explain Jewish attitudes to homosexuality and racism.

8.5 Women in Judaism

■ The role and status of women in Judaism

Christians and Jews share the belief that God created men and women in his own image (see Genesis 1:27). This means that men and women are regarded as having equal value and status. Traditionally, however, the **role** of women within Judaism has been different to that of men because they have different functions to fulfil. While husbands have often been seen as responsible for providing an income and dealing with matters outside the home, the role of wives has been primarily to do with the home and the family. Women's responsibilities have included bringing up the children in the customs and practices of the Jewish faith. To Jews, this is an important role because it ensures the survival of Judaism, even in a country where most people are non-Jews. Children are brought up to value their religion and to pass their knowledge and beliefs on to future generations. Jews believe that it is the mother who gives the children their Jewish identity.

Today, Jewish women in many households also have careers. They go out to work and take part in voluntary activities in the community. In addition to their religious beliefs, such roles may be affected by the need to support the family financially.

Another important duty for women has been ensuring that the Jewish food laws are kept. Only kosher food (food that meets Jewish laws) is prepared, and care is taken not to mix foods that should not be cooked or eaten together. This mainly applies to the eating of meat and milk products.

There must be a gap of three hours after eating meat before Jews may eat anything containing milk. Jews keep eating utensils separate, and they may have a double sink in their kitchens, so that things used for milk and meat dishes are not washed together. The wife also might prepare the challah bread for the celebration of Shabbat. The honour of welcoming in the Shabbat is also part of the role of the woman. She lights the candles, welcomes in Shabbat, and says prayers.

■ Orthodox Judaism

There is nothing in the Torah that prevents women from going out to work, or men from being responsible for the home and family. However, many strictly Orthodox Jews prefer a more traditional way of life. This does not mean that they wish to lower the **status** of women, but they emphasise the importance of providing the right environment for their children to grow up in the faith. This includes giving opportunities for prayer and the celebration of festivals.

In some Christian denominations, such as in the Roman Catholic Church, men are the priests and lead the worship. Similarly, in Orthodox

▲ *Blessing the Shabbat candles*

Objective

● Explore Jewish beliefs about the status, role and treatment of women within Judaism.

Key terms

● **role:** the actions a person performs; what they do
● **status:** how important a person's role makes them in other people's estimation

> " You shall not boil a kid in its mother's milk. "
>
> *Exodus* 23:19

Discussion activity

In pairs or small groups, discuss the following statement:

'There should be no gender prejudice or discrimination within religion.'

Judaism, men have the dominant role in synagogue worship. In Orthodox synagogues, the rabbi is male and the minyan only counts male Jews. Men and women sit separately, and women have the option to attend, whereas it is a duty for the men. However, in many instances, women have been asking for an increased role in synagogue worship.

■ Reform and Liberal Jews

Some Reform and Liberal Jewish women choose the traditional role of staying at home and nurturing the children, but others prefer to combine home duties with going out to work. Many Reform and Liberal men share the workload within the home, which makes it possible for their wives to have a paid job; as in many non-Jewish families, both parents may need to work outside the home in order to support their family.

In a Reform and Liberal synagogues, families sit together, and women are able to take leadership roles in worship. This includes carrying the Torah scrolls when they are paraded from the Ark to the bimah, and reading from them to the congregation. Although most rabbis are male, women are allowed to be rabbis. In fact the first woman rabbi was ordained in 1975 and there are now increasing numbers of women being trained. Jewish women who might not have considered a role in leadership in the past are now expressing an interest in taking a greater part in worship.

▲ A Jewish girl reading from the Torah at her Bat Mitzvah

The coming of age ceremony for girls, the Bat Mitzvah, is more important in the Reform and Liberal branches of Judaism than in Orthodox Judaism. In these traditions, young men and young women are counted as part of the minyan once they have completed their Bar Mitzvah or Bat Mitzvah ceremonies.

Activities

1 Explain the status of women within Reform Judaism.
2 'Every person should have the same status regardless of their role.' What do you think?

Activities

1 Why do Jews believe that men and women have equal value and status?
2 Traditionally, Judaism has given different roles to men and women. Explain, using examples, the main differences between the roles.
3 Explain how the role of women is seen in worship in Orthodox Judaism.

Links

For more information on the Bat Mitzvah, see Chapter 2, pages 48–49.

▲ Julia Neuberger, Senior Rabbi at the West London Synagogue

Contrasting beliefs

Use the Internet or books to find out about the status of women in Christianity. Compare Roman Catholicism with another denomination, for example Anglican or Methodist.

★ Study tip

It would be helpful to be able to compare and contrast the status of women in religion between Judaism and Christianity.

Summary You should now be able to explain Jewish beliefs about the status, role and treatment of women within Judaism.

8.6 Judaism and wealth

■ The right attitude to wealth

Jews believe that wealth is a blessing from God and a reward for following his commands. The Tenakh repeats on several occasions that God blesses those who are faithful to him. In the Torah it says that if Israel worshipped God and obeyed the law given to Moses, then 'The LORD will give you abounding prosperity' (Deuteronomy 28:11). This idea is developed in the scriptures. In contrast, there were times when the Israelites forgot God, and as a result, they fell on hard times. The responsibility is, therefore, not to focus on acquiring wealth but to focus on God, fulfilling religious duties and helping the community. God gave King Solomon a choice of any gift he desired, and the king chose wisdom in order to serve his subjects with justice. This pleased God, and he made King Solomon very wealthy as a reward. Solomon hadn't been greedy, so God said, 'And I also grant you what you did not ask for – both riches and glory all your life – the like of which no king has ever had.' (1 Kings 3:13).

Jews are constantly reminded to give thanks to God for all their blessings:

> ❝ Remember that it is the LORD your God who gives you the power to get wealth ❞
>
> *Deuteronomy* 8:18

Jews thank God by giving a **tithe**, a tenth of their earnings, and offerings.

> ❝ You shall set aside every year a tenth part of all the yield of your sowing that is brought from the field. ❞
>
> *Deuteronomy* 14:22

> ❝ All tithes from the land, whether seed from the ground or fruit from the tree, are the LORD's; they are holy to the LORD. ❞
>
> *Leviticus* 27:30

Some Jews today still give ten per cent of their income (once tax has been deducted) as a tithe and all Jews are encouraged to give to charity.

Jews and Christians are both taught that it is right to do honest work to earn money because laziness is not encouraged. The illustration of the ants in Proverbs 6:6–11 sums up this teaching by stating that ants do not need to be told what to do. They just get on with the necessary work. People should do the same, because poverty and hunger result from idleness.

■ The uses of money

In Judaism it is seen as perfectly acceptable to be wealthy, provided the riches are obtained in a moral and legal way. The wealth should be used for the benefit of others as well as themselves, and God must

Objective

● Understand Jewish attitudes to wealth and its uses.

Key terms

● **tithe:** one tenth of annual produce or earnings
● **tzedakah:** doing righteous acts; giving to charity; a religious duty designed to promote justice

▲ *Jewish people believe that having wealth is a blessing from God*

Research activity 🔍

Look up Proverbs 6:6–11. What does the illustration of the ants show?

Activities

1 Explain what the Tenakh teaches about the source of wealth.
2 What is a tithe?

not be forgotten. It is seen as important not to be selfish. From an early age children are encouraged to save money for charity. Many Jewish homes have a collecting box called a pushke. Members of the family put money in it so that it can be used to help those in need. Guests often put an anonymous gift in the box when they visit. Some are dedicated to a particular cause, such as the local synagogue or a Jewish charity. It is seen as very important to show kindness and do righteous acts to help the community.

Jews believe that to use money to show kindness is a religious duty called **tzedakah**. Tzedakah means justice, and tzedakah is a religious duty designed to promote justice. It is compulsory, not optional, and giving in the right spirit will bring spiritual rewards. Tzedakah, alongside repentance and prayer, is one of the three actions that will gain forgiveness from God. A tenth of their income may sometimes be given in tzedakah, providing that they have enough left over to live. Usually this is given to charitable organisations which help the poor, or provide health care or education. Some see tzedakah as paying a debt they owe to the poor because the most vulnerable members of society need help. Because voluntary donations are encouraged as an act of kindness when a need is identified, some Jews give more than ten per cent. It is usually seen as better to give the money to organisations rather than direct to poor people, because in that way, no one will feel humiliated by the gift. The Talmud says that the best way of giving is when neither the giver nor the recipient knows the other's identity. Tzedakah is used to help both Jews and Gentiles. The best form of charity is when it helps the recipient to become self-reliant and self-supporting.

 From a young age, children are taught to collect money for charity

> ### Discussion activity
>
> In small groups or in pairs, discuss the following statements:
>
> 'When people become wealthy it is easy to forget God.'
>
> 'Wealth is only useful for the good that it can do.'

Activities

1 Why do many Jewish homes have a pushke?

2 Explain the importance of tzedakah.

Contrasting beliefs

Use the Internet or a library to find contrasting Christian beliefs about the uses of money.

⭐ Study tip

Try to make sure you are able to compare and contrast Jewish and Christian beliefs about money.

Summary
You should now be able to explain Jewish beliefs about wealth and its uses.

■ Poverty

Worldwide, millions live in extreme poverty. Many of the problems caused by poverty are the result of circumstances that the individual sufferer is helpless to do much about. A major factor is the climate in many countries. For example, those who live near the equator have the problem of excessive heat, and in many African countries, the rainfall is unreliable or minimal. Drought conditions mean that there isn't sufficient water for drinking, supporting livestock and growing crops. Global warming is making the situation even worse. Regions that are already dry are becoming drier, and wet regions are getting even more rain. Deserts like the Sahara are expanding, and it is becoming increasingly difficult for those living on its fringes to make a living. Disease is also a major problem in many poor countries. HIV AIDS and diseases carried by mosquitos such as malaria are widespread.

Lack of health care, education and other factors mean that productivity is low. Often governments have to pay interest on loans, so they sell crops to other countries rather than using them to feed local people. Corruption, **exploitation**, war and population growth all contribute to the problem of poverty, especially in less economically developed countries (LEDCs). Even in countries where there are rich mineral or oil reserves, people may be poor because some foreign companies take the natural resources without giving much benefit to local people.

▲ *Children living in poverty in Nairobi, Kenya*

■ Fair wage

In some countries, many people are paid very little, and often employees are exploited. In extreme cases workers are forced to work very long hours for hardly any pay, but they have little choice or they and their families would starve. In Britain, the National Minimum Wage was introduced in 1999 to prevent the exploitation of labour. This fixed the lowest amount a worker could legally be paid per hour in the UK. A higher amount called the National **Living Wage** is being phased in between 2016 and 2020. Some Jewish synagogues, for example Finchley Reform Synagogue, have been pleased to be recognised as Living Wage employers. Jews consider it their duty to pay wages in full and on time.

> ### Objective
>
> - Understand the exploitation of the poor, including issues relating to fair pay and people trafficking.

> ### Key terms
>
> - **exploitation:** misuse of power or money to get others to do things for little or unfair reward
> - **living wage:** a wage that is high enough to cover the basic cost of living
> - **people trafficking:** the illegal movement of people, typically for the purposes of forced labour or commercial sexual exploitation

> ### Discussion activity
>
> In small groups or in pairs, discuss the following statement:
>
> 'Some people will always be exploited. It is impossible to stop it.'

Jewish business dealings must be focused on kindness, honesty and fairness, with no exploitation of anyone concerned. False weights and measures are strictly forbidden in the Torah and a fair price should be paid for a fair product or service. Workers must be paid on time for their labours. Obeying these ethical teachings should ensure that employers and employees are treated fairly and everyone in their communities benefits.

Excessive interest on loans

Often, desperate people are given loans at very high interest rates. Then they find that they are unable to pay off the debt. Interest rates for instant loans may be well over 1000 per cent. Families who borrow £100 may have to pay back over £1000 if they borrowed the money for a year. Low-income families are often targeted, and sometimes the lenders are linked to organised crime. If repayments are not made, they may threaten violence. Judaism forbids any interest on loans. Allowance is made for businesses or banks to charge interest but, otherwise, interest is forbidden because it is not fair on vulnerable people persuaded to borrow money. Some Jews give one per cent of their salary to a fund called the Pe'ah fund to help the most vulnerable and those facing financial crises.

People trafficking

Jews believe in the sanctity of life and the value of every human being, and so are opposed to **people trafficking**. The requirement to remember that the Jews were slaves in ancient Egypt and act towards others with this in mind has been a central part of Judaism for 3000 years. People trafficking is a worldwide problem and is often referred to as a form of modern-day slavery. People from poverty-stricken countries often pay people smugglers to help get them to developed countries, where they hope to have a more prosperous life. They arrive in a country illegally and find themselves exploited by criminal gangs. They dare not complain to the authorities for fear of being deported back to their country of origin. Others have no intention of leaving their homes but are kidnapped by criminals, transported abroad and then forced to work in the sex industry.

▲ *Protesting for fair wages*

Links

For more information on fairness, and the prophet Amos, see pages 156–157.

Activities

1 Design a diagram showing some of the major causes of poverty.

2 Which of these causes do you think results in the most poverty? Give your reasons.

⭐ **Study tip**

You might find it useful to make some mind maps or cards to include the main points that you need to remember.

Summary

You should now be able to discuss issues surrounding poverty, the exploitation of workers, excessive interest on loans and the problem of people trafficking.

Activities

1 Explain why Jews support the idea of a fair wage for a fair day's work.

2 Explain why Jews oppose excessive interest rates being charged on loans.

3 What is meant by 'people trafficking'?

Giving money to the poor

■ Responsibilities of those living in poverty

Although Judaism is a very charitable religion, it is understood that just giving money to the poor may not help in the long term. Jews recognise the need for those in poverty to try and overcome the difficulties they face and to avoid being a burden to others. People can become reliant on receiving aid, and those who are able may not make a real effort themselves to become self-supporting. If the poverty is caused by laziness, then Jews urge the people concerned to look for work. The Torah describes how the poor used to attempt to help themselves by gleaning corn from the harvest fields (see Leviticus 19:9–10). Proverbs 6:6–11 warns that laziness leads to hunger and poverty.

Wherever possible, Jews encourage individuals to make the effort to improve their skills and education, budget carefully, and try to obtain a good job so that they may escape the poverty trap. When someone is poor because of an addiction, such as gambling, Jews urge them to seek help. However, where there is a genuine need, Jews are encouraged to be generous and give as much assistance as they are able.

■ Giving aid

There are two main types of aid. First, there is what is known as **emergency aid.** This consists of resources given as quickly as possible as a response to a crisis which has occurred, such as a natural disaster,

▲ *The Jewish charity GIFT collects and distributes food to hundreds of needy families each week*

for example, an earthquake, flood or drought. The need is immediate and short term because there may be a shortage of food, drinking water, medical care and shelter. Second, there is aid which is designed to help people rebuild their lives, such as after a war or disaster. This is known as **long-term aid** because it helps with reconstruction projects or the setting up of projects which will enable people to become more self-sufficient, such as irrigation projects or the provision of training in better agricultural methods.

Emergency aid is given to Jews and Gentiles alike when people are suffering because

> ❝ When you reap the harvest of your land, you shall not reap all the way to the edges of your field, or gather the gleanings of your harvest. You shall not pick your vineyard bare, or gather the fallen fruit of your vineyard; you shall leave them for the poor and the stranger: I the LORD am your God. ❞
>
> *Leviticus* 19:9–10

of drought, earthquakes, floods or war. For example, in 2015 a large earthquake killed over 8000 people in Nepal, and World Jewish Relief (WJR) was one of the first relief agencies to send aid. Help has also been given to refugees fleeing from the Middle East and coming to Europe. This has been targeted particularly to assist Greece and Turkey who have received thousands of migrants.

Links

For more information on tzedakah, see pages 164–165.

For more information on the work of GIFT, look back to Chapter 1, page 23.

World Jewish Relief

World Jewish Relief (WJR) is the British Jewish community's international humanitarian agency. Their aim includes helping Jews in poor communities to overcome poverty. The work of the organisation is based firmly on Leviticus 19:18 'love your neighbour as yourself.' In particular WJR works in many of the former Soviet Union countries such as Belarus, Georgia, Moldova and Ukraine, where there is limited welfare support. In Africa, WJR supports people who are unemployed and living in poverty in countries like Rwanda. The organisation hopes to help 100,000 people out of poverty by 2020 by enabling them to become self-reliant. WJR provides courses to help people develop job-specific skills, vocational training and help to find employment. It has devised an employment programme specifically to support refugees from Syria who have come to the UK. Practical assistance includes providing food, medicine, homecare, and activities for the elderly Jewish population who would otherwise be suffering from loneliness.

A WJR homecare worker providing support as part of a WJR programme to help vulnerable elderly people in the Ukraine

Jewish Care

Formed in 1990, from a number of long-established Jewish charities, Jewish Care specialises in providing health and social care for the Jewish community in Britain, in particular in London and the south-east of England. Jewish Care helps around 7000 people and families each week, some of whom need financial assistance. Services are provided for people suffering from dementia, Holocaust survivors, people with disabilities, those who are bereaved and people with various illnesses. Other work includes youth leadership opportunities and cultural, educational and recreational programmes. Jewish Care has strong links with other Jewish charities, synagogues, welfare groups and youth and educational bodies, and has a vision to create a society where everyone supports and cares for each other.

Research activity

Use the Internet to find out more about World Jewish Relief. Record details of their latest projects.

★ Study tip

It is important to be able to explain the work that Jewish charities do. Knowing up-to-date examples of current or recent projects is useful. Remember that it is their faith that inspires them to help the needy.

Summary
You should now understand the responsibilities of those living in poverty and know how Jewish relief organisations help the poor and vulnerable.

Activities

1 Describe the work of World Jewish Relief, including how WJR helps with emergency and long-term aid.
2 Describe the work of Jewish Care.
3 Do you think that it is possible to create a society where everyone supports and cares for each other? Give reasons for your opinion.

Human rights – summary

You should now be able to:

✔ explain prejudice and discrimination in religion and belief, including the status and treatment within Judaism of women and homosexuals

✔ explain issues of equality, freedom of religion and belief, including freedom of religious expression

✔ explain what is meant by human rights and the responsibilities that come with rights, including the responsibility to respect the rights of others

✔ explain Jewish views about social justice

✔ explain Jewish attitudes to racial prejudice and discrimination.

Wealth and poverty – summary

You should now be able to:

✔ explain Jewish teachings about wealth, including the right attitude to wealth

✔ explain religious teachings about the uses of wealth

✔ explain the responsibilities of having wealth, including the duty to tackle poverty and its causes

✔ describe and explain the problem of exploitation of the poor, including issues relating to fair pay, excessive interest on loans and people trafficking

✔ explain the responsibilities of those living in poverty to help themselves overcome the difficulties they face

✔ explain what Judaism teaches about charity, including issues related to giving money to the poor

✔ explain similar and contrasting perspectives in contemporary British society to all the above issues

✔ explain similar and contrasting beliefs in contemporary British society to the three issues of the status of women in religion, the uses of wealth, and freedom of religious expression, with reference to the main religious tradition in Britain (Christianity) and non-religious beliefs such as atheism or humanism.

Sample student answer – the 12 mark question

1. Write an answer to the following practice question:

   'Racism is the worst form of prejudice.'

   Evaluate this statement.
   In your answer you:
   - should give reasoned arguments in support of this statement
   - should give reasoned arguments to support a different point of view
   - should refer to religious arguments
   - may refer to non-religious arguments
   - should reach a justified conclusion.

   [12 marks]

2. Read the following student sample answer:

   "There are many types of prejudice which are not good, but throughout history anti-Semitism has been a real problem. After the revolt by the Jews against the Romans in the first century CE, Jews were scattered to many parts of the world. Many people in those countries did not like people from a different race, with a different religion, language and way of life, living in what they regarded as their country. So whenever the country had problems, it was easy to make Jews the scapegoat and blame them. So Jews have often been picked on primarily because of their race. This was particularly so in Nazi Germany. During the economic depression, Hitler and the Nazi party blamed the Jews for all Germany's problems. This resulted during the Second World War in the Holocaust where millions of Jews were sent to concentration camps and murdered in

gas chambers. Never in history has there been such killing because of race. Surely this makes racial prejudice the worst form of prejudice, particularly as Genesis 1 makes the point that Adam and Eve, and so the whole human race, were created in God's image.

Others might argue that religious prejudice is the worst because thousands are persecuted and killed every year by people who believe in a different religion. Others may argue that sexism is the worst because that affects around 50% of the world's population. Others argue that colour prejudice is the worst because it resulted in apartheid in South Africa and the mistreatment of black people in America in the 20th century.

Personally I think that racism is really bad because you cannot change your race. You shouldn't be prejudiced against someone just because they were born in another country."

3. With a partner, discuss the sample answer. Is the focus of the answer correct? Is anything missing from the answer? How do you think it could be improved?

4. What mark (out of 12) would you give this answer? Look at the mark scheme in the Introduction (AO2). What are the reasons for the mark you have given?

5. Now swap your answer with your partner's and mark each other's responses. What mark (out of 12) would you give the response? Refer to the mark scheme and give reasons for the mark you award.

Practice questions

1. Which one of the following is the main religious tradition in Britain?

   a) Buddhism   b) Christianity   c) Islam   d) Hinduism   **[1 mark]**

2. Give two of the causes of poverty.   **[2 marks]**

3. Explain two similar beliefs in contemporary British society about what role women should be allowed in worship.

   In your answer you should refer to the main religious tradition of Great Britain and one or more other religious traditions.   **[4 marks]**

   > **Study tip**
   >
   > Make sure you develop the points you are making. This may be done by giving detailed information, such as referring to examples. Include similar beliefs in your answer. This can be done by referring to a Christian belief and a different view from another religion, e.g. Judaism.

4. Explain two religious beliefs about social justice.

   Refer to scripture or sacred writings in your answer.   **[5 marks]**

5. 'All religious believers must give to charities that help the poor.'

   Evaluate this statement. In your answer you:

   - should give reasoned arguments in support of this statement
   - should give reasoned arguments to support a different point of view
   - should refer to religious arguments
   - may refer to non-religious arguments
   - should reach a justified conclusion.   **[12 marks]**

Glossary

A

abortion: the removal of a foetus from the womb to end a pregnancy, usually before the foetus is 24-weeks-old

abuse: misuse; of the world and the environment

active euthanasia: ending a life by deliberate action, such as by giving a patient a lethal injection

adaptation: a process of change, in which an organism or species becomes better suited to its environment

addiction: physical or mental dependency on a substance or activity which is very difficult to overcome

adultery: voluntary sexual intercourse between a married person and a person who is not their husband or wife; in Jewish law, adultery is defined as voluntary sexual intercourse between a married woman and a man who is not her husband

agnostic: someone who thinks there is not enough evidence for belief in God

Amidah: also known as the 'standing prayer", it is the central prayer of Jewish worship

anti-Semitism: prejudice against Jews

Aron Hakodesh: the Ark – the holiest part of the synagogue, which contains the Torah scrolls

atheist: a person who believes that there is no God

awe: a feeling of respect, mixed feelings of fear and wonder

B

Bar Mitzvah: celebration of a boy coming of age at 13; literally 'son of the commandment'

Bat Mitzvah: celebration of a girl coming of age at 12, in Reform synagogues; literally 'daughter of the commandment'

benevolent: all-loving, all-good

Big Bang: a massive expansion of space which set in motion the creation of the universe

bigamy: the offence in the UK of marrying someone while already married to another person

bimah: a platform in a synagogue from where the Torah is read

biological weapons: weapons that contain living organisms or infective material that can lead to disease or death

Brit Milah: ceremony of male circumcision; the removal of the foreskin for religious reasons

C

cantor (chazzan): a person who leads or chants prayers in the synagogue

charity: 1. providing help and love to those in need 2. an organisation that does not make a profit, whose main purpose is to help those in need

chemical weapons: weapons that use lethal chemicals to poison, burn or paralyse humans and destroy the natural environment

circumcision: the removal of the foreskin from the penis

civil partnership: legal union of same-sex couples

cohabitation: a couple living together and having a sexual relationship without being married to one another

community service: a way of punishing offenders by making them do unpaid work in the community

contraception: the methods used to prevent a pregnancy from taking place

corporal punishment: punishment of an offender by causing them physical pain – now illegal in the UK

covenant: an agreement; in Judaism it refers to an agreement between individuals, often on behalf of the Jews, and God

creation: the act by which God brought the universe into being

creator: the one who makes things and brings things about

crime: an offence which is punishable by law, for example stealing, murder

D

death penalty: capital punishment; a form of punishment in which a prisoner is put to death for crimes committed

defensive wars: wars that Jews are obliged to fight if attacked

deforestation: the cutting down of large amounts of forests, usually for business needs

Design argument: the argument that God designed the universe because everything is so intricately made in its detail that it could not have happened by chance

deterrence: an aim of punishment – to put people off committing crimes

dietary laws: rules which deal with foods permitted to be eaten, food preparation, food combinations, and the utensils and dishes coming into contact with food

discrimination: actions or behaviour that result from prejudice

the divine: God, gods or ultimate reality

divorce: legal ending of a marriage

dominion: having control or mastery over something

E

educating children in a faith: bringing up children according to the religious beliefs of the parents

emergency aid: also known as short-term aid; help given to communities in a time of disaster or crisis, e.g. food during a famine, shelter after an earthquake

enlightenment: the gaining of true knowledge, particularly in the Buddhist tradition, that frees a person from the cycle of rebirth by seeing what the truth about life really is

environment: the natural world; the surroundings in which someone lives

equality: the state of being equal, especially in status, rights and opportunities

eternal: without beginning or end

euthanasia: killing someone painlessly and with compassion, to end their suffering

evil: the opposite of good, a force or the personification of a negative power that is seen in many traditions as destructive and against God

evolution: the process by which living organisms are thought to have developed and diversified from earlier forms of life during the history of the earth

exploitation: misuse of power or money to get others to do things for little or unfair reward

extended family: a family that extends beyond the nuclear family to include grandparents and other relatives as well

F

faith: a commitment to something that goes beyond proof and knowledge, especially used about God and religion

family: a group of people who are related by blood, marriage or adoption

family planning: the practice of controlling how many children couples have and when they have them

First Cause argument: also called the cosmological argument, the argument that there has to be an uncaused cause that made everything else happen, otherwise there would be nothing now

forgiveness: showing grace and mercy and pardoning someone for what they have done wrong

free will: belief that God gives people the opportunity to make decisions for themselves

freedom of religion: the right to believe or practise whatever religion one chooses

freedom of religious expression: the right to worship, preach and practise one's faith in whatever way one chooses

G

gender discrimination: to act against someone on the basis of their gender; discrimination is usually seen as wrong and may be against the law

gender equality: the idea that people should be given the same rights and opportunities regardless of whether they are male or female

gender prejudice: unfairly judging someone before the facts are known; holding biased opinions about an individual or group based on their gender

general revelation: God making himself known through ordinary, common human experiences

greed: selfish desire for something

H

hate crimes: crimes, often including violence, that are usually targeted at a person because of their race, religion, sexuality, disability or gender

healing the world: being involved in God's work to sustain the world; it can involve work to increase social justice or to preserve the environment

heterosexual: sexually attracted to members of the opposite sex

holy war: fighting for a religious cause or God

homosexual: sexually attracted to members of the same sex

homosexuality: sexual attraction to members of the same sex

human rights: the basic rights and freedoms to which all human beings should be entitled

human sexuality: how people express themselves as sexual beings

I

immanent: the idea that God is present in and involved with life on earth and in the universe; a quality of God

impersonal nature (of God): the idea that God has no 'human' characteristics, is unknowable and mysterious, more like an idea or force

J

judgement: the belief that God judges a person based on their actions, and either rewards or punishes them as a result

just war: a war which meets internationally accepted criteria for fairness

justice: bringing about what is right and fair, according to the law, or making up for a wrong that has been committed

K

kaddish: a prayer said by Jewish mourners that praises God and asks for peace

kindness to others: positive, caring actions that should be shown to all living things

kosher: food that meets the requirements of Jewish laws

L

living wage: a wage that is high enough to cover the basic cost of living

long-term aid: assistance given to a poor country over a long period of time that has a lasting effect

M

marriage: a legal union between a man and a woman (or in some countries, including the UK, two people of the same sex) as partners in a relationship

menorah: a many-branched candlestick that holds either seven or nine candles

mental illness: a medical condition that affects a person's feelings, emotions or moods, and perhaps their ability to relate to others

merciful: the quality of God that shows compassion or forgiveness to humans, even though he has the power to punish them

Messiah: 'the anointed one'; a leader of the Jews who is expected to live on earth at some time in the future

Messianic age: a future time of global peace when everyone will want to become closer to God, possibly through the intervention of the Messiah

minyan: a group of at least 10 adults; the minimum number of Jews required for a Jewish religious service

miracle: a seemingly impossible event, usually good, that cannot be explained by natural or scientific laws, and is thought to be the action of God

mitzvot (singular mitzvah): Jewish rules or commandments

monotheism: belief in one God

monotheistic: a religion that believes there is only one God

mourning: a period of time spent remembering a person who has died

mutation: the changing of the structure of a gene or chromosome that gives the life-form a different feature to that of the parents'; this difference may be transmitted to following generations

N

natural resources: the various materials found in nature – such as oil and trees – that can be used by people to make more complex products

nature: the physical world, including plants, animals and landscape; the environment or natural world

ner tamid: eternal light; a light that is kept burning in the synagogue above the Ark

non-renewable resources: things the earth provides that will eventually run out as there is a limited amount of them; examples include oil, coal, gas and other minerals

nuclear family: a couple and their dependent children regarded as a basic social unit

nuclear weapons: weapons that work by a nuclear reaction, devastate huge areas, and kill large numbers of people

O

obligatory war: a war that God commanded Jews to fight

omnipotent: almighty, having unlimited power; a quality of God

omnipresent: being everywhere at all times; a quality of God

omniscient: knowing everything; a quality of God

optional wars: wars that Jews fight for a good reason, and where all peaceful ways to prevent conflict have been tried

Orthodox Jews: Jews who emphasise the importance of following the laws and guidance in the Torah; they believe the Torah was given directly by God to Moses, so should be followed as closely as possible

P

pacifism: the belief of people who refuse to take part in war and any other form of violence

passive euthanasia: allowing a terminally ill or incurably ill person to die by withdrawing or withholding medical treatment

peace: an absence of conflict, which leads to happiness and harmony

peacemaker: a person who works to establish peace in the world or in a certain part of it

peacemaking: the action of trying to establish peace

people trafficking: the illegal movement of people, typically for the purposes of forced labour or commercial sexual exploitation

personal nature (of God): the idea that God is an individual or person with whom people are able to have a relationship or feel close to

Pesach (Passover): festival in remembrance of the Jewish exodus from Egypt that is celebrated in spring

pikuach nefesh: the obligation to save a life, even if doing so breaks Jewish law

polygamy: the practice or custom of having more than one wife at the same time

positive discrimination: treating people more favourably because they have been discriminated against in the past or have disabilities

poverty: being without money, food or other basic needs of life (being poor)

prejudice: unfairly judging someone before the facts are known; holding biased opinions about an individual or group

prison: a secure building where offenders are kept for a period of time set by a judge

procreation: bringing babies into the world; producing offspring

Promised Land: the land of Canaan that God promised to the Jews

proof: evidence that supports the truth of something

protection of children: keeping children safe from harm

protest: an expression of disapproval, often in a public group

punishment: something legally done to somebody as a result of being found guilty of breaking the law

Q

quality of life: the general wellbeing of a person, in relation to their health and happiness; also, the theory that the value of life depends upon how good or how satisfying it is

R

rabbi: a Jewish religious leader and teacher

racism: showing prejudice against someone because of their ethnic group or nationality

reconciliation: the restoring of harmony after relationships have broken down

recycling: reusing old products to make new ones

Reform Jews: Jews who believe the laws and guidance in the Torah can be adapted for modern times; they believe the Torah was inspired by God but written by humans, so can be interpreted according to the times

reformation: an aim of punishment – to change someone's behaviour for the better

remarriage: when a person who has been married before goes on to marry another person

repentance: saying sorry, and a way of believers acknowledging to God that things have gone wrong

responsibility: a duty to care for, or having control over, something or someone

resurrection: the belief that after death the body remains in the grave until the end of the world, before rising again when God will come to judge

retaliation: deliberately harming someone as a response to them harming you

retribution: an aim of punishment – to get your own back; 'an eye for an eye'.

revelation: an enlightening experience; a divine or supernatural experience in which God shows himself to believers

rituals: religious ceremonies that are performed according to a set pattern

role: the actions a person performs; what they do

Rosh Hashanah: the Jewish new year

S

same-sex marriage: marriage between partners of the same sex

same-sex parents: people of the same sex who are raising children together

sanctity of life: all life is holy as it is created and loved by God; human life should not be misused or abused

scriptures: the sacred writings of a religion a quality of God

self-defence: acting to prevent harm to yourself or others

sex before marriage: sex between two unmarried people

sex outside marriage: sex between two people where at least one or both of them is married to someone else; adultery; having an affair

sexual stereotyping: having a fixed general idea or image of how men and women will behave

Shabbat: the Jewish holy day of the week; a day of spiritual renewal starting shortly before sunset on Friday and continuing to night time on Saturday

Shekhinah: the divine presence of God

Shema: a Jewish prayer affirming belief in one God, found in the Torah

shiva: an intense period of mourning that lasts for seven days

social justice: the promotion of fairness in the distribution of wealth, opportunities, and privileges in society

special revelation: God making himself known through direct personal experience or an unusual specific event

stability: safety and security; a stable society is one in which people's rights are protected and they are able to live peaceful, productive lives without continuous and rapid change

Star of David (Magen David): a symbol of Judaism said to represent the shield of King David, who ruled Israel in the tenth century BCE

status: how important a person's role makes them in other people's estimation

stewardship: the idea that believers have a duty to look after the environment on behalf of God

suffering: when people have to face and live with unpleasant events or conditions

sustainable development: building and progress that tries to reduce the impact on the natural world for future generations

synagogue: a building for Jewish public prayer, study and gathering

T

tallit: a prayer shawl

Talmud: a commentary by the rabbis on the Torah – it consists of the Mishnah and Gemara together in one collection

tefillin: small leather boxes containing extracts from the Torah, strapped to the wearer's arm and forehead for morning prayers

Temple: the centre of Jewish worship at the time of Jesus; the meeting place between God and the priest

Ten Commandments: ten laws given by God to Moses over 3000 years ago

terrorism: the unlawful use of violence, usually against innocent civilians, to achieve a political goal

terrorist: someone engaged in the unlawful use of violence, usually against innocent civilians, to achieve a political or religious goal

theist: a person who believes in God

tithe: one tenth of annual produce or earnings

Torah: 1. the five books of Moses, which form the first section of the Tenakh/ Tanach (the Jewish Bible) 2. the Jewish written law

transcendent: the idea that God is beyond and outside life on earth and the universe; a quality of God

trefah: food that Jews are forbidden to eat; means 'torn'

tzedakah: doing righteous acts; giving to charity; a religious duty designed to promote justice

U

ultimate reality: the supreme, final, fundamental power in all reality

ultra-Orthodox Jews: Jews who are even more committed than Orthodox Jews to strictly following the laws and guidance in the Torah

universe: all there is in space, including planets, galaxies and stars; it encompasses all matter

V

vegan: a person who does not eat animals or food produced by animals (such as eggs); a vegan tries not to use any products (such as leather) that have caused harm to animals

vegetarian: a person who does not eat meat or fish

violence: using actions that threaten or harm others

vision: seeing something, especially in a dream or trance, that shows something about the nature of God or the afterlife

W

war: fighting between nations to resolve issues between them

weapons of mass destruction: weapons that can kill large numbers of people and/or cause great damage

wonder: marvelling at the complexity and beauty of the universe

Y

Yom Kippur: the Day of Atonement; a day of fasting on the tenth day after Rosh Hashanah

Index